Triple Jeopardy reveals many of the justice system. It crystallized the extent to which those who are sworn to uphold justice will go to make the justice system serve their individual cause. It's an alarming reminder that lady justice is often times not blind. It's entertaining and at times amusing but very insightful and informative. I applaud your courage for sharing this very personal experience.

Larry Hazzard Sr.
Global Sports of Boxing Icon

Once I began to read *Triple Jeopardy*, I could not put it down, reading it cover-to-cover until the sun rose. With dignity, pride and courage, Rita Ali combines her success in the world of business, boxing and beauty with the tragedy of unfair accusations against her; conviction, and incarceration, in a moving story that defines the grace she walks this earth on. *Triple Jeopardy* is a must-read and an education that everyone needs to acquire.

Flo Anthony
Celebrity Journalist/Bestselling Author

Triple Jeopardy chronicles a life well lived. Dr. Rita Ali's unfortunate circumstances that lead to time spent away from her family and friends, has propelled her to write a compelling work of art.

Kenny Gamble
Co-founder Philadelphia International Records
2008 Rock & Roll Hall of Fame Inductee

I have known Rita and her husband almost all of my adult life. She is an individual that has made planet earth a better place than when she found it. I welcomed her and her husband with open arms in the presence of Muhammad Ali. She was an individual that came with advice and didn't want anything in return. Her and her husband made Muhammad Ali a better business man. I truly enjoyed her book and I am sure the whole world is waiting to read it.

Gene Kilroy
Longtime friend of Muhammad Ali

This book is an absolute masterpiece. It will take you on an emotional roller coaster. You may cry, laugh and in many cases you might become angry, but what this woman has been able to do is to vividly depict the unfairness of the American justice system. Many know about it but only few have the courage to denounce it. This is a beautiful testimony of audacity, determination and resilience from a woman who I refer to as, Mom. This book must be read by the masses.

Fred "Frenchy" Madzimba
International Celebrity Agent

More than a memoir, *Triple Jeopardy* is a sizzling page-turner. You will laugh, you will be entertained but most importantly this book informs. It's a clarion call to pay attention to our criminal justice system and an opportunity to learn some seriously impactful life lessons. Thank you for your transparency, [Rita]. It's admirable and transformative.

Stacey C. Speller
International Speaker & Author

This memoir, Triple Jeopardy, Three Strikes But Not Out, sizzles! Each narrative therein is an engaging page-turner. The truth told on these pages may send searing tears down your cheeks and cause an irksome burn to stir up from your core. BUT, believe it or not, room was left for belly busting laughter, too! Get ready for a gusty ride as Dr. Ali whisks you through the halls of her star-studded history then straight into the halls of injustice, the American way. The author shows us all that survival not only belongs to the fittest, it belongs to the one who dares to believe that a trip to hell and back — three times — is a set up for your best good, ever. Dr. Rita Ali should be sainted!

Natalie "Nhat" Crawford
Editor for *Triple Jeopardy*, *Three Strikes But Not Out*

TRIPLE
JEOPARDY

TRIPLE JEOPARDY

3 STRIKES BUT NOT OUT

DR. RITA ALI

Gatekeeper press
Columbus, Ohio

Dedication

To the people I love eternally, both here and beyond, particularly...

My parents, Samuel and Marie Williams, to whom I owe my values and development.

My husband Shamsud-Din who is the epitome of love, devotion, patience and encouragement. You are a kiss from heaven and the best father that Azim and Kiki could've ever had.

My children without whom I couldn't stand. Lakiha Tyson, Mike Tyson, Jahaira Spicer, Azim Spicer, the late Rafi Ali, my grandchildren and great grandchildren.

Contents

Introduction

Intrinsically, life's journey is a complex series of events that contribute to one's growth and development. Our experiences are important, however, what we learn and how we grow from life-shaping events are determining factors to success, or failure. Generally speaking, most individuals have a plethora of stories that could be presented in the form of a classic memoir. My story is no exception.

Our ability to discern, analyze, and triumph over adversity requires the application of good judgment, planning, and effective execution. In considering the most essential message that I wanted to convey to readers, I concluded that my book should be informative and also motivational.

Inspiring others to reach their potential and overcome adversity has been a constant passion of mine. The ability to empower individuals to resolve issues and improve the quality of their lives requires proficient life skills. It is an ongoing process that renders better results, the more we practice and implement positive learned behavior.

The expression *experience is the best teacher* is a belief that is endemic in our culture. This view is generally perceived as an absolute fact and therefore taken literally. While this is certainly a concept I agree with, I don't acquiesce to the perception that we only learn from our personal experiences. To the contrary, we can learn from other's experiences. If we are open to observing their action, we can actually expand our knowledge, avoid repeating their mistakes, and grow from comprehending their experiences.

Years of personal and professional exposure have equipped

me with knowledge worth discussing. More imperative than awareness, is understanding. Simply knowing something does not automatically equate to understanding; the best strategy for achieving success is utilizing what you know in a matter that favors you.

I learned at an early age the relevance of how understanding trumps processing information; acquired knowledge is merely the first step. Evaluating the related information is the second level of thought. Ultimately, steps one and two lead to understanding the issue(s) at hand, which is essential to achieving desirable outcomes.

As an individual who has undergone one misadventure after another, as well as accomplished extraordinary undertakings, my story is deemed compelling. I was repeatedly advised with passionate emphasis, "Rita, your story must be told!" So, upon these pages, I've told!

This memoir differs a bit from traditional ones because it will also include life strategies from me — as a certified life coach.

In all, I have concluded that being convicted of crimes I did not commit is a relevant introduction to the journey you will embark upon with me as you read along.

TRIPLE JEOPARDY

1

THE VERDICT

Like the climax of a great movie, or a best-selling novel, there comes a defining moment in real life, too. My life's defining moment would occur at the age of fifty-seven when, despite our innocence, a federal jury handed down guilty verdicts for me, my son Azim, and my daughter Lakiha, affectionately known as Kiki.

I was convicted on twenty-seven counts. My children were convicted on substantially lesser counts against them. In the moment when the judge gaveled and confirmed what seemed like a life sentence, I was devastated for my family, friends, and members of the Islamic community who believed us to be innocent of all charges. Never did I imagine that we would be found guilty on something that we had not done, let alone that KiKi would be sentenced twice, and that I would be sentenced three times on virtually the same charges.

Triple jeopardy is unheard of in government legal proceedings. Nonetheless, the Feds manipulated the system by re-indicting me with a superseding indictment. We showed no emotion or signs of weakness even though we were fully aware that we had been persecuted by the Feds with the help of their media disciples.

Verbalization of the verdict drew emotional reactions from a courtroom filled to capacity with our supporters. With the exception of the U.S. attorneys and members of the press, everyone was shocked, disappointed, and disgusted with the unjust verdict.

Upon turning to face our supporters, many of whom were teary-eyed or showed their disdain for the verdict, I could see the hurt on their faces as they consoled us with hugs and words of encouragement. Mostly, they were outraged at how any jury could have found us guilty on every count based on trumped-up charges and overt lies.

The general consensus was this—even if the jurors wanted to throw the government an undeserved bone, based on the evidence, there was no way they should have found any of us guilty of *all* charges.

Azim, Kiki, my husband Shamsud-Din Ali (Shams), and I came into contact with more supporters when we entered the hallway to exit the courthouse. However, as we pushed our way through the hordes of people, Shams and I became blocked then separated from each other by several feet. Kiki worked her way toward Shams, Azim, and me to embrace us before leaving. She had several girlfriends with her who'd traveled from New York just to attend the trial. I remember wanting to spend more time with her but she had to get back to New York.

Azim and his wife, Jahaira, also embraced me before leaving. Although Shams and I had come to court together, my biological brother Mikal drove me home, along with my biological sister Zaynah Rasool and my Muslim sisters, Intisar Shah and Shaffeeqah Muhammad. Shams trailed us in a car with some of his most loyal brothers who were also members of the Philadelphia Masjid, where he was the resident imam (the person who leads prayers in the Masjid) at the time. There were also several carloads of supporters that spontaneously followed us home.

Entering the gated community we lived in, we couldn't ignore the presence of the media. They had actually beaten us getting home even though most of them had been either in the courtroom or among the press / camera crews stationed outside the courthouse.

We turned a deaf ear to the flood of overlapping questions from the press as we entered our house along with our many well-wishers, family, and friends. A host of concerned members of the Islamic community, more family, and neighbors continued to drop by throughout the afternoon and late into the night.

A morning that had dealt a negative blow morphed into an evening of prayer and delectable dining that would impress a king. Our supporters had supplied every morsel.

Seeing the last group of visitors to the door, I could hear Shams snoring from the library; no doubt all the excitement had caught up with him. Prepared to tidy up after everyone had left, I went into the kitchen and, to my utter delight, found that there was nothing left for me to do. The Sisters had straightened up everything. In retrospect, I should have known they would have cleaned up; this is typical conduct among Muslim women.

As I climbed the stairs to my room, I couldn't wait to crawl into bed, knowing that I would fall right off to sleep. I laid on the bed for what seemed like just a minute or so, and was jolted out of my state of comfort with the harsh reality of what had happened earlier. Thoughts of the indictment, trial, verdict, negative press, and everything associated with that time, consumed my mind. I found myself lying wide awake even when all I wanted to do was sleep. Normally, I would have attempted to divert my attention from such thoughts by reading, listening to music, or watching television until I drifted off to sleep. Such was not the case on that night; as opposed to drifting off to dreamland, I began to reflect on happier times. A flashback of memories of my childhood, teen, and young adult years began to dominate my mind:

EARLIER YEARS

My earliest childhood memories consist of a proud heritage as a member of the Cosby Clan. It had nothing to do with Bill Cosby being famous; it was because of the overall family bonding which was evident among us.

In fact, the most impressive member of the Cosby family was my two-time great Uncle Russell Cosby, Bill's grandfather. My grandfather, Daddy Zack, as he was affectionately referred to by his grandkids, was named after his grandfather Zack Cosby.

Zack Cosby and his wife Louisa were freed slaves and had eighteen children. Tears of joy filled my eyes when I first saw a photo of them, with one of their children seated at the feet of their mother.

Mesmerized, I stared at the faded photo of my great-great-grandparents and one of their children. I could see that they were distinguished and proud individuals. They were not shabbily dressed. In fact, they were very well groomed, which also indicated that they were persons of comfortable means.

It confirmed the countless stories I'd heard passed down from generation to generation of the Cosby's describing the legacy of educated family members. This is not to suggest that they were wealthy, but they were, however, landowners who grew their own crops, owned cattle, and were able to provide for eighteen children.

Moreover, I saw a remarkable resemblance between my great-great grandfather, Zack Cosby, and grandfather, Daddy Zack. Even more astonishing was the remarkable resemblance I saw between myself and my great-great grandmother. My great-great-uncle, Russell Cosby, and his sister, Annie Cosby, were two of the eighteen children of Zack and Annie Cosby.

Uncle Russell lived with his wife Gertrude around the corner from where I resided with my parents and siblings. Uncle Russell, who often referred to my grandfather as his favorite nephew, was my grandfather's mother's brother.

My grandfather's first name was Zack, but his last name was Allen because his mother, Annie, married an Allen, though her maiden name was Cosby. Upon moving to Philadelphia from Virginia, Grandfather Zack resided with Uncle Russell in Philadelphia.

Back then it was customary for many family individuals migrating from down South to live with relatives already established in the North.

Uncle Russell was a beautiful reddish-brown colored man and a longtime prominent member of the Corinthian Baptist Church located on 21st and Spencer Streets in the Summerville section of Philadelphia. To say he was warm and welcoming understates just how gentle and pleasant a man he was. Initially, Sunday afternoon visits to see Uncle Russell included my siblings, my mother, and me. Later, my younger sister, Shirley, and I frequently walked to Uncle Russell's home together without the rest of the crew. Aunt Gertrude was always happy to see us; she greeted us with fruit, cookies, and thirst-quenching beverages. While we never turned down the opportunity to indulge our insatiable appetites for sweet treats, there was also the opportunity to play the piano—another big interest of ours.

In spite of the fact that neither of us had any formal piano training, we were fascinated with creating what we perceived as beautiful music. On the occasions my mother attended Uncle Russell's home with us, she would always rush us off of the piano. We would hear Mother's voice rise above our plinking, "Girls, that's enough- you're playing too loudly and making too much noise." Uncle Russell would interrupt her, inserting, "That's all right. Let the girls play, they sound great."

Totally convinced that Uncle Russell was truly a fan of our musical genius, we were baffled by the lack of appreciation others had for our piano playing. Well, years later we learned that the reason Uncle Russell was not bothered by what I now realize was annoying, as opposed to alluring melodies, was because he was hard of hearing!

As a youngster I knew Bill's two brothers—my older cousins Russell and Bobby. While Bobby and I barely spoke, Russell and I were closer; he made it known how proud he was to call me his little cousin. I have vivid memories of hanging out with the younger sister of a girl he was dating. Russell's girlfriend lived near the corner of Spencer and Beachwood Streets, and her front porch was the place to congregate for much of the neighborhood youths. I perceived Bobby as marginally nice because he never seemed to embrace any interest in valuing me as family like Russell did. He seemed to barely want to speak. Perhaps that was because we didn't fraternize in the same circle of friends. That could be understood since he was considerably older than I. Cousin Bobby certainly proved that premise.

Rita's Rule # 1

Realize that family relates to blood ties; it does not guarantee bonds of friendship.

THE NEIGHBORHOOD

Summersville was located in the East Germantown section of Philadelphia, and was truly a family-oriented neighbor-hood. Parents were overseers of their neighbors' children, as well as their own. Just about anyone's mother or father could and would correct kids who got out of line at any time. In conjunction with keeping a watchful eye over the neighborhood, the adult population was very supportive of the youths.

Frankie Beverly, world renowned R&B singer, resided in Summersville during the early stages of his musical career. It was not unusual to hear him, sometimes accompanied by other neighborhood guys, singing throughout the neighborhood. Even then he was a showstopper. No matter what was occurring, when Frankie sang, everyone paid attention and every ear perked up. Sometimes groups would assemble on corners, or in front of someone's home, to hear Frankie sing. In the very early stages of his career he was in a group called Frankie Beverly and The Butlers. Among the most memorable assets to the group was their ability to execute precise harmony. Later Frankie's group was called Raw Soul before merging into Maze, which they are still referred to today. Many of the neighborhood gals had a crush on Frankie. Not only could he sing but he was physically appealing as well. I had a secret crush on him too, and was thrilled when he came to my house one day. However, my infatuation was abruptly shattered when I realized that he had not come to see me at all. It was my older sister. Fortunately, I got over it quick and simply turned my attention to the collection of other guys in my stable of cool dudes I also had crushes on. At age thirteen, I wasn't permitted to date, so having an innocent crush on guys was sufficient. Incidentally, my feelings for any individual were subject to change from one week to another. Years would pass before I would encounter Frankie again.

In the early '80s Frankie Beverly and Maze were honored in the mayor's Reception Room of Philadelphia and I was among the specially invited guests. I was sitting directly across from Frankie, and he acknowledged me with a nod and a smile. Until today, I doubt if he actually remembered me as the young girl from Wister Street. However, considering that he more than glanced at me, I think he found my face to be familiar.

Another heartthrob who emerged out of Summersville's array of golden voices was my longtime friend Ron Tyson, who, as of this writing, sings first tenor with The Temptations. Ron used to sing in a group called The Epics.

To this day, Ron remains a close friend of mine and my sister Shirley, as well as my son-in-law Mike Tyson. Mike is also very fond of Otis Williams, the founder and only surviving group member of the original Temptations. It is worthy of mention that Otis is still putting on spectacular performances, today.

Since I reside in Las Vegas, where The Temptations perform about four times a year, I try to see the show as often as possible when I'm not traveling. Even though Ron has been with the group for over thirty years, and participated globally, he never left his Philly roots. He stays in touch with home. The funny thing is even though we're all considered his old crew he's better informed of what's going on with the rest of them than I am. Whenever we talk, Ron apprises me of the latest news from Philly. That's just who he is—a Philly brother with swag.

It is precisely relationships like this that I carried into adulthood both personally and professionally. To advance in the public arena of Philadelphia politics, public relations, and media, required an attribute befitting of a people person.

Climbing the Ladder of Success

Success is subjective because it is contingent on a superabundance of circumstances, as well as one's perspective on what defines their accomplishments. By my mid-twenties I had achieved a fair amount of success. Introduced to the political sector by my "play brother," the late State Rep. David P. Richardson, Jr. (Brother Dave), I became well established in that arena. Most state and city elected officials were accessible to me. Those who were not could be accessed through all the politicians I had an established rapport with.

Entrepreneurship and public relations consulting are also part of my professional expertise. These positions were lucrative but it would be remiss not to accentuate the power of having political connections in a city like Philadelphia. Understanding the empowering resources derived from knowing elected officials should be acknowledged. Realistically, my relationship with a State Representative, the late David Richardson (Brother Dave), solidified me as a person of reckoning among the established professionals within Philadelphia. He introduced me to upcoming political forces, as well as those who already held prominent positions, like mayors and governors. One particular outstanding politician I have the highest regard for is Ed Rendell.

I was already a member of the WDAS radio family of personalities when Ed Rendell was running for the office of Philadelphia's district attorney. It was during WDAS's annual Christmas party, in December of 1977, when Brother Dave told me he wanted to introduce me to the then candidate. Being the people person that he was, he stirred himself into the crowd of predominantly African-Americans, as I watched intently. I was fully aware of who Rendell was and had been in his presence on different occasions, but this would be my first formal introduction to him.

After Dave introduced me to Rendell, the two of us chatted briefly. Professional, yet warm and engaging, best describes the gentleman I met on that evening. I took an instant liking to him because of what I perceived to be a genuinely honest, competent, and caring individual. Before concluding our conversation I asked, "So, tell me, what did you want to discuss, Mr. Rendell?" I was so engaged with the conversation and his aspirations to become the district attorney that I'd forgotten that my childhood friend's father, Judge Bobby Williams, was running for the same office. However, with a witty smile, Rendell's response to me was, "Thanks for the offer. What I need I don't think you can help me with."

Bobby Williams had become one of Philadelphia's prominent African-American judges. Undoubtedly, he would have made an excellent district attorney and would have been the first, from the African-American community, to do so. The majority of my friends from the Germantown/Mt. Airy community stood in support of Judge Williams, of course. Obviously, Ed Rendell assumed that I was a supporter of Judge Williams, too. And, as a result, I believe he showed some restraint in asking me to support him for the office of district attorney.

Since I produced the Georgie Woods talk show on WDAS, which incidentally was the number one show at the time, I thought he wanted me to book him as a guest. With that in mind, I offered Rendell an opportunity to state his case to the large segment of our regular African-American listening audience.

Baffled by his assertion, I asked, "What is it that you need, Ed?"

"Well, I doubt that it will happen," he said. "But an endorsement by WDAS would definitely help my chances of getting elected."

"I don't know but let me think about it," I said.

I was now officially torn; would I support my neighborhood friend Judge Williams, or Ed Rendell, who I'd just become acquainted with? Feeling I had done my due diligence in weighing the pros and cons of the matter, it was time to discuss it with the general manager, Cody Anderson. I had a great rapport with Cody. He always exhibited excellent leadership qualities. He was a fair-minded, true gentleman who was open to new ideas. Cody was always concerned about WDAS's image and the production of superb broadcasting. He insisted that the station contribute to positive social development in the African-American community and throughout the city at large. This was a serious priority for Cody.

Being the GM (general manager) of one of Philadelphia's largest and most affluent radio stations was a powerful position indeed. What made Cody such an accomplished GM was that he never used his position for personal gain. Not only was he revered by the staff, he was admired by everyone who was privileged to encounter him in any capacity. Overall, I had a good relationship with Cody during my tenure at WDAS, as well as outside of the station.

Nonetheless, it was apparent that the idea of endorsing Rendell over Judge Williams did not appeal to Cody. This prompted me to explain my rationale. I proceeded to provide a scenario wherein we could certainly endorse Judge Williams and strike a blow for African-American pride. However, given the political climate at the time, there would not have been sufficient support from the Democratic Party to elect Judge Williams. In that moment, Cody's facial expression indicated that I'd presented something worthy of consideration. Within a few days of our conversation, Cody did approve the station's endorsement of Rendell, who went on to become the district attorney. Cody and I did not discuss the matter any further; therefore, I can't say with any certainty that my suggestions and insight contributed to his endorsement of Rendell. However, Rendell certainly thought I had a lot to do with the station endorsing him — as told by his expressed sentiment the night of his victory.

Entering the Bellevue Hotel in Center City, Philadelphia, where the celebration was held, it took a few minutes before I spotted Ed standing beside his wife. No sooner than I saw him, he saw me too and beckoned me over. I quickly acknowledged his hand motions and jostled my way toward him through the flock of supporters. "Honey, I want you to meet Rita Spicer. She was very instrumental in getting me the endorsement from WDAS." His face was lit up with pleasure and gratefulness. His wife appeared to be as warm and kind as he was. We exchanged ladylike pleasantries typical of the socialites we were.

One thing in particular that remained in the archives of my mind is something that was said to me during our brief exchange that evening. Ed said, "Rita, I appreciate how you extended yourself even to the point of talking to Cody about me receiving the station's endorsement. Even more than that, I was quite impressed that you never asked for anything in return." I responded, "I never asked for anything because the only thing that I wanted was for you to be a fair and just district attorney. I had confidence in you from the beginning."

Rendell has never disappointed me. After his tenure as district attorney Rendell went on to become one of the greatest mayors in Philadelphia's history, exceeded only by him becoming an outstanding governor of the Pennsylvania Commonwealth. These days Rendell can be seen on network and cable TV as a political commentator. As a proud Philadelphian, and longtime admirer, it gives me great pleasure to see and hear him express comprehensive solutions to problems in today's chaotic and divisive political environment. With the exception of him and a few other politicians, gone are the days of respect for diversity of opinions. These are turbulent times fueled by far too many politicians who demonstrate more concern for a paycheck, and supporting their prospective parties, than caring for the welfare of our country. In spite of this, I believe in the resilience of the American people and our commitment to a free, fair, open, and honorable society based on the founding father's principles for this great country. Thus, I'm confident that we as a nation shall move beyond the adversity that plagues us at this current time. Honorable people, like Rendell, was the reason for my involvement in political campaigns.

My admiration for Rendell's politics, while primarily derived from my Democratic values, should not be confused with blind loyalty to the party. I have also voted Republican and supported independents on occasion. Avoidance of complacency with a single political party worked to my advantage as a public relations specialist. Developing relationships with influential corporations, unions, community leadership, and elected officials raised my public persona. Contacts of this caliber helped me to aspire to become a health and beauty columnist for the *Philadelphia Tribune*, where I provided health and beauty tips, became the producer of a morning show on WDAS radio, served a nine-year commission on the Pennsylvania State Board of Cosmetology under two governors, ran a successful public relations business, operated a prosperous unisex salon, and so on. Popularity has its perks, as well as its problems, which brings to mind an unpleasant and scary incident that occurred as a result of my photo being featured along with my weekly column.

Included in a stack of mail I received from readers was a letter from an inmate in a state penitentiary. Surprised to see a postmark from a prison, I reluctantly opened the letter. I hadn't known a soul who was incarcerated. Reading the words of the author moved me beyond surprise to shock and then fear. The writer began with a declaration of admiration for my weekly health and beauty tips. "...Your articles are so comforting and make me feel closer to home..." he'd stated. Then, in what appeared to be a flawed attempt to at a compliment, he rambled on about how beautiful I was and that I looked like his late mother. He wrote, "I'm basically an honest guy, considered very handsome, in great physical condition, with paper sack brown skin color, and clear light brown eyes. I very much want to have a relationship with you. I can't wait to meet you as soon as I'm released, but [until then] I hope you will write me back and start visiting me at the prison. I know we can have a meaningful relationship if you're willing to invest a little trust in me."

"WOW!" I hollered. "What the hell?!" I was now aware that my popularity made it relatively easy for anyone to find me, at will! I was frantic, so frantic in fact, that I was prompted to go directly to the office of Jim Cassell, editor-in-chief of the *Philadelphia Tribune* at that time. It was obvious that Jim found the letter — and my reaction to it — somewhat humorous even though he tried not to show it. "What's funny, Jim?" I asked. Looking up from the letter and directly into my face, Jim replied: "Sorry, I'm not taking the matter lightly. I'm just amused at this dude's descriptions of himself!"

Rita's Rule # 2

> *Notoriety is like a double-edged sword that cuts both ways. Each level of popularity mandates increasing your levels of security. The more public exposure you have, the more likely you are to come in contact with unsavory characters seeking to harm you. Set boundaries.*

WHO'S WHO IN '82

In 1982, the *Philadelphia Tribune* featured me in a full-spread story. The article was entitled *Who's Who in '82*. It covered my advancements in the professional, social, and political field. Beyond my interest in political campaigns, it outlined my involvement with various social and professional undertakings. As I mentioned, once I became a columnist for the *Philadelphia Tribune*, I'd written a weekly article including health and beauty tips. Concurrently, I was providing health and beauty tips on Philly's WDAS radio station while also producing the Georgie Woods Show. These venues provided me with writing vehicles that offered ample subjects to research and write about; added to that were celebrity interviews. This was as much an enjoyable time in my professional career as it was a foundation to advance in the political arena, make a name for myself in the world of cosmetics, and increase my social status. Hair shows helped with that as well.

Generally, performing on stage at international hair shows

conveys the perception that one is at the top of their game in the cosmetic industry. Companies select stylists who are savvy and exceptionally skilled in chemical applications, i.e. hair coloring, as well as advanced hair cutting and styling because these companies need to be represented well. Thousands of consumers pay a general admission price to walk the large convention facilities and observe platform artists at work. I recall workshops conducted by top stylists that were held in private areas. Admissions to these venues were costly and limited to paying consumers only, no exceptions. I, too, was featured in these private sessions. Achieving this level in the cosmetic industry elevates your status, your name recognition, and qualifies you as an expert in the field. Ultimately, it improves your earning capacity, too. Borrowing lyrics from late inspirational and multitalented Nina Simone, in my early adult years I can say that I was proud to be *Young, Gifted and Black*.

2

LIVING A DREAM: KNOWING MUHAMMAD ALI

"Float like a butterfly, sting like a bee."

— Muhammad Ali

Have you ever dreamed of something that became reality at some point in your life? If so, you know that feeling of elation. You'll understand when I say that knowing someone as great and amazing as Muhammad Ali is among the highlights of my life — to the extent where my life's story is incomplete without the mention of him. Factor into the equation that I had converted to the Islamic religion at the age of sixteen, so, in retrospect, it is clear why Muhammad Ali took an interest in me from our first encounter. Muslim or not, meeting "the Greatest," who undisputedly was the most noted person on the planet at the time, was surely a dream come true for me.

Being the polarizing, controversial figure that he was, many would consider me to be a conquest of his razor-sharp wit and undeniable charm. Don't worry, I've heard a lot of that — but none of that's true!

Muhammad Ali and I shared a unique bond. The man played a significant role in ensuring a successful entry for me into the public relations arena in the sport of boxing. He was the one behind the elevation of my career status from a television show producer to a successful media personality. He solidified and elevated me as a writer and consultant in the sport of boxing, as well as an event planner.

WHERE IT ALL BEGAN

It would not be improper if I say that I owe a major part of my success to Muhammad Ali. However, my relationship with that man dates back long before he became Muhammad Ali — before I ever met him; before he was even aware of my existence.

Growing up, I had no interest in any particular sport, let alone boxing. As a teenager, I vividly recall the day when I was sitting in the living room with my father, while I read a book and he watched boxing on television. I was suddenly distracted by the distinctive Louisville-Kentucky accent of a man named Cassius Clay fuming into the microphone of a reporter.

Every Friday night my father would hog the television to watch this intense sport. Sure, my hardworking father deserved to take his pleasure on Friday nights, in his own home, but it was the only television we kids had access to. The other TV was in our parents' bedroom, where we also had no access! Nonetheless, unfortunately, because of boxing that meant no television for us on Friday nights.

My siblings and I watched a lot of horror movies on TV in the living room over the weekends — after boxing of course. It was the only time we could stay up late. Frankenstein, Wolfman, and other creatures of horror were my siblings' choices, and although I never admitted it, I was not a fan! These movies scared me senseless. My eyes were wide and glazed over as I watched the TV screen; the scary music of pending doom made me shudder. I'd often position myself between my sisters or brothers to hide or find some kind of relief from the terror that blared from those horror flicks. But, hey, those were the bonding days of my siblings and I. I'll always relish them. But who knew that just around the corner of time during those teenage years, a man named Cassius Clay — the one who distracted me from my peaceful reading on that Friday—would actually have a profound impact on my personal and professional development.

I have to say it all began on a warm summer afternoon in July when that rhythmic enunciation… that distinctive voice radiated from the TV and demanded my attention beyond my book. I was captivated by this man's flamboyant delivery. He was alluring and I became temporarily hypnotized by his trash-talking rhetoric. My eyes and ears were peeled. Once I came back to myself I turned to my father and abruptly stated, "I'm going to know him."

Befuddled, my father said, "What? Why do you say that, daughter?"

"I don't know why," I said. "But I feel a spiritual connection to him. I just know that I'm going to meet him and have a relationship with him."

"That makes no sense, daughter!"

"Daddy, I know. It feels weird, but I really feel connected to him. I like him," I insisted.

"What do you mean you like him? You don't even know him. Do you have some sort of schoolgirl crush on this man?"

Frustrated for sure, my dad's tone was becoming a bit harsh. He was confused and I couldn't blame him. His brows were irreversibly crumpled as the exchange between us turned brash; not typical of our father/daughter time. I was about thirteen, and although we didn't have extremely conservative values as a family, keeping company with the opposite sex at my age was not permitted by my father. It wasn't even open for discussion.

Taken aback by my dad's harsh tone and the realization of where this discussion was going, I quickly said, "Daddy, it has nothing to do with any physical or romantic attraction." He nodded and said, "GOOD!" After that, he abruptly ended the conversation and left the room, but not before I got the chance to see his brows relax, and relief come back across his handsome face. I never got the opportunity to properly explain my feelings toward the charismatic Cassius Clay to my father that day. But there was one thing I was absolutely sure of-whatever I felt for that iconic boxer had nothing to do with a crush. I was attracted to his confidence. He seemed fearless—fearless to express his abilities, fearless to express his views. He exhibited the power that I had seen and respected in strong African-American men like my father.

In many ways Ali reminded me of my dad. They were both tall, attractive men with chiseled bodies that resembled the gods of Greek mythology. Both of them were charming, witty, and quite appealing to the ladies; thus their common trait—love of women.

Regardless of a woman's age, ethnicity, looks, or social status, Ali made every woman he met feel attractive and sought after. To be honest, it was not just the women. The Greatest—Muhammad Ali—could make absolutely anyone feel as though they were the most important person in the world.

Many years later, the man who blew the thirteen-year-old me away with his charisma and confidence changed his name to Muhammad Ali. Before his conversion he might have been the most celebrated heavyweight boxing champion of the world.Afterward he advanced to become a remarkable icon—a symbol of African-American pride.

African-Americans, and all nationalities alike, admired Ali's boxing capabilities and the extraordinary talent he had for marketing and promoting his fights. However, I knew this man represented a lot more. Ali's ability to capture global attention was a power to be seriously considered, whether he captured attention from admirers or individuals who harbored disdain for him. And, to think, I figured out this enigmatic ability of his at the tender age of thirteen. Nonetheless, this man was undoubtedly unique with a boxing style that befit his personality... *Float like a butterfly, sting like a bee.* Ali possessed the courage to stand for his convictions. Even when many Americans, both blacks and whites, lashed out in anger against him for denouncing his birth name (Cassius Clay), Ali persevered and emerged to the status of an American and international hero.

HOW I MET MUHAMMAD ALI

It was the summer of 1978. I was in my early twenties with a thriving career in the media industry. Today, I distinctly remember that evening. I was at the Philadelphia Art Museum for an event and there he was. Muhammad Ali — the global icon — the best of the best!

To think that I was in the same room with a legend of his stature was rather unbelievable, yet so real for me. It was a dream come true. My anticipation was being realized. The time that I'd hoped for was unfolding, which was to simply know this man, or at least get to see him once in my lifetime.

The thirteen-year-old me would have never imagined — not even in my wildest dreams — that I would be somewhere with Muhammad Ali *gawking* at me! Now, remember I mentioned that the great Ali had the power to make anyone at all feel like they're the most important person on the surface of this earth? Well, I felt the same way then. It's not that I was the prettiest woman present at the event, nor was I the most prominent personality in attendance. The Philadelphia Art Museum that evening was star studded. From elected officials to celebrities, all of Philadelphia's Who's Who were there that night, yet it was me that Muhammad Ali's gaze followed. Throughout the evening, I tried to avoid making eye contact with him, but Ali made his interest in me clear! At that time Ali was married to the extraordinarily beautiful Veronica Ali. On a scale of 1 to 10, I believe most men would have perceived her beauty as above the chart limit.

While I did not consider myself unappealing, I was intelligent enough to know that looks only take a woman so far. Hence, Ali's unexplained interest in me was obviously unsettling. As I continued to move about the large reception area as inconspicuously as I could, everywhere I went, I could feel Ali looking at me. While he mingled with notable personalities, I was determined not to catch his eye, to no avail. Ali didn't back down — he was determined to make sure I noticed him. I know this may seem like hyperbole, but I assure you, it isn't.

And, just to be clear, it wasn't like I was bothered by Ali's attention; on the contrary, it made me feel special even though I wasn't sure how to handle a situation like that. For goodness sake, he was a married man and this scene could be grossly misunderstood!

Of course I wanted to meet my hero and Muslim brother, however, I did not want him to have the wrong impression of me. I was already married with two children myself. I was also a successful businesswoman in my own right. I knew how important it was for a woman to maintain and present a professional demeanor in all aspects, and to be taken seriously by men in all walks of life—especially professional men. With that in mind, I continued to work the room. Suddenly, I felt a tap on my shoulder. "Rita!" someone happily said. I turned around to find a smiling dear friend, Andrea Shabazz, who greeted me with opened arms. Andrea and I had history and it had been years since I'd seen her. She and her husband, Minister Jeremiah Shabazz, had been traveling with Muhammad Ali.

Andrea and I had both converted to Islam as teenagers. We were both from the Germantown region of Philadelphia and shared a similar sense of humor. She was a pretty funny individual but kept it on the low when we were attending religious events, as we'd been constantly involved in activities serving the Muslim community of Philadelphia. Now, I'm not implying here that the Muslim community is against the idea of having fun or a good laugh. It's just that attending Islamic services and/or working on community projects required us to be serious and dedicated to the cause. Fortunately, Andrea and I had a sisterhood that exceeded religious ties.

Upon seeing her again my memory blessed me with the pleasant recall of when we would occasionally get together outside of the *Masjid* to relax and enjoy each other's company. Needless to say, I was pleased to see her again. Unfortunately, it was also getting late and I had to inform Andrea that I was preparing to leave. I had parked my car near City Hall, where I had attended a meeting earlier that day, and it would have taken me a while to walk there and then drive back home. She said, "We're getting ready to leave, too, and can give you a ride back to your car, if you'd like."

"*Perfect,*" I thought, giving her an affirmative nod. I had already seen her husband, Jeremiah, moving about the event, so I naturally assumed that by "we" she meant her and her husband.

Soon, Andrea and I left the event and went outside to wait for her driver to bring the car around, and for her husband to come meet us outside. Honestly, now that I was leaving for home, there was a part of me that was somewhat disappointed because I felt that I missed a golden opportunity. This could have been the first and probably the only chance to at least meet Muhammad Ali. "*After all, when will I ever have the chance to be in his presence again,*" I thought.

I didn't mention my disappointment to Andrea. I simply chalked it up to an experience that just wasn't meant to be after all. Just as I made peace with that thought, Minister Jeremiah and Muhammad Ali walked toward where Andrea and I were stationed. I was seated on a partition outside the art museum when Ali came and sat next to me.

Being the playful type, Ali started making frivolous conversation, which incited smiles and laughter. Within those few seconds of laughter between the two of us, we'd developed a bond. We were still laughing when he suddenly placed his hand on my thigh. Quickly, in mid-chuckle, I grabbed his hand and removed it. Obviously, there was no way I was going to let the Champ get away with that sort of inappropriate touching. At the same time I felt it was important to correct him in a way that would not offend him, if possible. If not, I was prepared to stop his unwanted and unsolicited advances at any cost.

We continued our verbal sparring with humorous jabs until Ali made another clumsy attempt at seducing me. Naturally, I rejected his advancement again. This prompted him to turn to Andrea: "She's a smart girl, isn't she? I bet she's a college girl, right?"

Before I had a chance to digest Ali's comment, Andrea responded, "Yeah, she's real smart. She has her own radio segment on WDAS radio and writes a column for the *Philadelphia Tribune.*"

Ali said, "I could tell she was big stuff from seeing her inside. It seemed like all the big shots knew her. So that's what it is. She's too smart for me," Ali interjected as he grabbed me around my shoulder with one arm and pulled me toward him. Pulling away from the Champ, I said, "It's not that I'm so smart, it's just that I'm not stupid enough to fall for your shit." It was not my intention to insult him, but I knew I had to put him in his place and stop his physical advances toward me.

As an ambitious columnist, TV/radio show producer and event planner, I was quite aware that developing a rapport with The Greatest would enhance my career. Thus, I wasn't sure that rejecting his flirtatious overtures would result in me being able to book him as a guest on the Georgie Woods Show, which I produced. However, I did manage to get Georgie an interview with Ali!

I knew Ali was a hot commodity and any chance of working with him would boost my career to new heights. Nonetheless, I still opted to establish boundaries—loud and clear.

Shortly after my verbal chastisement, I thought that there was no way a man of Ali's status would accept such rejection. To my utter surprise and absolute delight, the Champ was not turned off. As a matter of fact, he burst out in robust laughter. "You're all right, sister! I like you. That was pretty good!" he said, referring to my comeback statement about not putting up with his shit. Comforted by his remark, we continued conversing with each other, joined by Minister Jeremiah and Andrea.

Though the ride back to where I parked my car was short—less than ten minutes or so—it was a memorable experience that I never expected would lead to the development of a genuine friendship between Muhammad Ali and me.

Ali insisted on staying in touch with me. We exchanged phone numbers right before I got out of the car. Surprisingly, Ali got out of the limousine and walked me to my car, which was only a few feet away. "Let's stay in touch," he said, leaning over the top of my opened car door.

"Absolutely," I replied with a smile.

"I mean it, sister. I'm going to call you," he said. "Okay. I mean it too," I reiterated as he closed the car door for me.

Although I had been in the presence of numerous celebrities before, I had never been one to be caught off guard in a star-struck stupor. Meeting Muhammad Ali was no different.

Admittedly, I was overwhelmed with racing thoughts. Ideas of working with the Greatest literally seized my thoughts as I drove home. Without a doubt, I wanted the personal and professional gains of being associated with Ali, but it may shock some to learn that primarily I was more focused on what I could do with Ali to elevate the African-American and Muslim community.

From my perspective, the opportunity to merely hang around a celebrity was never appealing. Anything short of participating in some sort of activity that positively impacted the public was a waste of time, in my opinion. Moreover, I was no groupie nor did I ever want to be perceived as such.

Despite Ali's insistence that he would call me, I really didn't expect him to. However, he did follow up with calling me on occasion, extending invitations for me to attend Deer Lake (Ali's training camp in Deer Lake, Pennsylvania) and other venues in his honor.

In any event, Ali's demonstration of regard for me put me in the loop with his entourage. If not him, some member of his immediate group was sure to invite me to various events wherein Ali was featured.

Attending such events was interesting and wonderful, but it began to consume too much of my time. I just couldn't spare it being that I was still a working columnist and radio producer, not to mention a business proprietor. As a consequence, I could only attend certain activities.

BEING PART OF MUHAMMAD ALI'S OUTER CIRCLE

Working in the field of public relations and being a part of the Philadelphia elite, it was common for me to run into a variety of celebrities from the sports arena, music industry, and others. I knew many of them personally and/or professionally.

People, like the amazingly talented Teddy Pendergrass, Harold Melvin and the Blue Notes, Billy Paul, and Phyllis Hyman were often spotted going about their business through the streets and byways of Philadelphia. Even Philadelphia's pride and joy, the fabulous and legendary Patti LaBelle, had no problem running into fans throughout the city. I had been in her presence but never had the privilege of personally knowing the queen.

I would be remiss not to mention music legends Kenny Gamble and Leon Huff, who introduced the Philly sound of R&B music to the world. The ability to access individuals of this caliber definitely contributed to my success as a producer, columnist, and my public relations and event planning professions. Similar to Ali, these individuals treated admirers with respect and exhibited appreciation for the public at large.

It would be fair to say that my encounters with various celebrities from Philadelphia set a precedent for me when it came to interacting with other international figures. Nonetheless, I was ill-prepared for the level of enthusiasm Ali generated morale among people, particularly among other notables.

Undoubtedly, Ali was a star among stars. He brought out an array of famous people who sought to be in his presence no matter where he went. I witnessed this fervor firsthand when I attended an affair honoring the Greatest in Harlem, New York.

Minister Jeremiah and Andrea had invited me to attend a tribute to the Champ with them. As part of the extended entourage, we had attended several other events in his honor earlier that day before ending up at the Apollo Theater for the final tribute of the evening. The waiting room was packed with celebrities, as well as state and city officials. I could see Harry Belafonte, Fred Wilkinson, and Donna Summers from where I stood. Also present was LaWanda Page—the actress who played Aunt Esther with comedian Redd Foxx, who played Fred Sanford in the popular sitcom *Sanford and Son*. Seemingly, they were all just as delighted to be around Ali as the regular folk were. Looking up from a seated position in response to hearing someone call my name, I saw Eddie Kendricks, formerly a member of the R&B group The Temptations, come into view.

"Hey, Rita, what's up?" Eddie said, walking toward me.

"You!" I stated with a laugh.

The number of people I knew personally in that crowded room was limited to only a few, so I was ecstatic to see Eddie. I had not seen him in a few years. Prior to this encounter, I had only made his acquaintance on minimal occasions — but he was a familiar face and I was still happy to see him. Eddie coming over and holding a conversation with me took some of the edge off that I felt because of being around so many powerful people — some had relevance in my life, but most did not.

In our brief conversation, Eddie informed me that he would be coming to Philly soon and performing at a club there. "Why don't you come as my guest and bring your sister?" he asked.

Upon determining that I would be in town during that time, I happily accepted his invitation. We chatted a little bit more, mostly about professional undertakings and mutual acquaintances, until we were interrupted by a commotion from across the room.

"Oh, no! Y'all better hold me! I'm going to have to kill a nigger in here tonight!" we heard. Turns out, it was Ali contributing to the buzz of overlapping conversations already taking place in the room. I had never seen or heard Ali make such a scene. I was perplexed. What was this man up to?

I looked over at Eddie to see that he was just as confused as I was. We obviously discontinued our conversation and were drawn to the shenanigans of the Champ. By now he had captured the attention of every single person in the room.

Immediately several men from Ali's entourage rushed over to him. Surrounding the Champ, they pleaded with him, "Don't do it, Champ! Don't do it! It's not worth it!" They repeated their plea several times over.

In what appeared to be a true display of uncontrolled emotional posturing by Ali, he began to turn his focus in my and Eddie's direction. You could hear a pin drop among the numb crowd. By then, it was obvious that his outrage was directed toward us. Confirming our suspicion and to our embarrassment, Ali's performance was actually meant to get our attention. Ali proceeded to make it clear that he was talking only to Eddie now.

"Get up off your knees, nigger! I said GET — UP — OFF — YO — KNEES!" Ali chanted in a fiery cadence.

At this point he was standing directly over Eddie, who was kneeling down on the side of the chair I was sitting in, with one of his arms resting on the arm of the chair. Eddie looked up at the Champ with a frown and obvious dislike for his behavior. Eddie asked, "What are you talking about?"

"That's right, I'm talking to you. Look at you, on your knees trying to get with her," Ali blurted out. I was still trying to comprehend what Ali meant by that, when he roared again. "You can't have that! You can't get her. I'm the heavyweight champ of the world! Of the world! And I couldn't get her! And you ain't nothing but a little Temptation," declared Ali.

"Ah, get out of here, Ali, with that nonsense. It's nothing like that. I was just telling her about my show," Eddie said with a chuckle because he'd realized that the Champ was just messing with him, and with me for that matter. Suddenly, just as abruptly as Ali brought the focus of attention to Eddie and me, he turned and walked back into the crowd and took all that attention with him. "I'll see you in Philly, Rita," Eddie concluded. "Great, I'll see you then," I said as we parted ways.

Truth is I was a novice to some of Ali's comedic stunts. I was shocked because I had no idea that the guys holding him back were actually a part of the act. These men were used to picking up on cue and responding to Ali once he'd picked an unsuspecting person out of the crowd to playfully harass.

Just as I began to recover from being the target of Ali's theatrics, Ali came and sat on the arm of my chair. He placed his arm around the back of my chair and placed his hand on my shoulder. Suspicious now, I wondered what he was up to next. I braced myself for Ali's next antic but he sat silent, as I, too, said nothing. The next thing I knew, the press rushed toward us with a ton of questions.

"Who's the woman, Ali?" a reporter shouted.

Interspersed questions of the like filled the air. They became louder and faster. Suddenly camera lenses met my face and white flashes of light filled my batting eyes. Reporters were brutally curious. I'd never been more uncomfortable as everyone's attention was now focused on us. They were all pushing for an answer. I considered getting up and going to another area of the room. Somehow, I knew that wouldn't help and might make matters worse. Before I could collect my thoughts and figure out an exit, Ali blurted out, "She's the next Mrs. Ali."

On that note the press went into a frenzy like hungry sharks to fresh chum. Only this time, I was the bait and object of their interest. Everyone was startled by Ali's comment, including me!

Embarrassed, I nudged him with the butt of my elbow and insisted that he put an end to this immediately. I felt very uncomfortable and knew it showed in my face, which by now had turned red. "Ali, cut that crap out!" I said in a harsh whisper. "My husband will have a fit if he sees this!" Ali leaned in and whispered in my ear, "Shut up, fool. I'm going to make you a big nigger." Even though I was further shocked, something in me began to calm. In an instant, he turned to the press and said, "No, I'm just fooling around. She's a clean woman. She's my Muslim sister and she's smart too. She has her own radio show and writes a column."

In that precise moment, Ali had provided the curious press and everyone else in the room with a verbal résumé of my credentials — something that helped everyone around recognize the respect this man had for my virtues.

In reality he spoke so highly of me that no one questioned his word. They didn't question my abilities or me in any untoward way. Suddenly, I was known and I was accepted. Once he had pointed me out as a person worth knowing, he got up from the arm of the chair and circulated through the crowd again.

It had become quite obvious to me exactly what Ali intended

to convey. He meant precisely what he had whispered to me. He meant to make me a *big nigger* among the press and in the world of boxing. In fact, let's talk about that n-word.

It's easy to rush to insulting conclusions about this term. After all, it's been a contemptuous term used to insult black people at least since the eighteenth century. However, it is common knowledge that in the black community, *nigger* is used endearingly, giving it some neutrality. The sting from the term *nigger* returns when "outsiders" throw it at blacks as a negative, hate-laced term. But, as for Ali...aside from all the playing and his taunting me, my friend and brother in Islam simply wanted to boost my career, and he obviously didn't care about being publicly or politically correct.

More than anyone, Ali knew the difficulties women faced when trying to make their mark in the male-dominated sports medium and event-planning arena. It was a challenging hurdle to overcome, so he extended a helping hand to me by way of his renown. I was amazed by his love and consideration. Wow, he really wanted to help me. He might've had a rascally approach, but in retrospect I could see Ali's love and consideration for humanity, regardless. He'd consistently been a man who was selfless and devoted to helping individuals around him. I'm forever grateful that I was one of them.

Above all, his belief in servitude to Allah (SWT, *highly glorified is He*) was deeply held, which made him more phenomenal than ever. It was also evident that his interest in me did not stem from lust. No, it wasn't about my physical appearance-it was his recognition of my moral strength and the passion we both shared for helping others.

Relationships like the one shared between Ali and me don't go unnoticed. They attract both positive and negative attention. For as long as I knew Ali, there were and still are those who find it difficult to accept that our relationship was purely platonic. No explanation that I'll ever offer will be strong enough to raise the minds of these people from the gutter, but I'm confident that the pure in heart know the truth when they see or are confronted with it.

I was no stranger to the rumors and lies that our relationship generated — Ali and I were surrounded by half-truths, untruths and just plain lies on a continuum. However, the most hurtful slander came from members of Ali's entourage. That was something I wasn't prepared for, and it was quite disturbing. Despite how many times Ali confirmed that there was never any intimacy between us, I still became the target of hostility by those in Ali's camp. I recall the first time I was fully aware of the slander. It was during a trip to New Jersey.

I had accepted an invitation from Andrea to attend an event where Ali was to be honored. Jeremiah drove me and his wife to one of the locations where Ali was during the early part of the day. It so happened that the Champ was standing outside the hotel as we arrived. He was surrounded by a group of associates and fans seeking his attention.

When we pulled up and I exited the car, Ali showed his pleasure by acting up as always. When I took the first step in his direction, he began playfully pushing others to the side and panting as he headed full steam toward me. "I got to have her!" Ali chanted several times. When we made contact he reached out and pulled me into a great big never-ending bear hug. When he released me, he had a huge smile on his face as he officially greeted me with, "As-Salamu-Alykium sister" (peace be unto you). I naturally replied to him, "Walykium Salam."

By now, I had been in Ali's presence enough to feel comfortable with him making these moves on me and did not take any of it seriously. Others didn't see it the way I did. Not everyone could see or appreciate the humor or the genuine platonic bond shared between Ali and me.

It was on this occasion that I sensed Andrea's hostile attitude toward me. Throughout the duration of the day's activities and on the ride back home, it was obvious that she was giving me the cold shoulder.

It was during the same event that Andrea and Lana Shabazz, who was the official Chef for Muhammad Ali and author of a cookbook titled *Cooking for the Champ*, approached me to tell me something I obviously needed to know. "Everyone's saying that you're fooling around with Ali," she said. Lana seemed only too happy to offer that gossip.

I clearly recall how that affected me. It felt like someone had pierced my heart. It hurt so much that tears welled up in my eyes.

"No! No! How could they say that?" I responded.

On the ride back, in the car with Andrea and Jeremiah, I remained silent. We pulled into a gas station along the Pennsylvania Turnpike. When Jeremiah got out of the car to get gas, that gave Andrea an opportunity to scold me privately. "My husband and I are very disappointed with you!"

"Why?" I asked.

"WHY? You already know why! It's 'cause of the way you've been acting with Ali!"

"What? Ali?" My tone obviously suggested I had no idea what Andrea was referring to.

"Yeah. Letting him hug you and hit on you every time you get around him!"

"First of all, I didn't encourage Ali to do anything. You know that's how Ali plays with people," I said. "And you also know that there's nothing going on between me and him, with the exception of me being his Muslim sister and wanting to do the Muhammad Ali Day in Philadelphia. We are friends because of Islam!" I rebutted.

"Yeah, whatever. There's not going to be any Muhammad Ali Day in Philadelphia because my husband doesn't like you being around Ali with us!" she huffed.

"Okay," I said, trying not to show that I was extremely annoyed and insulted by her comments.

Regardless of my feelings at the time, I was aware that there was no reasoning with Andrea. Any attempts to discuss the matter further would surely lead to fire that we couldn't extinguish between the two of us. We'd had enough already during this short stop. By the time Jeremiah reentered the car, the conversation between Andrea and me had dwindled to nothing.

For the remaining forty-plus minutes of the ride back home, none of us said anything. The only verbal exchange came when I gave them the parting Islamic greetings, which only Jeremiah returned.

Once I was home, I mulled over the thoughts of not having any further contact with Ali. I felt a deep sense of disappointment for having to consider such a thing. The whole scenario was irretrievably messed up. Within minutes I'd lost my friend over virtually nothing, and I didn't even get a chance to accomplish anything major with the Champ.

Following that confrontation with Andrea, I was obviously not taking the whole situation well. The next day, I was at the beauty salon—the salon I owned. Now, salons are usually a place where women engage in conversations, both serious and frivolous. Until that day I had usually abstained from discussing my personal affairs with the staff and/or the customers there. But, that day I made an exception. I didn't care. I needed to vent. After explaining the situation in what turned out to be an open forum in the beauty salon, I was actually encouraged by the ladies' input.

The general consensus was that I shouldn't be dissuaded by the lies and gossip of those who may have negative agendas. These comments made me feel better, but what really jolted me back into a position of strength were the words of my sister. Zaynah, my younger sister, was also my business partner in the salon. And, by the way, her birth name was Shirley-her name was changed to Zaynah, an Islamic attribute for *beautiful*. Anyway, her styling station was on the other side of the room, directly across from mine. Unequivocally, she was a no-nonsense person and very protective of her older sister—*me*. As she listened to me rant on about the latest goings-on in the world of Ali and me, she took the verbal attack made on me, personally. Not to my surprise though.

"Let me say this," she interrupted the well-wishers commenting on the situation. "You've been around enough celebrities to know how people and their entourage huddle together to keep new people out. Ali's fondness of you obviously makes some people uncomfortable, even to the point of turning on you. This is the big league and if you're going to let innuendos and gossip crush you, then you don't belong in that environment. As long as you know the truth, don't worry about what anybody else says or feels. People are going to be jealous because Ali treats you special. Use that opportunity to accomplish your goals of doing something great for the Muslim community. That's what you set out to do. Now go ahead and do it. You've never been a weak person, so don't start being weak now. Go for it, sis!"

Her short speech was followed by the collective approval of everyone present. It was as if my sister's words awakened me. It was hard truth. It gave me the courage to take my power back and proceed with the Muhammad Ali Day Project in Philadelphia, come what may. I was going to make it happen with or without the support of Jeremiah and/or Andrea. Granted, I would have preferred to have their support, but their decisions to sever ties with me freed me to proceed without their interference.

Rita's Rule # 3

Never allow an impromptu verbal assault make you second-guess your values and therefore surrender your power to anyone, friend or foe. If you find yourself in such a position, take back your power even if it means severing close ties with friends.

OBTAINING ALI'S APPROVAL

Being relieved of the constraints of trying to accommodate the whims of others awarded me the opportunity to put my own plans in place for Muhammad Ali Day. I had to get Ali's signature on the agreement for his participation in the Muhammad Ali Day, and I found out that he was scheduled to be in Baltimore in a few days. *Excellent*, I thought. Baltimore was close, and this would be a good time to catch up with the Champ. Dreading making the trip alone, I called Porsche, who was a mutual friend of mine and Muhammad

Ali's. Having already discussed the matter with her, I'd gained her full support for the idea; she was a good person for the mission, and she was ready. "Well then, let's go down to Baltimore and get this done!" she said. In complete agreement, we headed to Baltimore. We had made arrangements to stay in the same hotel as Ali and his entourage.

As soon as we checked in and were headed to our room, we ran into Ali in the elevator. A surprised Ali hugged both of us. "As-Salamu-Alykium," he said to Porche before turning to me to ask where I was staying.

"I'm staying here," I replied.

"In my room?" was his comeback.

"Get outta here, Ali," I said. "No, fool, I'm not staying in your room. But I do want to talk to you."

"Yeah? What is it that you want to talk to me about?" he asked.

"I'll tell you later," I told him.

He was actually headed to his suite at that time, so he informed me of his suite number, and I told him, "I'll be down." At that point the elevator doors opened and Ali got out.

Before I got a chance to go down to his suite, Ali had called. "C'mon, you coming, sister?"

"Yeah, I'm coming," I said.

Porsche and I had barely gotten into our room before I had to rush right out. I thought I'd be able to just chill for a few. Considering that it was already after 10 PM and that Ali might be tired, I thought it best not to keep him waiting. I didn't even have time to freshen up a bit after the long drive before the phone rang again. It was Ali. "Are you coming or what?" he asked.

Okay, now I was really pressed for time. I threw off my coat, grabbed the room key, and quickly asked Porsche, "Are you coming?"

"Mmm, no. I need to shower first if I do. I had a little feminine accident during that long ride."

"Whew, girl. I understand that," I said. Presented with the choice to either delay an already anxious Ali and risk not accomplishing what I came down to Baltimore for, I opted to leave for Ali's suite right away. Right as I was getting ready to leave, my inner voice asked, *Are you cool going by yourself?* I said to myself, *Yeah. What's he gonna do? He won't do anything.*

Apparently, I was actually nodding my head or something as these thoughts rallied my mind. Porsche knew I was in deep thought about it. She laughed and confirmed my discernment when she asked, "Are you concerned about going to Ali's suite alone?"

"Not really, I'm sure he's harmless," I answered.

"I completely agree. Ali's nothing more than a flirt. You'll be fine," Porsche said.

I went downstairs and knocked on Ali's door. He opened the door with his robe on. Aside from being a bit taken by surprise at Ali's lack of attire, I was more surprised to learn that he was alone. Having been around him on several occasions, I had never experienced a time when no one was with him. Anyway, I couldn't tell whether he was wearing anything under the robe or not. But I knew he'd done a really quick change because I could see a shoe, a sock, pants, and underwear littered all the way to the bedroom.

Now this may sound crazy to some people, but even with everything that I was looking at, I didn't feel intimidated. Like most women, I had been hit on by so many men that I finally knew the difference between who was harmless and who was not. I wasn't afraid of Muhammad Ali. I wasn't the least bit fearful of Ali forcing himself on me or hurting me in any way—I knew he was never going to force me. In fact, I found the whole idea of it quite amusing.

Seeing Ali's clothes strewn about the floor, I smirked and said, "Really? C'mon, Ali, what are you up to?"

Like I said, Ali loved teasing people and I guess he really thought he had me this time with his latest stunt. "Sister, come on in. I'm just tired," he said.

I took his comment as an explanation for his questionable attire. I tried to conceal my amusement about his appearance, but it took all my strength to maintain a straight face. Admittedly, I still had no reservation about entering his suite. Respectful of Ali's acknowledgment of being tired, I was convinced that time was of the essence, so I proceeded to get right to the point. One moment I was saying, "Look, what I wanted to discuss was..." and the next moment Ali approached me for a romantic embrace.

"Okay, here we go," I thought. "Ali, stop fooling around! I'm not playing," I snapped at him.

"Oh. Okay. No problem, sister. I just thought that's what you wanted," he said as he quickly withdrew his attempt.

I nudged him on the shoulder with a soft fist and said, "No, fool. That's not what I want," and with that we both burst into laughter, which lightened the moment and brought our friendship back front and center. "I'm married," I managed to say, still laughing.

"Okay, good! I'm so tired I probably couldn't do anything anyway," he said in that infamous Muhammad Ali intonation. "So, what is it that you need?"

I told him about my agenda for coming to Baltimore, and he was very receptive to it. He was such a phenomenal person, and sought after by droves of women, so I believe, in his mind, he actually thought he was doing me a favor to approach me sexually. The propositions from women were endless, so I guess he thought that I was just taking a little longer than others to maneuver my way into his bed. I appreciated the fact that he respected my *no*.

Ali's taunting me was quite awkward for me in the beginning, but once I knew he meant no harm, his teasing became just another comical thing about him, to me. He kept me in stiches over his playful advances. One thing I can say is that the two of us enjoyed a great deal of laughter together.

I'm sure the obvious question is why would I, a married woman, willingly go to a man's suite at ten o'clock at night anyway if I wasn't hoping for, or at least, thinking about having sex with him? Friend or not, he was still a man. Friend or not, he was one of the most sought after men in the world. Friend or not, he was fine as hell, and...why not? He'd already asked me if I was coming alone — perhaps that was my clue. Why didn't I get it? Such questions are understandable particularly when you consider that many women have been sexually assaulted for doing less. Yes, I was shocked when he came to the door in his robe. And him being alone was the last thing I expected. I was fully prepared to talk about establishing Muhammad Ali Day with an audience of many — as usual. It wasn't until I saw the trail of clothes on the floor that I had a question about his intentions. It was obvious that he hadn't learned anything from his previous botched advancements toward me. By then, I still wasn't afraid because I'd come to handle business. Period. As opposed to feeling threatened, I felt empowered because I believed I held the trump card. To that point, I must assume some responsibility for Ali's mind-set, because my responses could have easily been perceived as flirtatious.

On a more serious note, I learned something about my friend Ali that day, and that is… he actually felt obligated to perform sexually for my benefit! Since he'd obliged a parade of others, he obviously believed that I'd feel rejected if I, a dear friend, wasn't ultimately included in the proverbial harem. In this regard Ali was no different than other famous powerful men who have their pick of feminine litters. At some point their experiences fueled by their egos suggest that all women want a sexual encounter with them.

I came to realize that Ali's constant teasing and taunting were a form of acknowledgment. I know from personal experience that Ali truly loved humanity and did his best to make the world a better place for everyone. That's just who Muhammad Ali was. He was a gentleman — one who was witty and humble. He paved a way for me in the world of boxing, holding my hand as I rose to a stature where I could write my own ticket to everywhere — whether it was to cover a boxing event or any other star-studded event taking place across the country or this world. My priority, however, was to see Muhammad Ali Day get off the ground. After attending a tribute to him hosted by boxing promoter Murad Muhammad, in Newark years before, I had to have this dream realized for my friend the Champ. All the other incidents paled in comparison to this.

3

A PREVIEW TO THE MUHAMMAD ALI DAY IN PHILADELPHIA

Murad Muhammad was an accomplished boxing promoter even though he mostly operated out of Newark, New Jersey. I had the chance to attend one of his charitable galas featuring Muhammad Ali as the celebrity guest. The event was concluded with a mock boxing match between then governor of New Jersey, Brendan Byrne, and Muhammad Ali. Totally astounded is the best way to describe my reaction to the entire production. The event also included a parade and a VIP reception attended by a distinguished array of A-list celebrities. I must say the event left me wide-eyed and inspired. Hence, Muhammad Ali Day was born, but it had to be done Philadelphia style.

In what seemed like an uphill battle, I was out to get Muhammad Ali the honor and recognition he deserved—*not that he needed it!* I just wanted him honored in the city hall of Philadelphia and celebrated as the monumental icon that he was.

Every now and then city officials would hold events in the mayor's reception room honoring worthy individuals. Muhammad Ali was a Muslim of world renown—and the most notable personality on the planet at that time. He deserved to be honored in City Hall.

I had connections. I knew people and wanted very much to put that to use to get that outcome for Ali. So, at one of the meetings with the Champ, I asked him if he would be willing to participate in a ceremony such as the one he had done in Newark, New Jersey, with Murad Muhammad. When he said yes, I was thrilled! Upon Muhammad's agreement, I took it upon myself to contact the city officials. This part was done before Andrea and I had our ill-fated fallout.

More determined than ever to pull off a spectacular event, I began developing all the plans for that day. First a Muhammad Ali Day committee was formed to oversee the planning and execution of the entire affair, of course.

Next, I commissioned a life-size and a half-sculptured bust of Ali. However, after the grand Muhammad Ali Day was over, although he loved and appreciated it, the sculpture did not go home with Ali. He graciously permitted me to donate it for a great cause. Today the magnificent works of art rest in the Philadelphia African American Cultural Museum, under the name Rita Spicer — my previous name.

Nonetheless, with Andrea gone because of our disagreement, I had no real allies from Ali's camp supporting me with the event, with the exception of Gene Kilroy.

At that time, Brendan Byrne was the mayor of Philadelphia. I was acquainted with the mayor because of my affiliations with city and state elected officials. After contacting Mayor Green about Muhammad Ali Day, I was put in contact with a member of the mayor's public relations team and received a cold reception from the front person, a woman who was not happy to hear from me. I was aware that I could not accomplish much over the phone based on her response, so I went over to meet her in person to discuss the details of the event. A couple of members of the Muhammad Ali Day committee accompanied me.

Just to be clear, what I sought to accomplish was to have the Pennsylvania commonwealth and the city of Philadelphia, proclaim a specific date as Muhammad Ali Day throughout.

The representative from the mayor's public relations team

insisted that the plan could not go forth if I did not provide her proof that Muhammad Ali would actually be present at the event.

"Okay, I can do that," I said.

Next, with a curt monotone, she asked, "So, who is the person that can offer this proof?"

"You're looking at the person that can offer proof," I responded.

"I need Muhammad Ali to speak to me personally about it," she said.

Unmoved, I said, "That's not gonna happen." Since I was the person representing Muhammad Ali on this occasion, my word was golden and it was final. With documented signatures of approval in hand, from Ali himself, I further told her, "Either you accept these or you don't."

Back then I was still working as a producer for the top-rated Georgie Woods Show. Georgie Woods was known for promoting major music events in his early career. During his tenure as a radio disc jockey, he was recognized throughout the country for elevating artists into the mainstream music industry—helping them make their music legendary in the city of Philadelphia and beyond. Ever since I'd come up with the idea of Muhammad Ali Day, Georgie was in the loop when it came to planning and the progress and he wanted to help however he could. Everyone at WDAS was interested in helping me promote the event however they could. In fact, that was the general reaction of whoever found out that I was pushing for the celebration of Muhammad Ali Day on the state and city level. But this woman, the representative from the mayor's office, seemed to remain completely nonchalant about the whole prospect. I'd become very annoyed with her condescending attitude.

Later, after contacting several people from City Hall, Georgie came to me and said, "Listen, Mayor Green will approve the day and he wants to be a part of it. He will agree to give Muhammad Ali the proclamation and present it to him at City Hall, but he didn't want to do it right now because he thinks it might interfere with some of the things he's trying to achieve."

I listened intently and became annoyed by what was purely nonsensical runaround. "All right, Georgie," I began, "since you just delivered a message to me from Mayor Green, give him a message back from me. You tell Mayor Green that I'm tired of playing games in this city and it doesn't matter whether they accept Muhammad Ali and give him the accolades that should be bestowed upon him; it truly doesn't matter whether they do it or not! I am going to have the leader of the Muslim community declare Muhammad Ali Day and then I'm going to use my media affiliates in radio and other associated press to ask the mayor why he refused to honor the most noted person on the planet who just happens to be a Muslim and African-American. They will have to explain that!"

Rita's Rule # 4

Always be willing to walk away from any negotiation, particularly if the other side is being unreasonable, or worse, insulting, especially when you know you hold the trump.

Worst-case scenario, I knew that I did not need for city or state officials to declare Muhammad Ali Day. He was such a phenomenal icon that the people would come to anything honoring him and line the streets just to get a glimpse of him. Holding firm to my conviction paid off. Soon after that encounter I got a call from City Hall. It was the deputy mayor, speaking on behalf of Mayor Green, saying, "The day has been approved. If there is anything that the mayor's office can do to assist you with Muhammad Ali Day, we'll do it." My demeanor was cool, but I was jumping up and down on the inside!

On the heels of this long-awaited for news, I was contacted by the mayor's representative of community affairs who then invited me to attend a ceremony that was going to take place in City Hall prior to Muhammad Ali Day just so that I could get an experiential idea of how to pull this off. I accepted the invitation. It was a lovely event held in honor of Patti LaBelle.

After the ceremony, the representative asked me, "Is there anything you can think of that you would want to do differently or something that should be added to Muhammad Ali Day? How would you like to proceed forward with the day?"

"No. Everything seems great," I said. "I liked the tribute to Patti LaBelle and the presentation, but I do feel you needed to beef up the security much more for Muhammad Ali. I'd also like a piano brought in, because I want to have someone singing 'The Greatest' — Muhammad Ali's song," I replied.

"Okay," she said. A few days later she called me back. "Listen, as for the security, the mayor in collaboration with the police department has that covered. They're used to doing it all the time."

"I appreciate that," I said. "I've been to Muhammad Ali ceremonies, and by comparison, the security they had at Patti LaBelle's ceremony would not have worked for Ali. So, again, thank you." Again, the representative assured me that the security would be adequately covered, so I decided to trust her on that.

Ali arrived in Philadelphia for Muhammad Ali Day accompanied by his entourage and his wife. I was there to receive them at the hotel. Seeing Veronica accompanying Ali for the event made my heart glad. I was pleased to see her there with her husband and that the event was something she obviously considered important enough to attend.

Later that morning I had to accompany Ali to McGonigle Hall on the campus of Temple University for an event open to the public where anyone and everyone could come and see the Champ. As we approached the area we saw hordes of fans already in place. More specifically, we spotted a crowd of kids on the corner of Broad Street and Vine. Seeing them Ali yelled, "Stop the car!" As soon as the limo came to a halt, Ali jumped out and began shadowboxing over the kids' heads. The kids couldn't contain their awe and surprise.

"WHAT? Muhammad Ali!" they shouted.

Their wide eyes told a touching story. It was obvious that they were living a dream in that moment as the Champ was in front of them playfully throwing punches. It was truly an amazing spectacle. Before long, droves more people rushed to the corner of Broad Street, and now there was a huge tight crowd circling around Ali, with more hurrying in from every direction. Ali always generated that kind of fervor among the people.

We reached McGonigle Hall and I noticed a woman there, apparently expecting us—obviously wanting to see Ali. She was of light complexion with attractive features. The reason I still remember her so clearly is because I'd overheard Ali and one of the members of his entourage discussing her. The part of the discussion I'd picked up on was Ali's past involvement with the woman. I didn't know the whole story, but it definitely appeared more than a joke among the men. She came over to Ali, talked to him in brief, then walked away. After that, Ali turned to me and said, "Hey, sister, do you have any extra tickets to tonight's event?"

"Yeah," I said.

Pointing to that same woman, he said, "You see that sister over there? Give her a ticket for tonight. Make sure she comes to the event."

"No," I replied.

"NO? What do you mean no?" Ali said.

"No," I repeated.

"I thought you said you have tickets," he said as confusion knitted his brows.

"I do [have tickets], but I'm not giving that woman a ticket to the event. You guys were just laughing about how you've been with her! For God's sake, your wife is here! Listen, she too is my guest and being a married woman myself, I wouldn't want my host inviting a woman that my husband has been with, in the past, to an event I'm going to be at," I explained.

Ali did not take kindly to my defiance. He did not like what I'd said or the force with which I'd said it. Never before this spat had Ali been upset or aggravated by me, or something I'd said. He'd always been genuinely kind toward me—until that day.

It was time to leave the venue and move on to the next agenda on schedule. As we were leaving the hall, Ali said, matter-of-fact, "You're just jealous."

"Jealous?" I said. "I'm not jealous!"

"Yes, you are. You're an old hag. You're just jealous that you can't have me, so you want nobody else to have me," he said.

"No. I'm not jealous at all," I said, trying to cool myself down.

He was really aggravated and it wasn't about the woman — there were plenty of them vying for his attention. It was more about the fact that I'd actually said no to him.

"Look, Ali, I'm not your pimp. That's something those guys would do. I'm certainly not one of them," I said.

"You know you're just jealous. You're just an old hag," Ali repeated, dismissing me altogether. He didn't even ride back with me in the limousine. He took the other limousine with other people who had accompanied us.

Rita's Rule # 5

A strong stand is always better than a weak fold. Principle matters even if it severs ties in the short run or permanently. Never permit anyone or personal ambitions to prompt you to lower your standards.

MUHAMMAD ALI DAY AT LAST

It was finally Muhammad Ali Day in Philadelphia and the Champ was being honored in my hometown. I was pleased that I had actually made it happen. Words cannot describe the sense of accomplishment I felt, but there was disappointment on the horizon that day too.

Amid the festivities, we were supposed to have lunch across the street from City Hall, but when we attempted to leave the mayor's Reception Room, we became wedged by the crowd; the hallway was packed with people. Our movement was completely hampered and exiting the room was impossible.

Although the police and our assigned security had designated a secret exit for us to leave City Hall, that became unlikely because it was filled with city employees. As a result it took us an hour to make it across the street—AN HOUR! The security arrangement was totally inadequate.

As we'd begun to make our way, the people were overzealous about seeing the Champ up-close and they began chanting his name; a cheerful frenzy overtook the masses of people. I must admit it was exhilarating to watch and hear.

I wasn't a novice in all this. I had witnessed similar scenes back in Harlem, where people flooded the streets and took down barriers just to catch a glimpse of their hero. It would take us double sometimes triple the amount of time to make it from one place to another. The mayor and his office finally realized that too—a bit too late for my liking—but eventually, I was proven right. They were obviously caught off guard, despite me giving them a heads-up about the situation and the serious need for adequate security.

So, the evening sessions went off without any further hitches. It turned out to be a beautiful event. Ali had a really good time. After the whole affair was over, we were assembled in the banquet hall along with the Muhammad Ali Day community, Ali, his wife, his entourage, people from the mayor's office, as well as my own family.

MUHAMMAD ALI & MY KIDS

Ali, his wife Veronica, and members of his entourage had arrived on the eve of Muhammad Ali Day. It was the first time they'd met my children, Kiki, who was barely four, and Azim, who was six. The Champ showed genuine love and affection for both children immediately. This wasn't unusual for him, as I had seen him positively engage other children numerous times. Upon being introduced to my kids, Ali began to hug on them and entertain them. My son was fascinated with Ali's illusion of levitating several inches off the floor. Ali had another trick that he continuously played on Azim. He would place his hand behind Azim's ear and create a buzzing sound like a bee. Somehow he even caused a juddering feeling, which made my little boy really think there was a bee threatening to get in his ear. Ali did it so well it often made people jump, too! When it came to Kiki, Ali couldn't resist covering her with kisses and hugging her tight with every opportunity. At age four Kiki wasn't having it. When she'd had enough Kiki would smash her little hands in his face and push him away and say, "Stop, Dahammad!" She couldn't pronounce Muhammad. Dahammad was the best my little girl could do.

"Y'all see that? She's a heartbreaker already," Ali said, grinning big. "She already knows how to break a man's heart!" There were many pranks and games he'd play with the kids all the time. Nonetheless, his love and concern for them was obvious.

*   *   *

During the dinner portion of Muhammad Ali Day, Kiki presented a bouquet of flowers to Veronica.

Kiki was so little, she had to be held up on the table so that the audience could see her flower presentation. Ali and Veronica's sentiment was made obvious by the expression on their faces. After that, Ali scooped Kiki into his arms and started kissing her. Once again she cried out, "Stop it, Dahammad!"

"She's just like her mother. She's learned early how to wrap men around her little finger. She's going to be a killer. She's a fox!" said Ali as he ignored her demands with continued kisses all over her little face.

Once everything was wrapped up, Ali sat next to me. The people were leaving and I was completely drained. Ali sat quietly awhile, then said to me, "Sister, I've been honored many and plenty times, but never with the love that you put into this event. Thanks, sister. It was a great day."

"You're more than welcome, and thank you," I said. He gave me a hug right before leaving with Veronica to retire for the evening in the presidential suite I had reserved for them. I made sure to see them off the next morning as they departed to return to Deer Lake.

FRIENDS, ACQUAINTANCES & FOES

It's interesting to add how Andrea wasn't the only one whose affection I'd lost. There were others too.

In the interim of organizing Muhammad Ali Day, I knew there would be many more occasions wherein I would see Ali. Of course this entailed being in a hostile environment comprised of Ali's immediate associates—most of whom were obviously not happy with me being around.

After my relationship with Andrea became strained, I felt distant from others in the group as well. I had nurtured a friendly relationship with most of Ali's entourage, but all that was reworked with time. Among others, who had suddenly turned hostile toward me, was Lana Shabazz. Remember, Ali's chef and author of *Cooking for the Champ*? Lana was one of two individuals in the entourage I developed a true affection for. She was like a mother to my sister, Zaynah, and me. The other was Ali's business manager, Gene Kilroy. He was a strong Irishman with international ties to some of the world's most powerful individuals. My relationship with him was comforting, particularly after the falling-out between Andrea and me. Again, I'd met Lana and Gene during my first visit to the Deer Lake training camp. The aroma of Lana's delectable nutritious meals filled the air from a distance; certainly on the way to the chow hall.

The Deer Lake Camp had a gym equipped with a boxing ring that was used by the boxers for sparring. There were also several cabins for visiting lodgers and a personal cabin for Ali and his family. Ali's lodging was situated in the mountains and structured in rustic log cabin style. The eating area had an extended dining table, constructed entirely of wood, and accommodated at least a dozen people during mealtime.

Though I never accepted Lana's invitation to join Ali and the staff for meals while visiting the camp, she always offered. By no means was I turning down her amazing meals, I was just always in a rush to get back to work, especially when I was pulling MAD (Muhammad Ali Day) together. I loved her dearly. So much so that I welcomed her with open arms to my home when she came through Philly. Staying in a hotel was out of the question. It was during those times that Lana developed a close relationship with my sister Zaynah even though we'd all known each other a short time. She even proclaimed Zaynah's daughter, Asia, as her godchild.

Zaynah and I spent hours listening to Lana's stories about her countless escapades while on the road with the Champ. We held Lana in profound regard right along with our mother. In fact, Lana was held in high regard by everyone in the camp, without exception. Lana was no stranger to my promotional abilities and professional standing, particularly in the Philadelphia area. When it came to promoting her cookbook, she recruited me to stir up some publicity for her. Without hesitation I gladly took that wheel! I booked her on exclusive local TV and radio shows in Philly. The written acknowledgment of appreciation for my efforts and helping her market her product spoke volumes about our close-knit relationship. At least I thought so.

It was during one of my visits to the camp that I sensed a cold new kind of reception from her. Initially, I didn't see any reason to take it personally, as there was no cause for her to be hostile toward me. However, her curt behavior persisted over an extended period of time, every time I was in her presence. She'd become a different person altogether.

Granted, Lana was obviously old enough to be my mother. I had to maintain the same level of respect for her that I had in my heart for my own mother. I wanted to maintain it but she was making it difficult. Strangely, while she appeared to increase a negative disposition toward me, she never failed to treat Zaynah with genuine love and affection.

Apparently, whatever was bothering her was directed solely in my direction. Finally, after more of her brute behavior towards me, she admitted her anguish to me.

"I've been meaning to say something to you for a while," she expressed, placing her hands on her hips.

"Really? What?" I asked.

"Well, people think you're after Ali," she began.

Annoyed by her comment, my response was firm, but respectful.

"People. Does that include you? I really expected better than that from you," I said. I shook my head and walked away, annoyed as hell. I knew people were talking behind my back, but for Lana to have a bit in it, too, was a major disappointment. I always believed she held a more respectable opinion of me than to even bring up such nonsense.

Leaving Lana behind, as I made my way to the parking area, I ran into Gene Kilroy. As usual, he greeted me. "As-Salamu-Alykumm sister. Where you rushing off to? Are you okay?" he said.

"Not really," I huffed and went on to tell him why.

"I heard it from a few people, too," he said. "Don't worry about it. A lot of people around [here] don't want to see positive and sincere people around Ali. Can you just imagine what I go through being a white man, trusted by Ali?" Gene really put forth kindhearted effort to convince me not to give mind to the dirty politics practiced by some members of Ali's immediate team. His comments managed to erase some of the grump from me and drew a smile on my face instead. "Thanks so much for those words of encouragement," I said as I turned to leave the camp.

The brewing negativity eluded me. My fallout with Andrea had been a hard pill to swallow, but severing ties with Lana would be even harder. Who would be next? Yes, in fact, Muhammad Ali and I had become close friends a little too soon for the liking of others in the entourage. Yes, in fact, Ali trusted me—blindly. And, yes, he was happy—more like thrilled to pieces—to see me each time I was in his presence.

TWO DOWN, HOW MANY LEFT TO GO?

It was during my visit to Deer Lake Camp to see Ali for a promo for MAD that Lana and I severed our ties and put distance between us. I'll never forget all that was going on around that time.

I had walked in with a contract dangling low in my hand. Members of the entourage were seated, scattered about the area, including Jeremiah Shabazz. I walked through them and found my way to Ali, my focus. I sat on the sofa next to Ali and I said to him: "Look, here's the contract I need you to sign." Without a thought, he took the contract and pen from my hands and was about to sign it when I interjected, "No, Ali, you need to read it first!"

"No, I don't need to read it," he replied.

"Then let me read it to you," I said, taking the contract from his hand. I began to read it to him until he interrupted me. "Sister, I don't need you to read it for me. I can read for myself. I don't need you to read the contract for me. I trust you."

I knew he wasn't merely sopping me with honeyed words. I knew he truly trusted me, but I still wanted him to read it for himself. At that moment, I could feel the tension resonating from the onlookers in the room. Ali seemed oblivious to it. "No, Ali, you still need to read it," I stressed to no avail. Ali ignored me nicely and signed the contract sight unseen. Or I should say, words unread.

That level of trust coming from Muhammad Ali was an honor that gave me pride and dignity. I cherish it still today. He was my brother who I never had intentions of harming in any way whatsoever. Unfortunately, what was a moment of pride for me became a moment of jealousy and disapproval from others in the room. It wasn't just Lana, or Andrea, or Jeremiah. By now I could sense the negative energy whenever I was in the presence of Ali's entourage, as a whole.

After Ali signed the contract, I rose to my feet as if I was the only other person in the room beside him, and walked out of the common area, past the staring faces...past the snivels...past the obvious, unspoken disgust. I could feel them peering at me as their stares followed me all the way outside. Once I was outside, the uneasiness didn't stop there. I'd nearly gotten to my car when I passed by this Native American guy named Lloyd Wells. He was a huge, tall, bulky dude with light brown skin and straight dark silky hair. I'd seen him before and never felt right in his presence. I'd always gotten ill vibes from him. He repulsed me in every way, so I'd never spoken to him.

Rita's Rule # 6

Never validate a fool as relevant by giving them any attention. Avoid looking at them, or even in their direction if possible. In this case, less is best. Only adhere to the minimum social norms of returning a hello if a fool offers it first. Your silence will speak volumes and relegate a fool to a position of insignificance.

As I walked past him I heard him whisper something, but by that time I'd learned not to pay much attention to those things. I didn't even bother to pursue any clarity. I didn't care what he'd said. The best part is, my chilling feeling toward Lloyd was later validated when I learned that his claim to fame was taking filthy pictures of women and setting up orgies, along with a number of other immoral, unethical activities. So, my inclination to never talk to him or warm up to him was right!

By then I just wanted to get in my car and disappear from every negative vibe in or around that camp. As far as I was concerned, Ali was the dearest thing in there.

Later that day, I got a call from a very excited Lana Shabazz, which surprised me since she had all but stopped speaking to me. "Girl! You will not believe what just happened," she said.

"What?" I asked, half curious.

"Gene Kilroy just knocked Lloyd Wells out!"

"W-H-A-A-T? What happened?" I asked.

Lana then narrated the whole story. Apparently, Lloyd had

said to Gene, "Rita thinks she's so high and mighty. She thinks everybody doesn't know that she's after Ali." To which Gene said, "No, no, she's a good sister; she's a clean, good Muslim sister." The two men got into a heated argument, which led to Lloyd throwing a punch at Gene. Evidently, Gene dodged the punch and took a swing at him with full reflex that knocked Lloyd unconscious.

That was one piece of gossip about me that Gene was not going to tolerate! The funny thing is Gene never told me this story personally, but he did confirm it when we spoke face-to-face later. "No, sister," he said, "I wasn't going to let anyone talk like that about you because I know better than that. I even told Lloyd that Ali emphatically states that he's never had any sort of sexual encounter with you. And everyone knows that Ali kisses and tells. That being said, Ali has never mentioned you in that way, so it's clear that he's never touched you! But, Lloyd, being the petty pervert that he is said, 'It was probably because the sex was so good, and you told Ali if he told anyone that you wouldn't give him no more.'" Evidently that disgusted Gene to no end and caused their arguing to escalate to fisticuffs.

Initially, when I heard Gene's account of what happened and what Lloyd Wells had said about me, I wanted to go back and slap him in the face. Defaming my character in that manner angered me to the point of wanting more than Lloyd getting knocked out by Gene. The audacity of this pig of a man speaking about any woman like that, let alone someone he knew nothing about, was appalling. Even more contemptible was that the men Lloyd said it to claimed to be Muslims and they allowed him to make such an unpardonable statement about a Muslim woman. If they were in fact Muslim, and that's questionable, there's no way they were from Philly. Regardless of what Islamic denomination, Philadelphia Muslim men would never have tolerated Lloyd's remarks about any Muslim sister. Lloyd would have learned an undisputable lesson. The message would have been so compelling that he would fear the mere mentioning of any women again. In retrospect, I'm glad I didn't act on my feeling and elected to just leave the camp. Had I gotten into any sort of confrontation with a man beneath my dignity, it would have made Lloyd happy. It would've conveyed a concept that he mattered. Instead of indulging Lloyd, I opted to ignore him altogether.

Rita's Rule # 7

You can't kill a thing by keeping it alive. Meaning it's important to let things go and move on with life. This has definitely been an empowering motto that I have applied throughout turbulent situations.

Gene going on the defensive on my behalf to the point of knocking out Lloyd was significant in my eyes. Some of Ali's entourage, and others around him, were misfits who had been ostracized from the Nation of Islam for their unscrupulous behavior. Yet they could deem Gene unworthy of Ali's trust and unsuitable to be Ali's friend because he's a white man? Regardless, Gene was close to Ali—closer than most other Muslim members of the entourage, which of course fostered jealousy and bouts of disrespectful behavior toward Gene. Elijah Muhammad, who was the leader of the Nation of Islam at the time, had been notified of how Gene was being mistreated by some proclaiming to be Muslims.

Apparently, the brothers in the Nation of Islam were not only being disrespectful, but they were plotting to harm him, too. So, the Honorable Elijah Muhammad made the effort to get Gene's phone number and put in a personal call to him. He told Gene to give Jeremiah, and other brothers from the movement, a message to meet him in Chicago the next day. According to legend, the next day, when the brothers met in Chicago, Elijah Muhammad told them that Gene Kilroy was an honorable man. Elijah made it crystal clear that anybody who harmed even a single hair on Gene's head would be answerable to Elijah.

Rita's Rule # 8

Never underestimate a perceived opponent, adversary, or enemy. Research opponents, identify their strengths and weaknesses before launching what may end up to be a foolish attack on someone who has more power than you.

Here's where the brothers made their mistake. They stereotyped Gene as a weak man void of any allies in their specific group. Therefore they underestimated his value to Ali, and never investigated what his relationship was beyond the entourage. Now this was remarkable. Gene was a white man who Ali loved and trusted. He was a decent guy, but the same type of jealousy that was directed toward him was directed toward me, too. From what I can tell it had more to do with the fact that we were both competent; Ali trusted us because we both delivered professional services that others around him couldn't.

The worst of the bunch were uneducated and had nothing much to do except hang onto Ali. Of course there were a scant few exceptions. But for the most part they were only around for a paycheck and free food. Most of their time was dedicated to spreading negativity, spinning stories, bringing parades of women before him, creating trouble between Ali and his wife. They were basically an unproductive, destructive crew.

That type of behavior is common though. I'd noticed it over my years of working with various male celebrities, from famous sports icons to renowned entertainers. They all had their entourage of sorts — people who they considered to be friends. These so-called friends were most always ruinous and weighty. They all seemed to bring the same strife. They bring women into the celebrity's life — women they control so in turn they can control the *commodity*, which is the star themselves. Ali was no different.

Gene was a gentleman and it was my pleasure to have developed a bond with him. He would visit me and my children at our home. My children were his godchildren, so you can imagine how tightly knit we were then and still are at the time of this writing.

At any rate, the disapproving glares and opinions didn't let up even when I brought forward a charity with the proceeds from Muhammad Ali Day being donated to the United Negro College Fund and the Stephen Smith Home for the Aging.

DIVISIVE CONFLICT

To my surprise, I'd gotten a call from Jeremiah Shabazz a few days after his wife Andrea had cut me out of her life. He wanted me to meet him at Adam's Mark Hotel for lunch to discuss the matter before leaving to travel with Muhammad Ali. Jeremiah had been the head of Muhammad's Mosque #12, which had several satellite locations throughout the city of Philadelphia. I had respect for Minister Jeremiah at that time, as he'd been a prominent member of the community. I had no problem accepting his invitation.

When I reached the venue I expected to see Jeremiah and Andrea. I thought it was a prime opportunity to iron out any misunderstandings that were severing our longstanding ties.

To my surprise, Andrea wasn't there at all. Instead, there was another gentleman, a giant of a man who stood at least 6'7" tall. I gazed up at him and realized I knew him—not personally, but I knew his name was Amin Jabbar. This was my first time seeing him in person, but I did know of the man through his legend. I'd heard many stories about him. While not all of the stories were true—I did know for a fact that Amin Jabbar was a person of reckoning. He wasn't one to be toyed with. Nonetheless, why was he at this meeting?

I took my seat at the table and Jeremiah made a formal introduction. He definitely wanted me to know who the guy was. For years people were convinced that Amin Jabbar was the muscle behind the minister's raft. People understood that the two of them had a brotherly alliance and that if anyone dared cause any trouble, or disrespect the minister in any way at all, they'd have to answer to Amin Jabbar. It had become obvious that I was supposed to find the whole scene intimidating, and though Jabbar's presence was unsettling to me, I was bent on not showing even a hint of fear. Despite the fact that I was not an active member of the Muslim community, I was one person who was afraid of nothing and no one except Allah (SWT).

I allowed Jeremiah to do most of the talking. I wanted to know without question what this meeting was about, especially in the absence of his wife, my former friend. He'd gone on and on about suggestions for Muhammad Ali Day. One such suggestion involved Ali making an appearance at a well-known franchise restaurant, which I quickly dismissed.

"We can't do that restaurant. That restaurant serves pork; there is lard in their hamburger rolls—we can't do that," I protested.

That apparently aggravated Jeremiah. Perhaps he'd already been in negotiations or made a deal with the restaurant for Ali to make an appearance. Whatever the reason, I was certain Jeremiah did not know the franchise hamburger buns contained pork. There's no way Minister Jeremiah would ever proceed with a deal that had any association with swine.

The meeting went on. I could see now why Jeremiah had called for this meeting. He wanted to show me who was in charge. He wanted to put me in my place—the place he thought I deserved. He wanted to show me he held a position of power in the community, and that that position should be respected.

That meeting was all about Jeremiah. He was visibly aggravated by our discord at the table, and how Ali had grown to genuinely trust me so. He was overtly bothered about it. "Well, thank you for the meet-up. I must be going now," I said, as I rose to my feet and left the table. It was time to leave this meeting behind me and move on.

A week or so later, while at home preparing to go to an event, my doorbell rang. I walked to the front door and saw a huge shadow of a person, obviously a man. His figure was blocking all the daylight in the doorway! It was Amin Abdul Jabbar—the same man I had met with Jeremiah at the Adam's Mark Hotel.

"As-Salamu-Alykium brother," I greeted him.

He returned my greetings and said, "The imam wants you to go up to the camp and speak to Ali about what's going on in the city of Philadelphia with Muhammad Ali Day."

By the imam, he meant Imam Shamsud-Din Ali. I was taken aback by the request.

"Okay. Well, when does he want me to do that?" I asked.

"Now," he said in a firm tone.

I nearly chuckled. Feeling sarcastic, I said, "Okay. Can I at least get my bag?" He allowed me that.

When I reached the car, I saw that the imam was in the front passenger seat. Jabbar and I got into the backseat, where Imam Adib Mahdi—another Muslim brother from my neighborhood, who I knew—was already seated.

There I was in the car with four men. Two up front and the two I was sandwiched between in the back. This was an awkward situation for me.

I'd only known Jabbar by way of stories I'd heard throughout the community, while I was only casually acquainted with the imam. That's why I was somewhat uncomfortable being wedged in a car with the pack of them. During the entire ride the men engaged in conversation among themselves. Not a word was directed to me or about me. I sat like a child among adults with no equality.

Once we finally reached the camp, my only anticipation or slightest excitement was being able to see Ali. However, he was nowhere to be found. The men had asked me to wait outside the room that was attached to the gym where Ali regularly trained. I waited there until Adib Mahdi came to get me. "Ali and the imam want you to come inside now," he said. *"Maybe now I can find out why I'm here,'* I thought as I followed Adib into the gym. Ali was there half clad in nothing but a towel wrapped from his navel to his knees.

As a Muslim woman, it was inappropriate for me to be in the same room as Ali because he was dressed like that. I felt quite uncomfortable. It was worse than when he had on the robe in his hotel room, earlier.

Jeremiah Shabazz was there in the gym, along with a couple of other men from the camp who always accompanied Ali, as well as the brothers I rode up with. Before I could make out what all this was about, Brother Adib Mahdi spoke up and said to me, "Tell Ali about what's been going on."

"What do you mean?" I asked.

"Tell Ali about the meeting you had with Jeremiah and Amin. Tell him about how Jeremiah has been sabotaging Muhammad Ali Day and trying to exploit the situation."

Given the chance to finally speak, I relayed everything that had happened over the past weeks until Jeremiah interrupted and said, "My wife never said anything like that! She never said that we didn't want anything to do with you or that we thought you were inappropriately involved with Ali!"

I was shocked and retorted, "With all due respect, Minister Jeremiah, you can tell me what you did or what you didn't say, but you were not privy to the conversation I had with your wife. You cannot tell me what she said to me, because you didn't hear it—I did! And before Allah (SWT), that's exactly what she said to me! Plus, you wanted me to proceed with scheduling Ali to appear at a fast-food chain, which I declined because I discovered they had swine in their rolls. That was apparently the other reason that you happen to be angry with me."

Expeditiously, Jeremiah forcibly shot back, declaring, "I didn't know anything about the restaurant having products with pork in them."

"I know," I said nodding my head.

In that moment I was reminded that I had such respect for this man—always—even after the episode with the fast-food chain and his attempt to intimidate me. There was a time when I would not have ever disputed Minister Jeremiah. But by now, I'd had it with being bullied by him or any of Ali's entourage. So, on that day, something inside me snapped and I welcomed the opportunity to set the record straight. It was Imam Shamsud-Din Ali who took over the conversation from there.

"This is what has been going on, Ali," the imam said. He then addressed the minister, saying, "Jeremiah, you need to clarify the reasons for your actions, because you ain't nothing in Philadelphia! What do you have to say?"

Jeremiah seemed flustered when he responded, "No, no, no. I'm not, I'm not," real pathetic like.

"You need to tell Ali. Do you run Philadelphia? Do you have anything to do with running the Muslims or organizing or anything in Philadelphia?" the imam continued.

"No, no, no," Jeremiah said.

It seemed like *no* was the only answer Jeremiah could come up with. Admittedly, it was too weird seeing Jeremiah Shabazz—a giant of a man in my eyes, a man people were afraid of—cowering like he was. Was this the same man who one could lose their life over if they crossed him the wrong way?

In the midst of Jeremiah's pitiable moment I could've sworn I heard him ask for everyone to wait. In that same instant I heard a loud, sharp rebuke come from Mahdi, the smallest one in the group. "Shut up, Jerry! Don't you ever speak while the imam is talking!" he'd said. It was startling; I couldn't believe it.

The group of men continued talking amongst themselves while I remained quiet like a fly on the wall. Suddenly, I realized what the brothers were trying to do. They wanted to make sure that Ali ended any hold Jeremiah Shabazz had over him by ensuring him that the former Minister Shabazz had no power in the Muslim community. Furthermore, they wanted Ali to know that the Muslim brotherhood stood with him.

I was glad to confront the issue pertaining to me, but I was also done listening to the men go on and on, so I walked outside. At that point, I felt like there was a burden removed from my chest— it was a liberating feeling. However, I pitied Jeremiah; I felt like he was emasculated because the brothers had chastised him in my presence. Perhaps that should've just been a guy thing. In all this chaos, I felt that I'd been blindsided; I should have been informed of what was expected of me. I didn't agree to get in the car and come to the camp to see a man dethroned, so to speak. And, I certainly hadn't wanted Jeremiah Shabazz to feel like I planned and plotted all that against him.

Personally, I wasn't bothered by the actions of Jeremiah or his wife enough to wish them harm. Apparently, the brothers who confronted him that day were of a different opinion about it. Of course the brothers had an obligation to protect their Muslim sister, me, which I appreciated. However, it was obvious to me that they had other concerns to confront Jeremiah about, completely unrelated to me.

My mind was still reeling from the aftermath of what I had just witnessed and experienced. The fresh air outside seemed like a good idea — it helped me lighten up a bit and it wasn't long before the brothers joined me outside, as well.

The imam stood near me quiet while Mahdi began to chat with me.

"Are you okay, sister?" the imam asked.

"Not really," I said.

"What's wrong?" he asked.

"I feel bad…like somebody died," I told him.

Adib interjected, "Actually, it was the assassination of a character that was not real, and Ali had to know the truth about how he was being used by Jeremiah. You shouldn't feel bad that you were a part of what just happened in there. Besides that, that wasn't the only issue we discussed with Ali about Jeremiah."

Nonetheless, I couldn't shake the sadness I felt for him. Although Mahdi's words were true, they brought little comfort. The memory of successfully pulling off Muhammad Ali Day, despite all the negativity that surrounded me, was my real comfort. As I said before, MAD was a tremendous day. Neither Jeremiah nor Andrea had showed up despite getting formal invitations. Besides, it was their town too. An intimate thread of familiarity runs through Philly; everyone knows everyone or about everyone. I didn't want them to feel unnoticed in their own city.

It was common knowledge that Andrea and Jeremiah Shabazz

were dominant members of Ali's entourage; they'd traveled the world with him. How could they have not been a part of that auspicious day? I'd even thought of Lana. Ideally, she should have been present, too.

Neither Andrea nor Jeremiah made their presence known prior to Muhammad Ali Day, but the best news is, to their credit, we managed to resume our friendship shortly after the Ali Day event took place. Both Andrea and Jeremiah expressed regrets for getting caught up in the negative politics practiced by some of Ali's hanger-on losers. I also apologized for anything I'd unintentionally done to contribute to the rift between us. Anyway, no one was more pleased than I was to resume a relationship with two of my longtime friends.

Confirmation of our resumed friendship was evident during the numerous times that Andrea and I hung out together. She'd often stop by my beauty salon. I'd do her hair, and later we would go out for a bite to eat. It was as if we had never missed a beat or had a glitch in our relationship. Naturally, I didn't see Jeremiah as much, but when I did he was always pleasant. The confirming factor of his forgiveness came on a day I was doing an interview with the owner of a local gym in Philadelphia. The gym smelled atrocious with the smell of funky sweat and whatever the staff was cooking on a hot plate in the office that was stationed above the gym. Jeremiah was there for some reason, hanging out with the owner when I arrived. We politely exchanged the traditional Islamic greetings to each other, and proceeded to chat briefly. I was wearing a mid-length silver fox coat which I took off and laid on the arm of a padded chair that was located in the office. Jeremiah, who was sitting on the other side of the room, quietly got up and walked over toward me.

"Sister Rita, you may not want to lay your coat there, or anywhere other than on your lap. I saw roaches over in that corner earlier. That's why I moved across the room," he whispered.

I was aghast. Immediately, I felt as if something was crawling on me. I couldn't help my reaction. "Eww! That's disgusting! Let me move!" I blurted out. I snatched my coat up and thanked him for the warning. "Good looking out, my brother," I said, flushed now with discomfort. With that Jeremiah and I both chuckled softly. The owner of the gym had stepped out for a minute and we did not want to be caught in an outburst of laughter when he returned.

Rita's Rule # 9

Never allow bitterness to define who you are or overcome your sense of humanity because of the actions of others. Misunderstandings can only be resolved through communication.

Allow me to backtrack for just a few. Remember, I said I'd also thought of Lana. Even though our ties had been severed as well, I still missed her and hoped to rekindle our friendship. Well, just a smidge before Muhammad Ali Day, I received a call from Lana.

"Hey, Lana, what's up?" I said as if I'd spoken to her just yesterday.

"Listen, I'm here at Billy Crystal's house," she began. "We just finished the show." (It was a show to pay tribute to Ali. Billy Crystal was an actor/comedian who'd imitated Ali unlike anyone had ever done before. He was just amazing.) At any rate, Lana continued, "Something just told me to call you, Rita, and apologize to you for treating you the way I did. I am going to help you, sister. I am going to make sure that I talk to people and help you gather support for the day because what you're trying to do is really nice for Ali. It was horrible of me to fall into that mode," she said.

I was overwhelmed. Overjoyed by Lana's voice in my ear, and even more so to hear a heartfelt confession from her. "Thank you, Lana!" I said. "It has done my heart good to hear from you, my friend. I accept your apology and your offer with open arms." I had gotten the miracle I'd hoped for. Three great friends and I were back together. Certainly we could do more together than apart.

*   *   *

Though most of my events and media activities went off without a hitch, there were a few incidents that were uncomfortable, to say the least. Perhaps, for the sake of clarity, I should preface the occurrences by acknowledging a particular hang-up I had early on in my career.

As part of the Who's Who of Philadelphia, I consistently attended events with the city's elite. In doing so, naturally I'd run into many of the same people. Without fail I was asked about what project I was working on. That often meant—What celebrity are you working with? It made me feel uncomfortable, actually. My responses were always determined by who was asking the question because I was strict with confidentiality. Not to mention being accused of name-dropping and bragging. I just thought it was best to keep my lips sealed.

During a conversation with Ali I mentioned that some people seemed to be turned off or thought I was name-dropping after answering their curious questions pertaining to my latest project(s). In another noteworthy moment of receiving a dose of Ali's witty wisdom, he turned to me and said, "Sister, if it is true, it ain't bragging. Never be afraid to speak the truth about what Allah (SWT) has blessed you with. He has given each of us something special and instructed us to not worry about what he has given someone else. Just do something with what He has blessed you with. As long as you do that, don't worry about what others think, say, or feel."

Such empowering words coming from the Champ comforted me and reshaped my mind-set about the blessings of being in the unique position of working with high-profile individuals.

4

ONLY THE HEART KNOWS

One thing I was immensely thankful for was that no matter which way my relationship with individuals in Ali's entourage swayed, the friendship I shared with him never faded.

No matter where we were or who was around us, Ali was his same cheerful, playful self. Whatever occasion allowed us to be in the same location—be it riding in the car together or him seeing me standing somewhere as he looked on from the car, he would just jump out of it and spout his famous line: "There she is; I have to have her!" To a clueless bystander it would definitely seem like something completely different. It became a standard practice for Ali to mess with me for two reasons: first, he realized that it would get a rise out of the crowd. Secondly he wanted everyone to know that I was, as he said, a good Muslim sister and a good friend of his. He never cared what anyone thought of him. He enjoyed life, laughter, true friends, and good people. I knew without a doubt, this was Muhammad Ali—my friend. He was just funny like that! Thanks to him I learned not to be concerned by most anything anymore, just like him.

Looking back, I'm confident Ali thoroughly enjoyed annoying some of those around him, too, even when they showed their dislike for it. I think it was his way of showing them who was in charge and that his entourage could not pick his friends.

PRIVILEGE BEGETS PRIVILEGE

This was sometime back in the early '80s when people like me found it a major privilege to obtain media credentials to cover major fights ringside, particularly so for those representing a local African-American newspaper — that too, being a woman of color. That was something I owed to Ali and will forever be grateful to him for. He saw my spark and ambition and knew just how to ignite it, letting me evolve into a firework in the boxing world.

Today, in retrospect, I feel my gratefulness is inadequate for having known the Champ up close and personal. What a life privilege. What an honor to have called him friend. How many people get to have a dream fulfilled? I was a thirteen-year-old girl when a knowing came over me that he'd be in my life. I'm better to this day because of his wisdom, too. How he oozed wisdom always at the right time. And whether I saw it coming or not, I got many doses of it from him.

I remember one such time after an event, my dear friend Lana Shabazz, knowing how close I was to Ali, asked me for a personal favor. "Rita, ask Ali to buy me a house," she said. "He promised to buy me one since I've been working for him for so long, but he hasn't done it yet." She had this feeling that I could somehow remind Ali of that promise and convince him to buy her a house. She went on to say, "He loves you, so if you ask him...you know, just put a word in to him for me...I think he'll go ahead and buy me a house."

So that same night I decided to talk to Ali about it.

"Listen, Ali, Lana has asked me to ask you to buy her a house. She said you promised her that," I said.

His response surprised me. I'll never forget it. Ali simply stated: "Sister, let me tell you something. In life you only get but so many favors from anybody. Don't burn up yours for someone else for what somebody wouldn't do for you or somebody else. Lana has been with me for years. She has traveled all over the world with me. Every time I fought, I gave her a bonus; I think I already paid for the house Lana lives in. If she didn't get that by now, it's not my responsibility."

With that, I left the matter alone, but I did tell Lana what he'd said.

There was another instance that same night, when a reporter had caught up with us to get answers for his questions. Enthusiastically the reporter spouted, "Wow, how did you get him to do this? How did you get Muhammad Ali—a man of this reputation—to do this?"

"Oh, it was nothing," I replied. "He's my brother in Islam and that's why he went ahead and agreed upon doing this event."

Once the reporter was gone, Ali turned to me and said, "Listen, don't ever tell anybody that it didn't take anything to get me to agree to something. Always say it took a lot to get me. I just happened to do it for you because I care about you and I care about the message that you were trying to put out. It's not easy to get me. People all over the world are trying to get me. Don't ever say that again."

Laws of Power's Rule

"Never Outshine the Master" is one of the most profound rules of engagement offered by Robert Greene's book The 48 Laws of Power.

If you don't see already what my mistake was, in innocently blurting out how it was easy to get Ali to commit to a tribute, let me explain. In the moment, I made the issue more about me than I did about the master (Ali). I conveyed to the reporter the impression that Ali acquiesced to my request because of some powers that I had. Not only was this not true, it was an insult to Ali's phenomenal accomplishments and being a person of superior relevance in that situation.

I got what Muhammad meant. However, after this exchange, there was just one thing racing in my mind. I thought that he felt like I was in some way diminishing the relevance and significance of bringing a person of his stature in for the event. I obviously didn't mean it that way. My answer to that reporter was based subconsciously on the fact that the Champ had always made everything so easy for me, so I guess it came out all wrong.

I got what he was saying. I knew he wanted me to realize and acknowledge how big of an achievement it truly was. So, I went ahead and admitted my mistake. "I stand corrected," I said.

There were a lot more incidents that afforded Ali to impress wisdom and life lessons upon me. It was all because in addition to helping me, he wanted me to grow as a professional and as an individual. In retrospect, he treated me as if he thought I was his adopted sister. Why else would he go to such lengths for me? I know for a fact he wanted to help me reach the stars.

There was never a need for me to be in his presence every day like some others. Our relationship and my assistance to him were not based on that kind of reliance—to the contrary. I met up with Ali on occasion, but our friendship was perpetual. After the aforementioned event a great deal of time passed before we met again.

A TRUE FRIENDSHIP

Several years passed since I'd seen Ali and he was no longer married to Veronica... I'd gone to Atlanta, where I was a featured stylist in an international hair show...and that's where I ran into Ali again.

One of his associates came excitedly in my direction. "Muhammad's here!" the associate said. No sooner had he got the words out, Ali walked up in my direction. It was obvious from the way he beamed that he was happy to be there. We were equally happy to see each other again. "As-Salamu-Alykium, sister, I want you to come up to meet my fiancée," he said. "Okay!" I said. Then he, my sister, and I played catch-up and shared plenty of laughs over lunch.

After our meal we followed him into the elevator and up to his suite, where he proudly introduced us to Lonnie—his fourth and last wife. She had a youthful radiance about her and a beautiful full head of reddish blonde hair, and cute girlish freckles. Anyone seeing how Ali glowed when she was by his side had to know that she was exceptionally special to him.

"This here is Sister Rita. She's a good sister," he began as he introduced us. Before I could return the greeting or shake her hand, he continued with my introduction by reciting my entire résumé to her! He told her of my accomplishments, from the radio station to the hair salon to Muhammad Ali Day, and so on. "She is an honest, clean sister. She's the kind of sister that will make you a true, good friend," he said as he finished.

Lonnie didn't respond to that statement, but was polite. I liked her because Ali liked her so much. Next, Ali went on to brag about his Lonnie. "Lonnie is smart. She has a master's degree," he said. "And she's a hometown girl, too. I've known her since she was a young girl. There was no doubt in my mind that my friend Ali was over the moon being with Lonnie. That made me extremely happy.

Lonnie was genuine and Ali loved her. She and I never really developed a relationship of our own, but I did find her to be a valuable person in her own right. Unfortunately, after meeting her, I was rarely ever in her presence again. I was just pleased with the fact that Ali had found "the one true love" of his life and was unquestionably happy. That's what mattered most.

Ali was a brother to me. He inspired me, lifted me up, or helped me to move ahead like he did. He made me reach for everything that I had dreamed of. Ali showed me just as much support when I married Shamsud-Din-Ali. Anytime he would see us together, he would yell out, "Shamsud-Din Ali, that's a bad man! You got the right one this time, sister!"

Sadly, the last time I saw my friend Ali was at Smokin' Joe Frazier's funeral in November 2011, in Philadelphia. Although it was a sad occasion, it was uplifting to see Ali with his wife Lonnie and her sister, his ex-wife Khalilah, one of Ali's daughters, and other members of the Ali family all assembled to show their respect to Ali's longtime rival. Leon Spinks, Larry Holmes and his lovely wife Diane, James Binns — the former attorney for the WBA, Don King, and a host of other legends from the boxing world were also in attendance.

As I gazed upon my old friend, the deterioration of his health was quite evident. His dexterity and mobility were severely challenged. But he was in good hands. Seeing the genuine love and respect that Lonnie and her sister showed as they attended to the Champ was heartwarming.

After Jesse Jackson's electrifying eulogy and the service concluded, Ali and his family, along with other VIPs and dignitaries, retreated to a private room across from the assembly room where the service had been held. Still grief-stricken from the loss of my dear friend Joe Frazier and saddened to see Ali so physically challenged, I didn't go into the VIP room with them. I didn't want to crowd Ali or make him feel compelled to exert any energy on my behalf. I just didn't want to be an extra weight of sort.

While standing in the corridors of the church, my longtime friend Francis Jones, who had coordinated the events for Joe Frazier's funeral, located me and said, "They want you to come inside of the VIP room. Gene Kilroy and others are looking for you."

"Okay, thanks," I responded to Francis. It was just to show appreciation to her for finding me and passing on the message. But I knew I wasn't going to go into the room, so instead, I waited for Gene Kilroy to come out.

"What happened?" Gene asked. "We sent for you to come to the VIP room. Why didn't you come in?"

"It was just too crowded in there," I said — my cover answer for the truth.

I was overwhelmed at the sight of my longtime, vibrant, fast talking mentor and friend. Seeing him in a deteriorating posture, quiet, in need of constant assistance, was too much for me. I knew in my heart that this day would definitely be the last time I'd get to ever see my friend again. Despite that fact, I was comforted to know that he was being cared for in such an affectionate way by his wife and her sister. It was also a pleasure to see the entire Ali clan there as a cohesive unit.

My good friend and mentor Gene Kilroy and I had flown in to Philadelphia from Las Vegas and were staying at the Loews Hotel in Center City. In true Gene Kilroy fashion, he never let me pay at check-in, or anything. He paid for my room at the Loews Hotel and checked in on me constantly to make sure I was okay, that I had eaten, or if I needed anything at all.

Directly after the funeral I went with Gene Kilroy to the repast, which was held at a large banquet hall in South Philadelphia. Upon arriving I saw many other acquaintances; two of my many young home girls, as I like to call them, were present, too: Kathy Sledge — the former lead singer of Sister Sledge — and Lynn Carter, who became one of the first female boxing judges. It was great seeing them because they were among the people who always stood by me, in spite of having the unjust title of felon bestowed on me.

Well, as it turned out, that day was indeed the last time I saw Muhammad Ali alive, in person. He may have been a lot of different things to the world, but to me he was a gem. His ability to lighten situations that made people feel better about things in order to give them a better perspective about situations, inspired me to become the best I could be. And in doing so, in being so, he never really diminished the value of things. He just had this way about him that was intrinsically captivating for those around him.

LOSING MUHAMMAD ALI

How likely was it that a local reporter/columnist and radio personality from Philadelphia would meet a legend and develop a close bond with him? Who would've thought I'd make the accomplishments and strides that I did — and with the help of a legend like Ali, no less? It's not common to meet a sought-after legend and develop a brother/sister bond that would change a life forever. I'm all around better for having known him. Allah (SWT) truly smiled on me.

So, five years after I sighted him at the funeral, I received news that Muhammad Ali, my dear friend, had died. The news belted me in the gut. My heart was stricken with untold grief. If my flesh-and-blood brother had died, the pain would not have been any different. My daughter was with me and we both cried together.

As is typical of the media, after Ali's death, they showed scores of pictures of him for days. His image was all over, everywhere. My daughter, Kiki, and I didn't miss a moment of television coverage as we cried through most of it—that is until we were able to share one humorous moment in the throes of it all. As one Muhammad Ali image after the next flashed across the screen, at one point we turned to each other and commented on how gorgeous old man Ali really was. I quipped, "Wow, it's a good thing that Allah (SWT) blinded me back then and didn't let me notice how extremely handsome he was in the early years of our friendship because perhaps I would have fallen for his undeniable charm!" I know in my heart that I would never have gotten involved with Ali. I guess Allah (SWT) protected me by not allowing me to see what was right before me all those years. Ali was not only wise and very smart, but he was fiercely handsome!

Nonetheless, reality brought us back around and we watched more coverage and shed more tears. Kiki's husband, Mike Tyson—Mike to us—actually attended the funeral as he'd been asked to be a pallbearer for Ali. The funeral was during the time of one of Mike's six-week performances of *The Undisputed Truth* at the MGM Hotel. Mike took his two older sons Miguel and Amir with him, which was an amazing experience for two young men who grew up loving and admiring one of the most adored legends of all time. It was short notice to get to Louisville, Kentucky, in time for the service and private burial, but he did it—of course. I feel like Mike and the boys represented all of us. I badly wanted to be at the funeral, too; I wanted to be there for Ali as I'd been there for him in life, during those years long before, but things don't always work out the way you want them to. Just knowing that Mike was there and that he was one of the pallbearers for Ali's funeral made me quite happy. Knowing how Ali loved Mike, I'm sure that's what the Champ would have wanted.

We prayed for his family, particularly Lonnie, knowing how difficult it had to have been for her. It was June 10, 2016, the day of Ali's funeral. I was glued to the television. Thirty thousand people were jammed into the Ali Center in his home in Louisville, Kentucky. I was amazed by the attendees and pleased by the reflection of the Islamic faith most prevalent throughout the long lavish ceremony. What struck me deeply was when Lonnie made her entrance being escorted by President Bill Clinton, who like Ali was an extraordinary humanitarian. It was also a reminder of the fact that not only was she the wife of a great man, Lonnie was a distinguished, accomplished woman in her own right.

When she took the podium she exuded poise and was well-spoken as she expressed her passion about her faith, her husband's life, and all he stood for on behalf of the poor and disenfranchised, Caucasians, African-Americans, and other people of color around the country, and the world. He'd been a fighter inside and outside the ring. He had fought and beaten the system—without putting up a fight! No one had ever done that before, and that's why he gained recognition for being a mega hero. By the time the celebration of his life had ended that day, it was clear that there were many more like me who had benefitted from knowing him; who had become wiser and taller because Ali had touched them in one profound way or another. There were many more forlorn people with potential, not yet actualized, whose ears he'd whispered some knowledge and wisdom into, that enriched their lives.

An entire chapter of my life ended with the death of Muhammad Ali. My friend and brother taught me, guided me, and pushed me forward. I know my life would have been incomplete without him, just as the worth of this book would wane without a chapter depicting his life as it intertwined with mine.

SPEAKING OF BILL CLINTON

Shamsud-Din and I had affiliations with a host of affluent individuals throughout our involvement in civic affairs, social events, and the boxing and entertainment industry. However, President Bill Clinton was one of the most impressive individuals I'd ever met, not because of his notoriety and swagger, but because he struck me as a very sincere man of extreme intelligence. He possessed a unique quality that was limited to very few. Like Muhammad Ali, who is by far one of the most charismatic persons I've ever encountered — who always made me feel important and relevant — Bill Clinton has the quality to make others feel as though they are extremely relevant, also.

Call it what you will — savvy, swag, charisma, charm, or personal magnitude — like Muhammad Ali and Mike Tyson, President Bill Clinton has it. Meeting him was one of the cherished moments of my life. It was during John Street's first campaign for mayor of Philadelphia. Polls were tight, which was rare for a Democratic candidate running for mayor against a Republican in Philadelphia. La Salle University sports arena was packed beyond capacity with many supporters of John Street. However, given the enthusiasm of the crowd, it was obvious that the vast majority were there to get a glimpse of President Clinton.

In true Bill Clinton style, coolheaded and at ease, he delivered a rousing speech that turned skeptics into enthusiastic believers. His smooth comments were assertive and genuine, yet captivating to every listener present. It was electrifying as told by the intermittent eruptions from the crowd as he spoke; they stood to their feet and gave raucous applause and earsplitting cheers. Clinton's words were obviously taken to heart, but one comment stood above the rest. And I paraphrase: "Let's be honest...if it weren't for the fact that John Street was a black man running as a Democrat for the mayor of Philadelphia, there's no way this race would be even close."

His heartfelt discernment had a terrific impact on that racially diverse audience of thousands that day. Only Bill Clinton could have pulled that off. Caucasians loved and admired him as one of their own, while people of color loved and admired him because, to them, he was affectionately considered a brother and the first black president.

I was among the privileged VIPs who were able to meet President Clinton in a private setting after the campaign rally. His aura filled the room. Before I even approached him, I felt him as I waited in the reception line to meet him. As the only woman dressed in Islamic attire, admittedly, I wasn't sure how he would receive me. Not because I thought he might be anti-Islamic, but I wasn't sure if he would feel comfortable shaking my hand. I wasn't sure if he knew that some Muslims suggest it is inappropriate for men to shake a Muslim woman's hand. I was about the tenth person in line, so I got to the front quickly. What a rare opportunity it was to be standing in front of the most powerful political leader in the world. I was delighted at the thought of making his acquaintance. I was keenly aware of his indisputable humanity and inclusive nature. Yet I thought that he might still be uncertain of the protocol regarding how to greet a Muslim woman. With that in mind, I initiated the introduction; I extended my right hand to him and said, "It is a distinct pleasure to meet you, Mr. President." Looking directly into my eyes, the President gently placed his left hand on my right upper arm, moved slightly closer toward me, and said, "No, ma'am, the pleasure is all mine; I am so honored to make your acquaintance." That millimeter of a second stood still, while I relished the warmth of the President's impactful compliment. I'll cherish that moment for life.

Mingling with some of the political leaders, community activists, members of the media, and other VIPs who remained in a private reception area after President Clinton had departed the building, I conversed with some of the women. We talked about how elated we were with the President's speech and how it had motivated us to step up the get-out-and-vote movement. We shared our experiences with meeting him as well, which revealed that we all had similar lasting impressions of how the President treated us. He had actually made each of us feel as though we were the most important person in the room at that moment. We collectively shook our heads in amazed disbelief and concluded that our political idol was extraordinary, charming, and a great humanitarian. Our emphasis wasn't so much on what the President had said to each of us — on the contrary. It was the manner in which he expressed his regard for us. We took his comments to heart assuming they came from his, too. Simply put, President Clinton possessed a unique quality. In this regard his personable interaction with the public is consistent with phenomenal leaders who have the ability to make everyone they encounter feel special in real-time.

5

DWIGHT BRAXTON VS. MATTHEW SAAD MUHAMMAD

James Binns and I were not personal or professional acquaintances. However, I was fully aware of his position as the boxing commissioner for the Pennsylvania Commonwealth and the attorney for the World Boxing Association (WBA). Also acclaimed for his immaculate tailor-made blue pinstriped suits, Binns wore a different pinstriped suit every single day. You could tell each suit was different by the dimension of the stripes. On a visit to his home for dinner and a personal tour of his lavish home in Center City, my husband and I saw what had to be no less than a hundred blue pinstriped suits hanging neatly in his mega closet.

As the boxing commissioner for the Pennsylvania Commonwealth, James Binns, Esq. was responsible for sanctioning fights. Murad Muhammad was in the process of promoting the Matthew Saad Muhammad vs. Dwight Braxton championship fight. Saad being from Philly and Dwight from Camden, New Jersey, the fight was a natural for Philly. However, Murad was being courted by the mayor of Jacksonville, Florida, to stage the event there. He offered Murad every possible means of support in order to bring the fight there.

Philadelphia was known for producing some of the world's greatest fighters who exhibited that Philly fighting flare. I knew the fight was right and it belonged in Philly. Determined to achieve my mission and to get the fight in my town, I called Murad.

"Murad, the fight belongs in Philly," I insisted.

"It's too late for that," he said. "The mayor from Jacksonville is flying in to Newark to meet with me later today. We are scheduled to close the deal at that time."

I couldn't hear of it. "Please, please, give me a shot at this," I begged.

"Sorry, sis. It's a done deal, and besides, there's simply not enough time to facilitate such an enormous undertaking and get all the licenses needed to do it in Philly," he said.

Nonetheless, somehow, I landed the opportunity! I'd have to say he had mercy on me. While I had been involved with working with several fight promoters, Murad gave me the biggest opportunity and took the biggest chance on my proposal to house the fight in Philadelphia.

Promoting this particular venue was a natural for me, particularly as it relates to media coverage because I was a member of the press. I knew key players like Elmer Smith, sportswriter for the Philadelphia Inquirer, as well as other sports commentators. My affiliation with WDAS radio station was an added advantage. Thus, I knew all of the tricks of the trade to get the most gain for our advertising bucks. I put together a package that included purchasing radio time and giveaways. Savvy promoters often engage in the practice of ticket giveaways to media outlets in return for receiving free promotions in addition to paid-for spots. Ideally, the station would promote the giveaways with each of the radio hosts, which gives the production extraordinary exposure. In some respects, it could've been viewed as overkill—repeatedly hearing the same advertisement, the same theme music being recycled day in and day out until the event had occurred.

That type of near harassment advertising is intended to secure a mental register of the promotion no matter how else you may be occupied. The theme music will pierce through! And that is the precise approach we needed to promote the Matthew

Saad Muhammad vs. Dwight Braxton championship fight in Philadelphia.

Listen, I brought the first championship fight to Philadelphia in an over thirty-two-year gap. While I can bask in the overall success of the promotion, my encounters with Dwight Braxton were uncomfortable to say the least. He showed blatant disrespect and contempt for me pursuant to my event planning strategies. My best recollection is that he didn't reveal any animosity toward me until after Matthew Saad Muhammad did a promotional interview on the radio show I produced. Dwight was also scheduled to come in to the station, or call in, during the same time slot. For some reason he reneged on it and every other appearance that I'd arranged for both fighters. That was baffling to me until I learned from others that Dwight was disturbed with me because, supposedly, he thought I was biased toward Saad when, in truth, I'd actually favored Dwight. I didn't even know Saad. However, after working with Saad one would be hard pressed NOT to favor him. He was a soft-spoken, kind, and modest gentleman. As well, members of his entourage were civilized and professional. My experience with Dwight's people was the complete opposite.

THE HORROR AT THE BARCLAY HOTEL

I had arranged temporary residency for key personnel of the boxing event planning team. Promoter Murad Muhammad and essential members of the team moved into the five-star Barclay Hotel in Rittenhouse Square, Philadelphia. It was palatial-a place for the refined upper-class people of the world. There were even permanent elite residents who occupied several condominiums on the high floors. How I managed to convince the hotel manager, who herself was a resident of the hotel, to accommodate our boxing industry parties baffles me to this day when I think about it.

All was going well when members of the promotional team were limited to just a few essential staff members. Barclay residents and hotel guests seemed fascinated by our presence initially, but that would drastically change on fight night, at the after-party. It would be held in the main ballroom, a place fit for a royal gathering.

Since I was essentially the spokesperson for the event, naturally I took my place in the hospitality suite to handle a few preliminaries, then headed to take the elevator down to the lobby. I had great anticipation as I glided down to the lobby floor. The fight was on my mind as was the after-party, all just twenty-four hours away. However, as soon as the elevator door opened, before I could step out, I was pushed and shoved by about ten people bum-rushing the elevator. "Yo, motherfucker, hold the elevator!" someone yelled. I couldn't believe what I was experiencing. Was I dreaming?

At any rate, when at last I'd escaped the elevator and the apparent low-lifers who overtook it, I entered the lobby only to hear the raised voices of a crowd of apparently very unhappy people. They were slinging profanities to no end. It was coming from people I'd seen with Braxton and assumed them to be members of his entourage. Hopefully, they'd figure it out and just calm down. But it should have been a warning that the worst was yet to come. The rowdy crew was not done yet. I knew I should go back to the hospitality suite—our temporary main office—to inform Murad of their disorderly conduct, but I didn't follow my mind and rushed on out. I was relieved to be out of their presence anyway.

These people were out of their element and would surely be problematic. Regardless, I had to stay focused. There were a number of time-sensitive tasks I needed to attend to before the fight, which was coming up fast. Regardless of how tough the crowd was, fight promoters like Murad were used to dealing with individuals of this sort. Sufficient security would be on hand during the preparation stages for such events and even more at the venue. Still, it was a big mistake on my part not to alert the proper personnel right away of what had taken place. My focus, however, was on the many other matters I had to attend to, quickly.

Our production team worked until sunrise, the morning of the fight. The day of a major promotion is always hectic and requires all hands on deck, all boots on the ground. Every final detail must be attended to. But what was up ahead would be all the fault of my own.

After the devastation of Saad losing the fight—who, admittedly, I now favored over Braxton—I headed straight to the lavish Barclay Hotel. Arriving there thirty minutes before the event was to start, I was the only member of the promotion team there. The main ballroom of the Barclay Hotel with all its ornate chandeliers, candelabras, textured wallpaper, and soft lighting was the perfect celebratory atmosphere. Bartenders and their open bar setups were stationed in the four corners of the room, ready to accommodate guests with food, cocktails, and soft beverages. Waiters and waitresses were decked in black-and-white tuxedo-style uniforms ready to serve the specially invited guests. I was in place, too, and ready to host the event and check off my guest list at the door.

Some of the VIP guests began arriving a few minutes early. That was to be expected. I welcomed them with a smile, hugs, handshakes, and what have you. They continued to trickle in when suddenly, to my dismay a crowd of about sixty rowdy persons barged into the area of the ballroom. Standing in the entrance of the venue, I extended both arms out in an effort to block them, asserting, "This is a private affair. It's invitation only." My attempts to stop them were futile. "Excuse me, please verify your invitation" I said with my list in hand.

"Fuck you, we're with Dwight Braxton," yelled a man in a deep, intimidating voice. Several others followed his lead with similar declaratives. One after the other ignored my requests. They had no intention of honoring a silly list, in their eyes. They would provide no proof at all. It quickly became obvious that I hadn't invited them. I was just trying to stall until security arrived. This crowd was getting louder and more unruly by the second. They were pouring in past me like I wasn't standing there at all. Their ears were deaf to my voice. My authority was disregarded as they bulldozed past me. I was literally knocked out of the doorway by several men followed by the women with them. Had I put up any further resistance, I know they would have physically attacked me.

With no viable option I was relegated to watch the slew of uninvited rogues rush the room and dismantle all that we had planned. Within minutes the posh room fit for royalty was diminished and filled with pandemonium. There were now people behaving more like animals than civilized individuals. Tearfully, I looked on as they tore into the food and guzzled beverages like *humites* (my coined word for human termites). To my horror, and disbelief, I watched as they ate and drank everything in sight. They cursed and talked loud and endlessly. They consumed everything like ravenous animals. There was no stopping them. That is until Barclay management called in the Philadelphia police.

Seeing law enforcement was an enormous relief even though they shut the party down completely. We couldn't even recover and commence with our original plans. It was also a relief that the nightmare ended with the ballroom still intact, too. Not one candelabrum or chandelier crystal was harmed. No walls were desecrated. No dish or glass broken. Phew! Thank Allah (SWT) I didn't have to live knowing my event ended with the destruction of any décor in one of the city's landmark hotels.

Many of the invited guests and promotion team members arrived as the police were dispersing the crowd; therefore, there was little to no reason for an explanation. What did bother me was the look on the face of the woman who owned the hotel. The look on her face was frozen in extreme disappointment and I understood why. I had unintentionally betrayed her confidence in me, and as time has proven, my resourceful contact with her and with the Barclay Hotel became irretrievably broken as a result of an event gone embarrassingly awry.

Rita's Rule # 10

Always attend to details and be prepared for the worst as well as the best scenario that could occur.

Incidentally, I never did understand why Braxton despised me so. The explanation I received from a small dark-skinned, musty, chick should suffice, I guess. She wasn't bad-looking really. She was polite...always spoke to me even when Braxton didn't. But, lord, did she smell. My nose knew when she wasn't far off. My eye would always catch up a few seconds later. "Yo, I just wanted to let you know that I think you're nice even though Dwight hates you and says you look like a canine," she blurted out to me.

Startled by her sudden presence and offensive odor, I wasn't fazed by her comment. I lifted my neck and turned away as if to rescue my nose from any further vexation. I stepped back, smiled, and responded, "Thanks, but I have to check on something, ASAP!" and briskly walked away. Right as I started to leave, I couldn't help but notice her proud look of accomplishment. She wore a smirk instead of a smile. Was it because of a botched compliment? Or was she simply content to think she'd brought me down a notch? I'll never know.

I did, however, run into Dwight Braxton while I was at the Stadium in Philadelphia. It was the evening of Mike Tyson's return to the ring when he fought and annihilated Bruce Sheldon. I nearly missed him. Nonetheless, when we spotted each other, he hollered, "Don't touch me!"

Since I had never touched Braxton before or indicate that I was going to right then, his demand made no sense. For him to harbor such hatred, after many years, suggested a psychological condition that is beyond my ability to fix. Admittedly, his attitude toward me did arouse my curiosity. It was puzzling to witness a man who had initially been kind and welcoming to me change so drastically. As for my final sentiment on the matter, I'm not now nor was I ever in the least bit bothered by Braxton's attitude toward me. The topic is only included in the book because, number one, it happened, and number two, like other negative experiences I've overcome, it was worth sharing. With enough said on that, I'm pleased to move on to discuss the pleasant experience I had upon meeting former heavyweight champion Larry Holmes.

Rita's Rule # 11

Observe both positive and negative encounters by assessing what went right and what went wrong so you can grow from each situation and keep moving forward.

6

INTERVIEWING LARRY HOLMES

Unlike the contemptuous treatment I received from Braxton, Larry Holmes was more genial and there was no strife in our encounter. It was 1978 and Larry was at the top of his game in the sport of boxing. He was the heavyweight champ at the time I sought to interview him. This would be another tremendous opportunity for me as well as for my paper, the *Philadelphia Tribune*. Obtaining an interview with Larry wasn't easy. He wasn't readily available for even some of the most established media because he was in such high demand. More than likely Larry granted me an interview because I was introduced to him via a mutual associate.

With only a day's notice it was too late to have a *Philadelphia Tribune* staff photographer accompany me for my interview with Larry. Uncertain if I'd ever have another opportunity to conduct a one-on-one in-depth interview with the sought-after heavyweight champion, I was determined not to blow the interview. Going without a photographer was not an option, so I had to come up with an alternative plan, quick. "Hmm, who can I get to fill in…who can I pass off as a professional photographer at the last minute?" I said, having an external conversation with myself.

My sister Zaynah was nearby and had heard me. I was jolted out of my pondering when she suggested that I do it myself with a new camera I'd just gotten and had even used to cover events. Zaynah was right! I had taken photos at fights, other sport venues, political and social functions. But, an interview on this level, this was different. During events, and such, I would take candid photos of celebrities and activities. It didn't matter if they were perfect. *"But the interview pictures had to be perfect,"* I thought to myself.

"No, that won't work because I need to be in some of the photos this time. Readers seeing me in the pictures with Larry will add more validity to the story," I told her.

She said, "Sure, that makes sense, but who can you get at this late hour, when your interview is tomorrow morning, particularly since it's a workday?"

At this point Zaynah, who always looked out for me, had taken on my plight now. She was brainstorming with me especially since it was already after seven on a Thursday evening and we were still in the beauty salon finishing several patrons. Desperate to find someone for the mission—preferably a man—we continued to ponder. Suddenly, like a high moment in a movie drama, the door of the salon flung open and in walked the answer to my dilemma—I hoped. Norman, our longtime friend and popular Mount Airy Avenue resident, entered the salon.

"Hey, Rita and Shirley, what's up!" he began.

I greeted Norman casually as he continued to greet the patrons as well.

Meanwhile, my mind was racing with possibilities. Maybe, just maybe Norman was a candidate for the next day's assignment. *"As a matter of fact, why not?"* I thought. Fully aware that Norman was unemployed, homeless, and primarily living out of his car, I knew he'd be available. I'd known Norman since high school, so I was privy to personal information about him. It was a well-kept secret that Norman had recently fallen on hard times after his wife kicked him out of their house. Norman had given her ample reason to-one being that he chose to quit a well-paying job to pursue a career as a piano bar player. Oh, did I mention that he'd never played a piano before? Now, that was the final act of foolishness that prompted his beautiful wife to call an end to the marriage, and any further chance for him to father their young son.

Norman had made nightly runs from one piano bar to the next to observe how it's done. Surely it couldn't be that hard, he thought. Unfortunately, his nightly vicarious piano lessons cost him dearly in bar tabs, too, further robbing his family's needed finances. So, Good Time Charlie became Homeless Norman—with lots of time on his hands.

Living out of an old car in need of repairs and washing up at the 30th Street train station didn't seem to bother Norman in the least. He was charming and jovial, nonetheless. He'd be perfect for what I needed. Surely, he could stare into a camera, focus, and click. And, the fact that he was quite articulate was a bonus!

"Hey, Norman, what is your schedule tomorrow?" I asked.

"It's flexible, why?" he asked, frowned up.

Sighing a sigh of relief I hollered, "Great! I need you to help me tomorrow morning by taking some photos for me at an assignment that I'm doing for the *Philadelphia Tribune!*"

"Whoa!" Norman replied. "I'm not a professional photographer. You know that, right? What do you need the pictures for? Is it for your health and beauty column? I might be interested if it involves taking pictures of women as pretty as the women in this salon," he said. The unsmiling stern look on my face conveyed to him that I needed a serious answer, and his joking was ill-timed.

"Hold up, you're serious, aren't you?" he said. "I didn't mean to make light of your question, I'm just not sure that I could do justice to your project. It's probably best that you get somebody else. Really, even though I said my schedule was flexible, I have a lot on my plate tomorrow, as well. Actually, I have some must-see clients that I shouldn't postpone meetings with. Sorry, I just can't do it," Norman said in his best serious tone.

Annoyed by his conflicting report, I shot back, "Okay! Okay! I got it. You can't do it!" My frustration was spilling over for sure now. I knew damn well he didn't have a job, much less clients to tend to.

"Wow, it must be a pretty important interview," Norman interjected.

"Yeah, it's real important. I have a chance for a one-on-one interview with Larry Holmes."

Norman was suddenly infused with new life. "Larry Holmes! Are you kidding me? Hell, yeah, I'll do it. A chance to meet the champ? I'd be a fool to pass up a chance to meet him!"

Norman's enthusiasm was a bit too much, in my opinion. Zaynah agreed as told by the scowl she gave from across the salon.

"Okay, then, Norman, so you're in? Thanks so much. Meet me at my house tomorrow morning at eleven and we'll go from there," I said, grateful.

As soon as he left, my sister and I talked further about it. "I don't know, Rita. You might need to postpone the interview," she said. "Norman may not be able to pull this off. Look at him, he's a homeless drunk, Rita!"

"Zaynah, I just don't want to risk not ever getting this opportunity again. I would never be able to reschedule it."

"Look, Rita. Norman, is going to get in there and embarrass you in some way. I just know it."

"I know he lives in his car and drinks a little too much, but he wouldn't dare be foolish enough to insult the heavyweight boxing champ of the world. Besides that, underneath it all, Norman is a nice guy and he idolizes Larry," I said.

"Okay then. You'd better lay down some rules of engagement for our friend then. Number one: absolutely no drinking any alcohol!" Zaynah said.

INTERVIEW TIME

At 7:45 on the morning of my much-anticipated interview with Larry Holmes, my kids had just left on the school bus, so I went to prepare for the day ahead of me. Quite unexpectedly my doorbell started ringing and gonging like crazy. Was there an emergency? Perhaps one of the kids left a book or something. Startled I rushed to the door still in my nightgown. "Who is it?" I asked.

"It's Norman!" the voice said.

What! "Why are you here so early?" I asked him through the closed door. "We're not scheduled to leave till eleven."

"Well, I just wanted to show you something and go over a few details with you," he insisted. I ran to put on a jogging suit and opened the door. Shivering from the morning chill, rubbing his hands together, Norman stepped inside, thankful to be out of the cold.

"Woo! It's really cold out there! I know I'm early but I really wanted to show you this camera and go over exactly what is expected of me," he said. I appreciated his eagerness to get things right. By no means was I an expert on cameras, as I could barely operate my little Canon Sure Shot, which I used to capture events as best I could. However, I'd been around enough professional photographers and had seen enough commercial cameras to recognize that Norman was working with the real deal. Dressed in a pair of blue jeans, plaid button-down shirt, blue sports jacket, and Western-style boots—which were so run over to the sides it made him appear bowlegged—he was ready. And they just happened to be the clothes he wore the night before. Other than that sad detail, Norman looked the part. Although he was doing me a favor, somehow I was returning the same. I was happy for him. "Oh, by the way, that's an awesome-looking camera," I said with a big smile. "I didn't know you were into photography."

"It's not my camera. I borrowed it from my main boy. He loaned it to me when I told him that I was going to accompany you to take photos of Larry Holmes. As a matter of fact, he wanted to do the photos himself, but I told him that wasn't possible, so he let me borrow the camera under the condition that I give him a photo of Larry Holmes. Not a bad deal, right?"

"Sure, that's a good deal, but I just need to run a few things by you as it relates to this project today," I said.

"Okay," he responded.

"Norman, you really need to conduct yourself in an unquestionably professional manner. I understand you're hyped about meeting Larry Holmes, but you need to tone it down and act professional. Under no circumstance are you to ask Larry for an autograph or to take a photo with him. Your conversation should be minimal; it should not exceed greetings and salutations unless absolutely necessary. And the most important thing, Norman, is that under no circumstances are you to consume any alcohol on the trip, even if it is offered to you. Got it?"

"Okay, got it," he said.

"Good. Now I have some things I must tend to before we go. I'll see you back here at eleven sharp," I said.

"Me, too. Got some things to do. I'll see you back here at eleven. Thanks!"

*   *   *

I put on a mid-length gray skirt with a long-sleeved black button-down silk blouse and black suede pumps. For the chill outside I donned a red fox fur jacket, then draped a Louis Vuitton bag over my shoulder and carried a matching briefcase. About 10:55, Norman was honking the horn. We had agreed that he would drive my car because there was no way his old rundown jalopy would make it. Nor could I take the chance on being seen in such a beat-up vehicle. As I was approaching, Norman exited his car and walked toward the passenger side of my current model dark metallic gray Mercedes-Benz, which I had already unlocked with the automatic key. Like a gentleman, he opened the door for me. *How nice*, I thought. When he got close to me, I smelled alcohol. "Have you been drinking?" I snarled.

Slurring slightly, he said, "Na, not really. I just had a few beers."

I let out a long sigh of disgust. "That's it! I'm driving!"

With that, I stormed off to the driver's side of my car, which was parked right in front of Norman's bomb (car). My disappointment with him was unmistakable. He said nothing further and knuckled beneath my instructions. So off I went accompanied by my makeshift photographer and a calculated risk. I was determined. Less than fifteen minutes into the trip Norman was dead to the world, snoring like a bear. With a travel time of at least an hour and forty-five minutes, in good traffic, I figured Norman would have slept off his buzz by then and be in good shape to work. Unfamiliar with the narrow winding roads leading to Easton, I was frightened at the thought of accidently careening down one of the many cliffs along the way. I drove like an old lady clenching the steering wheel, staring straight ahead without batting an eye. As if this wasn't bad enough, about an hour into the drive, Norman suddenly woke up, grabbed his camera, and added to my anxiety with repetitive click noises of his camera as he vigorously started snapping pictures of me. When I commanded him to stop, he said nothing and quickly turned the camera toward the window on the passenger-side and fired off at least ten more rounds. "Will you please stop taking pictures, particularly of me?" I demanded. "Now, what the hell are you taking pictures of the landscape for anyway? And how much film do you have?"

"Don't worry, I have a whole extra roll. I was just taking some shots to get used to the camera," he said.

I shook my head. "Norman, we're going to need more than another roll of film. Now we have to stop and buy more." This interview was my big chance. It was important to me to be prepared especially since Larry was gracious enough to grant me extended time at his home with his wife and family, as well as a visit to a hotel he had recently purchased. After stopping at Wal-Mart to purchase several more rolls of film, we proceeded to the destination.

We pulled into a parking lot across the street from Larry's office building, which was located in the main area of Easton. Following my instincts, I reminded Norman one more time to be cool and not act like an overzealous fan. Assuring me that he had it covered, we proceeded on to Larry's office, where we were greeted by one of the members of his staff, just outside. After a brief wait, we were escorted in to meet Larry. His office was huge and tastefully furnished. It was more like a presidential suite with every accommodation of home. From the initial introduction, Larry was quite the obliging host. "Welcome to Easton," he said, extending his hand to me. Realizing that Norman was standing right next to me, quiet, I introduced him to Larry. He extended the same grace to Norman, with a welcoming hand. I could see the spark in Norman's eye. Well, after slapping his hand to Larry's hand, with a force so hard it sounded like a pistol went off, Norman said, "Larry motherfucking Holmes, my man! I can't believe I'm really standing here with you! You're a bad motherfucker, man. Oh, man!"

Shocked and dismayed I tried to make light of the situation and said, "WOW! That was quite a handshake, Norman! Just remember you're not here to spar with Larry, just to take photos."

Obviously, getting the hint to knock it off, Norman quickly responded, "My bad, man, I just got a little carried away."

Apparently amused with Norman, Larry laughed and said, "No problem."

Delving further into the interview, I got to observe Larry Holmes the superior athlete, the man, husband, father, friend, and revered resident of Easton. The interview would span not only from his office but would also include other businesses he owned The final stop would be at his home with him and his wife.

By now we were two hours into the interview and the next stop was Larry's home. Architecturally, I would describe the house as a mid-century modern style compound. The exterior and interior consisted of modern lines. The home was exquisite yet welcoming. His wife Diane welcomed us. I had seen her on other occasions—boxing events, I'm sure—but had never been properly introduced. Aside from her physical attractiveness, she was spiritually beautiful, as well, and extremely hospitable. I vividly recall her touring us around her home and ending up at their indoor pool. Without reservation I can say Diane Holmes impressed me as one of the most pleasant women I'd ever met. There was not an untoward word about her anywhere, from anyone. No matter when or where you encountered her, she was friendly, and delicate in her mannerisms.

The last stop before leaving the Holmes's house was a tour of Larry's fleet of expensive and rare automobiles. They were housed in a huge garage, several times as large as the average three-car residential garage. The facility was immaculately kept, as were the cars. It was a good thing I brought along a tape recorder because I was collecting so much material, it would have been impossible to take notes.

By now, I felt really comfortable with Larry, Diane, and their staff. But, it was getting late and I didn't want to overstay our welcome. After thanking Larry and Diane for their time, Norman and I had packed up our equipment and were about to leave. The plan was averted when Larry reminded us that we had yet to see his newly purchased hotel. Naturally, I was more than happy to include a visit to the hotel, get some photos, and check out the venue. Norman and I trailed Larry, and the two men accompanying him, to the hotel. Arriving at the facility, I was expecting to see a small establishment, but that was not the case at all. We pulled up to an edifice that would rival a Marriot hotel and its grounds. It was impressive to witness Larry Holmes' business objectives to accrued properties. Deliberately, I avoided asking exactly how many properties he owned or the collective value of them. Along with an office and clothing store, Larry owned other properties in a prime location of Easton. That was proof enough of his entrepreneurship and business savvy.

Upon completing the tour of his recently renovated hotel, Larry invited us to join him for a meal. He led us to one of the restaurants in the hotel. Joined by the two men who had been accompanying us throughout our visit, we sat in a booth. Norman had been a gem throughout our visit, capturing images and being very discreet with conversation. I was really proud of my friend because he did a great job. However, I got a bit nervous when Larry ordered a glass of wine and insisted that we join him for a glass of Blue Nun with dinner. Larry described it as a very light semisweet-tasting wine that he felt sure we'd enjoy. Under no circumstance would I have ever indulged in alcoholic beverages on the job, not even light semisweet-tasting wine, as Larry put it, so I politely declined his offer, expecting Norman to do the same. Not only was I concerned about Norman drinking too much and engaging in loose behavior,

I dreaded driving back to Philly. Recalling the winding roads and narrow passages going around cliffs that could easily be driven off of, I never wanted to drive that route again. I was actually comforted by the thought of Norman driving us back to Philly. Obviously, that would not be a consideration if he started drinking. My hopes of relaxing during the journey back home was shattered when Norman abruptly reached for the bottle of wine, poured himself a glass, and said, "Hell yeah, man, I'll try it; I need a drink after taking all those photos!"

Nervous that I could experience a debacle within minutes of every swig Norman took, I shot him a look of disapproval and held it relentlessly. And by no means would he make eye contact with me. He just continued to drink his fill, glass after glass after glass, all the while carrying on a conversation with Larry and dropping one F bomb after the next. In an effort to minimize any further damage, I interrupted the flow and announced that I needed to get back to Philly.

Fortunately for me, Larry was not the least bit disturbed by Norman's language. Primarily, I think it was because of Norman's delivery. He had laced it with so much humor that Larry was laughing during the whole meal. The best part was that Norman wasn't saying anything out of kilter; there was actually realistic substance coming out of Norman's mouth.

Under different circumstances, wherein it wasn't a professional environment and I wasn't trying to pass Norman off as a professional photographer, his language wouldn't have been as disconcerting. All in all, I had to admit things went well that day and I couldn't have done it without the help of my homeless buddy. Norman rescued the project and was indeed an asset. For that I will always have a note of gratitude to Norman, who still remains a good friend.

✶　✶　✶

On a follow-up trip to Easton, Zaynah accompanied me. In spite of earnest efforts, most of the photos Norman took did not come out clear, if at all. Even the photos that could've passed weren't usable for my article. So, I decided that I would just use my Canon Sure Shot camera to get some more photos. Granted, it wasn't an extravagant-looking camera with zoom lenses and all the added pieces, but it took great pictures and was easy to use. In addition, since I only needed more photos to complete my article, I figured between Zaynah and myself, it'd be easy to do, then get right back to Philly, which we did.

Ultimately, the article was a success. There was extensive interesting information about Larry and his family life that made for eager reading. And as if that wasn't wonderful enough, the *Tribune* featured the article as a multi-page pullout in the weekend edition of the paper, instead of the expected, traditional magazine layout.

Over the years, Larry, his wife, and I maintained a good rapport between us. Whether I was at press conferences, a weigh-in, sparring sessions, or covering one of Larry's championship fights, Larry always looked out for me and treated me with the utmost respect. Like being associated with Muhammad Ali and Joe Frazier, knowing Larry definitely had its perks. Special treatment was something I had grown accustomed to pursuant to obtaining press credentials and having all-access passes to events and after-parties. A few occasions where Larry really looked out for me come to mind.

At the last minute I had decided to cover a championship fight held at the Wynn Hotel in Las Vegas, Nevada. The ability to secure a room at the facility where the venue was being held was a great advantage for someone covering events. You simply had to travel from your room to an area in the hotel where a specific activity was taking place. Typically, it required making reservations well in advance. The Wynn and most of the surrounding hotels/casinos were completely booked, which meant I had to get a room that was quite a distance away. Well, as fate would have it, I ran into Larry and members of his entourage, and what a pleasure, as always! We chitchatted for a few then somewhere in our exchange I mentioned my hotel dilemma. Before I knew it Larry and his folks were getting me a comp room at the Wynn. Not only did they secure a room where I needed to be to have the best coverage possible for the fight, they also gave me ringside tickets to the fight. There were press agents who didn't have the seating arrangement I had! And, what likely made me appear more prestigious was being escorted to my seat by Wynn security, which happened to be smack next to Don King and Steve Wynn. The two gentlemen had companions seated with them. A middle-aged Caucasian couple, and a beautiful young blonde who couldn't have been more than twenty-two years old were seated on the other side of Don. I assumed she was the couple's daughter. Within minutes we had all exchanged hellos and made brief light conversation, which I quickly exited, leaving them to talk among themselves. It was obvious their eyes were on me, perhaps wondering who in the world I could be.

I'd observed many details around me. One being that the assumed mother and daughter were clad in a blinding array of diamond jewelry. Don and the gentleman—the father, I guess— also illuminated the area with their Rolex watches and Don's gaudy gold ring. If I had to guess, I'd estimate the collective value they'd donned was at least a million dollars. There I was, an unknown, surrounded by all this wealth and affluence. They had to be wondering if I was in the right seat. As I discreetly observed them I couldn't help but notice the touchy-feely manner in which the young blonde rubbed all over Don's back. Seemed seductive to me at first thought. Or, perhaps, it was the kind of affection a young woman might have for a grandfather, and Don was certainly more than old enough to fit that bill. Perhaps she was coming on to Don? As for Don and her parents, they appeared to be oblivious to the young maiden's behavior, even when she started becoming loud, teetering on obnoxious, as she got drunker. I felt that a young woman of her stature and privilege should have behaved with more decorum in public. At any rate, minding my business was the order of the hour. After all, it wasn't my daughter, Don was not my father, and they weren't my guests, or friends. To the best of my ability I focused my attention on the fight despite the young lady's verbal outbursts. It made me think about my own daughter and feel a sense of pride at what a classy young lady she was. Under no scenario would my daughter ever act like that. Was her conduct acceptable to her parents, Don King, and/or Steve Wynn because she was the daughter of wealthy parents? I wondered, as the last round of the fight concluded.

When the fight was over I immediately left the area and headed toward the press conference, where I ran into a Philadelphia colleague covering the fight for another news outlet. She had a local TV show in Delaware she was gathering news for, and like me, she had also failed to secure reservations at the Wynn, a perfect opportunity to offer her the other bed in my newly acquired room, which she gladly accepted. It just goes to show that good deeds beget good deeds.

Rita's Rule # 12

Whenever and wherever possible, extend kindness to others, without expecting anything in return. Releasing good energy attracts good energy in return.

PROMINENT WOMEN AFFILIATED WITH THE SPORT OF BOXING

Since the existence of boxing, men have been the face of it. However, a feminine line has been cast throughout the sport, as many women have contributed to the sustainability of boxing. Promotional event experts, sports commentators, and countless other women attend to the operational concerns within the world of boxing. Most of them are hardworking, dedicated individuals who remain anonymous to the millions of fans who frequent boxing events. Considered by many to be the unofficial First Lady of boxing, Mariam Muhammad is a phenomenal icon and boxing official. She's an extremely competent and knowledgeable person with a well-earned status in the boxing industry. Long before I ever covered my first fight, she was immersed in the sport. Early on she worked with Bob Lee, president of the International Boxing Federation (IBF). I met her while working on fights with boxing promoter Murad Muhammad. Mariam was well versed in all aspects of official sanctioning of fights, ranking fighters, and was media savvy. Her expertise and leadership skills earned her the position of IBF president in 2001. To say I've always admired her is an understatement. My admiration spans beyond her outstanding accomplishments. She was a supportive person who looked out for me upon my initial involvement with the sport. Unlike some who blocked women access to press credentials, interviews with fighters, and/or the ability to obtain information, Mariam was very supportive. In essence, she pioneered the paths for numerous women to advance their careers in the boxing industry. Additional women like Cora Wiles, who became the boxing commissioner for Washington, DC, and Lynne Carter, boxing's first African American official female judge, are also worth mentioning. Columnists, event planners, PR specialists like Flo Anthony and me, who operated on the fringe of the boxing industry, also contributed to promotional aspects of the sport.

Brutal is the word often associated with the sport of boxing. As someone who was privileged to have affiliations with a profusion of champions and aspiring fighters, I can personally attest that brutal is not befitting for most boxers. Consistent with the occupations in general, there are the good, the bad, and the ugly. In my experience, whether pertaining to fighters, basketball players, baseball players, football players, corporate executives, entertainers, and so on, most of the men I've encountered are decent guys. However, far too often these men are forgotten as a result of coming in contact with counterproductive others that make the workplace uncomfortable and unbearable for women.

Ranking high among the list of decorous gentlemen in the sport of boxing/sports commentating is the incomparable Howard Cosell. Most would agree that his unique style of covering events contributed a lot to the elevation of sports. The memorable exchanges between him and Muhammad Ali are what made me first take notice of Mr. Cosell. Once I began covering fight promotions, I was in his presence on numerous occasions, but had only spoken with him a few times. And it was always around something related to boxing or Muhammad Ali. While attending one of the Phillies baseball games, which Howard Cosell was commentating for, I ran into sports historian "Bert" Randolph Sugar. We were engaged in a substantive conversation about an upcoming event, when he said he was headed to the press area and suggested I walk with him so we could continue conversing. Once we were in close proximity to the press box, I could clearly hear Cosell's voice. I told Bert that I always enjoyed Cosell's interviews with Ali. Bert insisted that I come in and say hello to Howard. By this time we were right at the doorway of the press box, and it was my intention to just turn around and leave Bert to return to my seat. Before doing so, I softly said to Bert, "No thanks, that's okay. I'm not even sure Mr. Cosell would remember me."

Suddenly I heard Howard Cosell utter the words in his choppy speech tempo, "Rit- ta! Rit-ta of course I remember you. Who could ever forget the lovely maiden Rit-ta Rit-ta. Come on in. It's good to see you. How have you been?" He ran off the above inquiries in a matter of seconds. His welcoming gesture relaxed me enough to respond to his questions and chat with them for a few moments before leaving the press box. What may seem like a small gesture to some was a big deal to me. Being acknowledged by the legendary Howard Cosell was an honor. Though it was only a few words, the fact that he remembered me, out of all of the many people he came in contact with in the sports world, was significant. It was verification that I had arrived in the boxing world as a serious public relations consultant and columnist.

7

ENCOUNTERS OF MANY KINDS

As my numerous encounters with celebrities go, so goes an awkward one I had with members of the Jackson Five. Let's start with Tito Jackson and an incident that took place in Philadelphia.

As the producer for the Georgie Woods Show, I assisted with various concerts and productions beyond my normal duties. Attending to details for entertainers' performing venues in Philadelphia was a natural for me, and something I had done for Georgie on numerous occasions. Georgie informed me that Michael Jackson wanted to attend the Phillies baseball game. While he did not mention Michael's brothers, I assumed that this venture would include all the Jacksons. I contacted Mayor Greene's office to request the mayor's private box at the stadium, for their privacy and comfort. His assistant answered his calls of course and immediately recognized my voice. "What a coincidence," she said. "The mayor is walking towards me right now. I'll ask him. Hold on." She neglected to mute the call, so I overheard the conversation between them and heard when the mayor said, "Sure, Spicer can use the suite. By the way what is a Jackson?"

The assistant replied with a few bars of "ABC," the 1970 #1 hit by the Jackson Five. "You know that song, sir!" she said, keeping time with the tune.

"Oh, you mean Michael Jackson and his brothers," responded Mayor Greene, as he finally saw the light!

After securing the mayor's suite, I learned that Georgie had not made any preparations for sufficient security. As a result, I called two of my friends, John Anderson, who was a member of city council, and Philadelphia's first African-American deputy mayor, George Burrell, Esq.

What started out as a request for me and the Jacksons to be accompanied to the stadium ended up in abashed pleading, on my part. After all, I had called two high-level intensely busy city officials in the middle of the day, and requested to be accompanied with a small group to the stadium. What else should I have expected?

After I didn't let up, and had explained a hundred times my need for high security, I finally got a yes — a reluctant one, but a yes just the same. This was important because at that particular time I did not know anyone in charge at the stadium, and that particular area of South Philadelphia was known to have some racist tendencies. It was important that the Jacksons' trip to the stadium was pleasant and free of incidents.

Gary Maddox and Gary Williams were major stars of the Phillies baseball team at the time. Gary Maddox was also someone I had secured as a guest on the Georgie Woods radio show. So, I reached out to him and requested that he meet Michael Jackson and his brothers, along with some other ball players. I wanted the Jacksons' experience, that day, to be a memorable one.

John Anderson and George Burrell showed up with the police escort that I had requested and were waiting for us outside of the hotel. Shortly after Georgie Woods informed me that Michael wasn't going to the game, after all, so I was even happier to have a member of city council and the deputy mayor with us. It was time to head out to the stadium; our police motorcade was revved and ready to go. My plan was to drive or ride with John or George in one of the city cars. However, Georgie Woods was insisting that I ride in the limousine with the Jacksons. I quickly declined. "I don't know them like that. I'd be very uncomfortable," I explained.

"Just walk over to the car and meet them so they know who's escorting them," Georgie instructed.

"Why aren't YOU riding with them?" I asked.

"I can't! I've got a lot of stuff to do before the show tomorrow," he said. So Georgie insisted that I at least permit him to introduce me to them.

"Fine. Let's both go for an introduction," I said.

We arrived at their limo on the side where the door was already opened. Tito was seated on the backseat across from Jackie, who was seated with another male that wasn't one of the Jackson siblings.

Still not planning to ride with them, I leaned in the car as Georgie made the introduction. Suddenly, I felt a nudge in my back as I was thrust to the floor of the car and Georgie said, "This is Rita Spicer, she's going to ride with you and be your host for today."

I didn't want to make more of a spectacle of myself, so I got up quickly and sat near the window in the backseat of the limousine across from Tito. I explained to them that I had secured the tickets for the baseball game, then attempted to make light conversation, for about thirty seconds, without a peep from any of them when suddenly, Tito exclaimed, "Do you even know anything about baseball?"

I was quick to pick up on his arrogance and realized the hostile environment I was in. I was more than annoyed, particularly since I felt as if Tito's actions suggested that I was some over-the-hill groupie impressed with them. Never being one to back down from rebutting against being disrespected, I turned toward Tito and shot back, "Gary Maddox! That's the extent of what I know about baseball! Do I detect a problem here? At this point I'm really not in the mood for any attitude!"

The car was already rolling when Tito said, "Stop the car! I want her out of here!"

I responded, "First of all, there's nothing I would like better! But before we do that, there's something you should know," I said, trying to compose myself. "You see that police escort and those two city official cars containing a member of city council and the deputy mayor? They are compliments of Rita Spicer — yours truly.

So when I get out of this car and I leave, so does all that," I said, pointing. "And y'all can go down to the stadium on your own, get in line, purchase your tickets, and sit in the stadium like everybody else. And guess what else? Some of those racist people down there at the stadium don't give a damn about a Jackson shaking it down to nothing! Y'all will be just another group of niggers. You have no idea what it takes to get the accommodations I secured for y'all. So what's it going to be? Do we go to the game or do you want me to get out?"

There was silence until Jackie finally spoke up. "No problem, let's go to the game, thank you."

As a few of the ball players had promised me, right before the game Gary Maddox and Gary Williams, along with a few more Phillies baseball players came to the mayor's suite and brought the Jacksons a few signed souvenirs. Jackie, Tito, and their associate sat right down in front of the suite.

Still miffed by the limo incident, I searched out a seat in the very back of the suite as far away from them as I could get. Of course John and George detected that something was wrong and asked me about it. I explained the limo ride in detail. They were annoyed at how I'd been treated and insisted that we leave then, which we did without saying anything to Jackie or Tito. However, in all decency, we did leave them with police security and the limo so they could get back to their hotel safely.

That evening my sister Zaynah and I were having dinner when a middle age Caucasian male named Freddie joined us. Freddie was identified as the point person for the Jackson Five, so I'd been communicating with him during the weeks leading up to the promotion. Since he did have a relevant role with the Jacksons, he expressed his disgust in regard to how I was treated and vowed to tell their father about it. It made no difference to me at all if he told Joe Jackson or not because at that point I wasn't even going to go to the show, which was scheduled for the next night. I don't know if he ever told Joe Jackson or not, nor did it make any difference to me. I was done.

Setting aside my insult and fury for just a moment, I had to remember that as a professional in a world of celebrities, I had to go to the show, my presence was important. I had responsibilities to tend to. I kept my anger under wraps and went anyway. Engaged in my normal routine of working at the venue, I ensured that celebrities and notables attending the event had their credentials and VIP seating.

The show was already in high gear when I had to go to one of the VIP suites to escort some guests. Michael was at the height of his performance, with his brothers backing him up of course, when he abruptly ripped off his shirt. In spite of him having the smallest chest I'd ever seen on a man, his theatrics and extraordinary stage presence electrified the crowd and widened my ears and eyes, too. I became oblivious to Tito's actions toward me in that moment. I marveled at the extraordinary talent that played out before my eyes. Michael Jackson was astonishing. On the whole, I had to give all the Jacksons their just due. As a unit, they were like a machine whose relevance called for the support of each other. And support they did. And that's the making of icons.

In retrospect, I also put myself in their shoes when it came to the limo incident. A strange lady is introduced to them and thrown into the car at their feet. How does that come off as someone you should respect? And once I rose from the floor in utter embarrassment, that was a ticket to ride—me! They might've thought I was some kind of nut, not an entertainment professional. Not trying to make excuses for their treatment of me, I'm just trying to be fair to both sides of view. But, you know what? I'm sure today they don't even remember me, nor that incident. Admittedly, I thought pretty highly of myself at the time and was used to flattery from men. So, to be reminded that I wasn't the most sought-after woman in the world knocked me off my game. *Hilarity emphasized!*

I only had one more Jackson encounter in my life. But before that and like countless others, years later, I was shattered by news of Michael Jackson's death, which I learned of before it was made public. My son-in-law, Mike Tyson, had confirmed his death via a call he received from Joe Jackson. My heart was broken for my son-in-law, the Jacksons, friends, and fans. It was such a phenomenal loss to the world and I mourned along with millions of others.

I got to see Tito in a different light in the throes of obscene grief. He was gentle. Humble. While the world was blaming the doctor who supplied the fatal dosage that ended Michael's life, Tito displayed a level of humility and understanding that made him stand out. Basically, he reminded us that it was God's will and he did not disparage anyone at that time. Having lost loved ones—two siblings to violence—I was particularly moved by his comments. He was obviously a reflection of the strong family values he grew up with. That's how I shall always regard Tito.

Rita's Rule # 13

While first impressions are impactful, they're not always correct.

In October 2017, I was in Whole Foods in Green Valley, Las Vegas, when I ran into Jackie Jackson, the peacemaker back in the limo, all those years ago. It was a coincidence for the ages. We passed awkward glares between us for a moment or two. I actually wasn't sure if it was him or not, initially, because his look had changed from back in the day. He finally gave a quick "Hi" and looked away. I did the same. His voice was familiar, even confirming. Was it really him?

I had gone to Whole Foods that day for the sole purpose of making a salad to go. And that's where Jackie was, too. I guess we were destined to collide that day. "Jackie?" I said softly.

"Yes," he replied in an even softer voice. His face was crumpled.

I had a flashback to the limo ride all those years before; my clumsy entrance…mine and Tito's fallout…and Jackie's peaceful resolve in the end. *"Oh no, here we go again,"* I thought. *"He must be thinking I'm some ancient groupie."* Desperate to dispel such a thought, I quickly said, "I'm Mike Tyson's mother-in-law." I could see the relief come over him.

"Oh, okay! How's Mike?" he said, suddenly awakened.

"Mike is great. Busy with the new version of his one-man show," I answered.

"Please tell him I asked about him," Jackie said.

"Will do," I replied as I started to walk away.

Later, I conveyed Jackie's well wishes to Mike, which he graciously received. Then in a manner only Mike could deliver, he jokingly commented, "Ah, name-dropping, hum, Mom?" to which I replied, "No, just telling the truth."

Mike likes to playfully instigate and burst people's bubbles, particularly those close to him who understand his sense of humor. Admittedly, it toyed with my self-worth just a little because I started questioning whether or not I was really viewed that way. On second thought, I knew better. There was no way I was one whose self-worth depended on knowing a celebrity, or two. Then I snapped back to reality and consoled myself with the fact that some names are worth dropping. In fact, celebrity or not any name is worth dropping if there's a reason to do so.

Rita's Rule # 14

Never doubt your self-worth or think that you are of lesser value than anyone regardless of someone else's lofty status.

FALLING FOR SMOKEY ROBINSON

Smokey Robinson was scheduled to receive a commemorative china bowl scripted with the official seal of the city of Philadelphia. I was standing back stage in clear view of the performance, with Deputy Mayor George Burrell and others, when George insisted that I present the bowl to Smokey on behalf of the city. "No," I said. "I don't work for the city."

"So what. You don't have to work for the city. You can still do it. It's better that you do it than a man," George countered, meaning him.

I totally got why George, or any man for that matter, wouldn't want to present the award to Smokey Robinson, especially if there was a woman available to do it. Not that it mattered to him, but in his own right, George Burrell was quite the heartthrob for most ladies. He was quite attractive, above average height with a light brown complexion and a face that boasted keen features. He could not get through a crowd without being noticed, that's for sure. He had been a prominent attorney and was now the deputy mayor. George had what I would describe as professional swag in personal magnitude. Aside from being one of the most powerful men in the city, he was always a gentleman and someone I could respect.

George kept on until I agreed to make the presentation. After all what could possibly go wrong, right? Well, aside from being extremely clumsy — a condition I never overcame since childhood. To make matters worse, I was wearing heels this day. Not my norm. Fully aware of my 5'8" height and my tendency toward clumsiness, I generally wore flats. Literally, I could be standing around with a group of friends, or by myself for that matter, when suddenly, for no apparent reason, my ankle or leg would buckle, nearly toppling me over. So you can imagine how concerned I was about falling on stage in front of a crowd of more than twenty thousand people.

Well, the time had come to make the presentation. With the china bowl in hand, I proceeded toward the star of the show. There was a pause in Smokey's performance to announce the presentation of a city tribute to him. Just about the time I was in my comfort zone and a few feet away from Smokey, I tripped over my own feet. Instinctively, I was conscious not to drop the bowl — which I was more concerned about breaking than my neck. Midway between the floor and a standing position, I felt the strong grip of hands on both of my upper arms. Instantaneously, in the midst of a roar of laughter radiating from the packed stadium of onlookers, I made eye contact with the individual behind the firm grip that spared me from crashing to the floor—it was Smokey Robinson.

With the warmest, most comforting smile, and softest voice he said, "Are you all right?"

Still somewhat dazed from full-blown humiliation and looking directly into Smokey's beautiful hazel eyes, I nodded yes. Trust me, I know that when you err in the face of 20,000 strong, you don't live it down. You're tagged as a joke. An oaf. Maybe even as someone who was so stars-struck that she couldn't hold her composure and stumbled into the arms of her fantasy crush or something.

After that day I continued to think about the experience. It was thoroughly embarrassing, but being saved by Smokey Robinson was thoroughly comforting. My friends, family, coworkers and strangers talked about it for months on end. I was teased at work, on the streets, by friends, you name it!

It was a while before I could really laugh about it, but it's so easy to find the humor in it now. For countless women around the globe, meeting Smokey Robinson—let alone being rescued by him—would be like a fantasy come true. However, I am willing to bet that no woman on the planet would have sought to meet him the way I did. What a unique experience anyway. There is not a dark side to it, just laughter and excitement. It was much better than meeting Bill Cosby, who I happened to be related to.

*　*　*

GOOD OLD COUSIN BILL

It was the winter of 1980. Philadelphia had just elected their first black mayor, Wilson Goode. The city was bursting with pride for having accomplished this major victory, which took place directly after Mayor Bill Greene's departure from the office.

Democrats seem to be the party of inclusion, particularly

after defeating the controversial former mayor, Frank Rizzo. The inauguration for Mayor Goode, and for state and city officials, took place at the Philadelphia Academy of Music. Peter Liacouras, president of Temple University, and Bill Cosby were also being honored at this time. The concert hall was befitting for the occasion, as it was indeed lavish. The ceremonies were long and verbose but necessary, I'm sure. Nonetheless, I left to take a breather in the lobby.

Within seconds I ran into two acquaintances of mine who also knew I was a member of the Cosby clan. Bill Keyes and Ed Ford were good people. We were in the midst of a nice chat session when we noticed Bill coming out of the main concert room and walking toward us. Suddenly, out of nowhere Bill kissed me on the lips while also scooping me up into his arms in a big warm embrace.

"How are you doing?" he asked.

Confused by Bill's action, I pulled away and said, "Fine?" *What was that?* I thought.

Honestly, from the delighted expression on Bill's face I believe he thought I was someone else. Even though we were related, I'd NEVER seen him as an adult, so the mistake was easily possible. From there he went on to very enthusiastically greet and hug Bill and Ed, too. To some extent I wanted to introduce myself properly as his relative, but the three men were thoroughly enjoying their time together, so I returned to the venue.

Departing the Academy of Music through a side street reserved for the VIPs, I ran into the same two acquaintances from the lobby and walked with them. Bill and his beautiful wife Camille were walking about three feet ahead of us. One of the men I was walking with said, "So, did you tell Bill you were his cousin?"

"No," I replied.

Before I was able to provide a reason why I was not informing Bill of my Cosby heritage, Bill turned toward us and said, "What? Who's my cousin?"

"I am," I answered.

"Really?"

"Yes," I said and began to explain how.

Then Bill turned to his wife and said, "See that, Camille, I told you everybody in my family wasn't ugly. Look at her, beautiful, just like you."

Obviously used to her husband's comedic ways, Camille simply smiled and acknowledged me with a nod. That was my "in" to a proper introduction to her. She was extremely pleasant, classy, and distinguished. It was my pleasure to meet her.

Unlike Bill's appeal, which was one of notable intelligence with a brush of brandish comedy, Camille's brilliance was evident in a more subtle way.

"Let's talk more, cuz," Bill propositioned. "Are you going to the reception at Temple?"

"Yes, I'm headed there now," I said.

"Good. We'll see you there," he said, while Camille confirmed with a nod and simple smile.

The reception room at Barbara's Hall, located on Temple University's campus, was packed with dignitaries, politicians, Temple faculty members and students. Bill was mobbed by the crowd. It was obvious that most of the people were there only to get a glimpse of him. Nonetheless, he still found moments to briefly chat with me. Inasmuch as we seemed to establish a good rapport, I finally mustered up the nerve to ask for an interview with him at some point in time. His response disappointed me.

"I don't generally give interviews unless I have something to say. But I'm going to give you my manager's info so that we can set up something."

"Okay, thanks," I replied. I knew I would see him later at a fund-raiser for Ira Davis, who was a close friend of Bill's and was running for city council on the Republican ticket. Normally, I didn't attend too many Republican events, but I knew Ira Davis from the neighborhood and wanted to lend my support.

Ira was among the many individuals who occasionally stopped by our family home and chatted with us on the porch. In addition, he had the status of a local celebrity who had a promising future as a result of running track at La Salle University, which was located a few blocks from our home.

Later that evening I arrived at the fund-raiser. Bill was already seated at the dais (seats of honor), which was elevated about two feet from the floor.

I was happy to see him again, particularly because there was the prospect of landing an interview with him for my newspaper and perhaps even booking him on the Georgie Woods radio show. Eagerly, but not obnoxiously, I walked toward Bill and made eye contact with him. I smiled at him, but did not receive one in return. "Hey, cuz, how you doing?" I said, trying to be lighthearted about it.

He gave me a stern look square in the face. I didn't catch the hint though. There was no way someone who'd treated me so warm and kind just hours before could switch up and ignore me like this. So nervously, I pressed on.

"It's me, your cousin…from earlier today."

I was certain I'd get a positive response now. But, no, not at all. Instead, he withdrew his gaze from me and turned his head as far as he could over his left shoulder, ignoring me once again. Well, there was no mistaking that he wanted nothing to do with me at that point. Admittedly, I felt humiliated and was curious about what had happened to make him behave like that. However, as fate would have it, I never got the opportunity to find out about it on that evening or any other occasion where Bill and I were under the same roof, at the same time, attending the same affair. Simply put, his basic disregard for me as a person, let alone a member of the media, was a turn-off. It didn't matter what his reasons were for his sudden change of attitude toward me, nor did it matter how accomplished he was as a person or that his interview would have added to my status as a columnist for the *Philadelphia Tribune*. I would never subject myself to the possibility of him treating me with such disrespect again.

Bill Cosby's negative response was more of a shock than anything. I'd known so many prominent people who had treated me, and other members of the media, with so much more regard.

Rita's Rule # 15

Immediately take the hint and remove yourself from someone at the first sign of them not wanting to be bothered by you. Never give anyone a second chance to disregard you.

Not only did Bill not connect with me as a family member, there wasn't even a Philly connect. Generally, there's a special bond or at least some small regard Philadelphians have toward each other. My relationship with Philly's pride and joy, Earl the Pearl Monroe, is a perfect example. Phenomenal star basketball player though he was, he treated people well, always receiving them with warmth and responding to fans with respect and wit. Equally, it's how he always treated me. I grew to expect this kind of treatment from celebrated people in general.

I met Earl when he was the Rookie of the Year for the Baltimore Bullets. He was an astoundingly adept basketball player, and a real cool dude from south Philly. Not only was he smooth, his swag extended on and off the court as did the broad, winning smile on his face. Watching him play reminded me a lot of the Harlem Globetrotters when it came to moves and tricks he'd pull on the court against his opponents. The only difference was that Earl was not mock playing, like the Globetrotters do for entertainment purposes. Earl's moves were real!

His mother, Rose, had a beautiful home on Haines Street in the Germantown section of Philadelphia. She was among the women who greatly impacted my development during my transition from teenager to womanhood. My sister Shirley and Earl's younger sister Teresa were friends and schoolmates. After becoming friends with Earl, I met his mother Rose, who I visited on occasions. It had little to do with Earl. He wasn't around most of the time. I was simply fond of Rose. She was uncompromisingly wise. Being around her allowed me to see where Earl got his wisdom and charm from. Although we didn't see each other daily, monthly, or at times for years, we shared a friendship that was not impaired by time or geography. But whenever we'd see each other, it was always great. In fact, while attending one of the Don King Production fights, and hanging out with his son, Carl King, Carl mentioned his admiration for Earl the Pearl and that he was his favorite basketball player. He said he would love to get a signed artifact from the Pearl for his son, Carl Jr., and himself.

I hadn't spoken to Earl in several years and had to get his phone number from his sister. As always, Earl was happy to hear from me, and willing to honor my requests. Fame and fortune did not deter him from his people. He was an ultra-proud African-American who never shied away from his roots. While he was a phenomenal ballplayer in the NBA, his prowess reigned supreme in the Baker League, too. He really showed out there! Fans could be heard screaming his various titles throughout the stadium. Some called him Black Jesus, so some were screaming, *Jesus! Jesus!* while others were screaming, *The Pearl! The Pearl!* For me he remains my true friend, Earl.

SMOKIN' JOE FRAZIER, BACK IN THE DAY...

My sister and I had met Joe Frazier during a performance at Ciro's Nightclub on Ogontz Avenue in the West Oak Lane section of Philadelphia. It was our friend's birthday. She was dating a drummer in the group called Joe Frazier & the Knockouts. Yeah, that's right. Joe prided himself as an R&B kind of down-home singer. Needless to say, he loved the public and the public loved him. Well, apparently, Joe was impressed with us, too, as told by his visits to our table every time the band took a break. Joe invited us to come check out his club, Joe Frazier's Knockout Room at 15th and Fitzwater in South Philly. Since we already had no business being in any nightclub because we were underage, we were hesitant to say yes. After some persuading, which included sending a car to pick us up, we consented to go. Besides, that night would just happen to be his birthday party.

From the time the three of us arrived at Joe's club, it was obvious to everyone that we were special to him. He kept referring to us as pretty girls and telling everybody to look out for us. Joe was a real party guy; he loved to dance, sing, and engage the crowd. In spite of Joe going out of his way to make sure that we were accommodated in every possible way, the crowd that had gathered at the club was a little too raunchy for us. We didn't want to hurt Joe's feelings, so we made the excuse that I wasn't feeling well, which prompted him to have his driver take us home. After all, we were young and underexposed and this crowd was out of our league. In no way did our exit negatively impact our relationship with Joe; we maintained it quite well over the years. In fact, it became normal for him to just pop up at our place any time, unannounced. My sister and I shared our first apartment in Chestnut Hill, which was in route to Joe's mansion in Whitemarsh Pennsylvania, and like many young single girls we had our share of parties where we entertained a slew of friends, some of whom were NBA players and other celebrities. It didn't matter who was chilling at our apartment at the time, they were always impressed by seeing Joe Frazier. His stays were never long-he was just checking on his friends. In later years, Joe frequently stopped by our beauty salon at 7108 Germantown Ave, which was also close to his home in Whitemarsh.

I'll always remember Joe's greeting as he entered the shop. It didn't matter that our shop had an affluent setting filled with predominately professional, moneyed clientele demanding services that included everything from massage to hair and scalp treatments, to facials, and relaxation time in our recessed hot tub, all while sipping wine and champagne, of course. None of this pomp stopped him from entering with, "What it look like, ladies? They tryin' to get me, y'all!" Of course he commanded attention and invoked a roar of laughter every time. Above all, it was a fun environment, which was right up Joe's alley. Joe's love for my sister and me was reciprocated; we loved him dearly. I can't think of anything he wouldn't do for us, or most people for that matter. He was simply a kind, big bundle of love who cared about the well-being of others.

*   *   *

It was in the early 1970s when the Muslim community was sponsoring a citywide bazaar. I happened to stop by the office of community affairs, which I was affiliated with, and learned that the committee had been trying to get Joe Frazier to attend the event, to no avail. Knowing that I knew Joe, they asked me to try. I made no promises, but sought to see what I could do.

I discovered that Joe was training fighters at his gym at Broad Street & Lynnwood Avenue and paid him a visit. After asking him about attending the Muslim event, he blurted out, "I'm not going around those A-R-A-B-S. They don't like me!"

"Oh, stop it, that's not true," I rebutted.

"They're Ali's people," Joe insisted.

"Okay, okay. So will you go? That's all I want to know," I said.

So, after some back and forth I convinced Joe to attend the Muslim event. Much to his surprise, Joe received a hero's welcome from the Muslims and everyone else in attendance. I had personally greeted Joe upon his arrival near the entrance and walked him in.

Joe thoroughly enjoyed himself that day. He was so impressed that it set precedence for Joe's ongoing support and attendance at future Islamic fund-raisers that I would later host for the Sister Clara Muhammad School.

*   *   *

Time had taken up wings and I was turning forty! Joe showed up at my birthday party driving his own limousine, which he drove right over the hedges of my next-door neighbor's house. It was a cold day in January but my single dwelling split-level home was filled to capacity; everywhere you looked, up or downstairs, there were people. Tucked away in one corner was a jazz trio. On the lower level was a custom-built bar to rival any commercial bar setup, cocktail tables, and so on. My guests were at every turn, but left room for dancing.

The party was in full swing by the time Joe arrived, and as

always, he made quite an entrance. Making his way through the crowd, he sniffed out the bar. He picked up a tall glass and said, "Hey, mister bartender, pour me a shot of every liquor you got — right here." Of course that was not possible because the bar was stacked with far too many top-shelf brands of alcohol to go into one glass, regardless of how tall it was. With a laughing smile, the bartender did his best. "We'll see what we can do," he said with a cordial smile.

Glass in hand, Joe chugalugged the concoction of mixed liquors down, blew out a loud extended breath, and took to the dance floor, where he boogied all night.

* * *

Joe was actually more active in my life on many occasions than even my good friend Muhammad Ali. I guess you can say he was more accessible. One matter comes to mind where Joe lent a helping hand, concerning my son. When he was only seven he was the victim of neighborhood bullying. I was beside myself and kept pressing my son to handle the situation; he had to fight back! It didn't matter that we lived in an upper-class community. He needed to protect himself and send a strong message to the three boys who were at the center of his problem, which meant it was now my problem, too! Well, I called Joe to help my boy learn to defend himself, and he did! My son soon had no more problems from those young bullies.

Rita's Rule # 16

Control yours fears; never permit fears to control you.

Another time that comes to mind is when I took Joe Frazier to Cheltenham High School to speak with the students during an assembly. During Joe's approximately thirty-minute speech, he talked about the values of hard work, dedication, perseverance, and integrity. He provided examples of how such characteristics were fundamental to growth and development, even in him becoming the heavyweight champ of the world. It was obvious that the students really connected with Joe and thoroughly enjoyed his candor. I already had been in his presence enough and witnessed how he affected audiences all over.

Later that day we stopped by the Cheltenham Township Police Department. Again, Joe impressed those in attendance with his warm and engaging persona. He was cordial and agreeable; taking pictures, signing autographs, and shaking hands. However, Joe drew the line when the officers asked him to go inside one of the jail cells and pretend that he had been arrested. "Hell no!" he said, "I'm not going inside no damn cell. You white boys might forget that it's just a joke and keep my black ass locked up." The place erupted in laughter. I laughed and shook my head. That was Joe for ya.

A HEARTBREAKING FAREWELL

My last encounter with Joe was during a low point in my life. I spotted him seated with his son Marvis in a restaurant lounge area as I was passing through from the main dining area. His back was toward me but Marvis spotted me as I approached. "Here comes Rita! Rita!" he announced. Joe whipped his head around and saw me. It was heartwarming to see him again and experience his warm embrace.

With concern in his eyes he dug in deep. "Rita, how are you coming along? I really hate the way they have been treating you in the paper," he said.

By now there'd been an extraordinary amount of negative press about me. I was subjected to media harassment daily since the press identified me as a subject of a federal investigation. I could tell Joe was truly hurt. I attempted to comfort him by insisting that I was okay. He reached into his pocket and pulled out a humungous wad of money and started peeling off hundreds one by one. "Joe, what are you doing?" I asked, assuming the money was intended for me.

He turned to me and pulled me in close enough to kiss my cheek and said, "Here, take this. I want you to have this." I became overwhelmed and shook my head, no.

My eyes began to well up with tears, and with that, I gently pushed Joe's hand away. "I can't take any money from you, Joe. Thanks for the gesture, though. I really appreciate it," I said as my voice cracked. Joe's love and care for me preceded him. He wouldn't take no for an answer but I just couldn't. It certainly wasn't that I didn't need the money. I needed it terribly because by that time I was in a state of financial ruin and had already lost my properties, and nearly everything else I owned. Anyone under federal indictment can attest to how expensive it is to defend yourself. Add to that, being pounded all day, every day, by media lies, and so on. There is no way not to be adversely affected by it. I was on the verge of losing everything I ever owned or stood for. My self-respect and a healthy sense of pride were all I had left.

ADVANCING MY PROFESSIONAL CAREER

Currently, in the news, there are repeated reports rising up from the past, of sexual harassment and other violent sex acts posed against women in particular. Violators are being exposed left and right, and with every victim who comes forward, awareness is ignited all the more. What a blessing that there really isn't any statute of limitation on exposing these sexual predators. It is, however, unfortunate that some get away with their perverse conduct due to statutes of limitations to file criminal complaints. These violations date back ages, even for me.

Numerous women that have served as my motivation have encouraged me to reveal unprovoked sexual aggression acts made against me. Unfortunately, I'm restricted from exposing the names of the lowlife wolves in sheep's clothing who committed the crimes. I was made aware of this disappointing limitation during conversations with potential publishers.

Three separate representatives from different publishing companies cited strict ethical standards which preclude me from mentioning their names without proof of an incident. By proof they were referring to a written or taped confession, a legal conviction or perhaps formal statements from person(s) who actually witnessed the act in real time. Under constraints of this sort it's virtually impossible for victims of sexual aggression, assaults, and/or rape to prove what occurred. In spite of that it's imperative that I tell what happened to me, anyway. I really wanted to expose the creep but I didn't out of fear or even being sued by him. However, without hesitation I would submit myself to a lie detector test administered by law enforcement, and I would pass. I'm completely confident that the perpetrator would not subject himself to the same procedure. I even explained to the publishers that my account of the incident is factual and I'd be eager to take a lie detector test to confirm my recollection. Nonetheless, each prospective publisher maintained the same position out of concern for their policies and being sued. Consequently, I'll leave it up to each reader to discern the credibility of the following story:

Naturally, the opportunity to be contracted to work with one of the most successful individuals in the sports entertainment industry was a major conquest of mine. Although I had been around this person of renown on numerous occasions, I had never formally met him. I'll call him Mr. Arnold.

I attended a press conference in Philadelphia for an upcoming promotion. While there I had the good fortune to run into Brother James, a prominent member of the Islamic community who just happened to be affiliated with the promoter, Mr. Arnold. He was happy to see a Muslim sister as an official media representative. We extended Muslim greetings. James remembered me for the work I'd done on projects for the Islamic Office of Community Affairs and the Muslim TV show *Muhammad Speaks to Philadelphia*. He'd also seen me at Muhammad Ali's Deer Lake Camp and at other events where Ali was in attendance. James had always expressed high regard for me, as did many in the Muslim community because of my work, and he was absolutely always a gentleman.

"My sister, what are you doing after the press conference? I'd like you to join me, Mr. Arnold, and a few friends for lunch," James said.

"I don't know about that. I'd feel awkward just showing up at a group meal since I've never been formally introduced to Mr. Arnold."

My answer surprised James. "What!" he shrieked. "I thought you knew Arnold! Well, that changes today, sister. I'm going to introduce you to him right now," he said as he beckoned me to follow him. However, after only a few steps he stopped and said, "You know what, sister, you wait right here while I bring him over here to meet you. You're a respectable and accomplished Muslim sister with top-of-the-line credentials, and I want to make sure he has a right impression. He needs to know that he has to respect you." James's comment made me feel really good and confident as I waited for him to bring Mr. Arnold to me.

Upon making my acquaintance, Mr. Arnold was extremely polite, verbally engaging, and respectful. Immediately, he showed an interest in my professional skills as a columnist and public relations specialist. Graciously, Mr. Arnold extended an invitation for me to join him and his entourage for lunch, which I enthusiastically accepted. And because it was a professional environment, it didn't bother me that I was the only woman there among his crew, which included a younger Caucasian male introduced as Mr. Arnold's public relations/media rep specialist. Also present was a man claiming to be the manager of a South African sports icon.

Primarily, my spiel was directed at Mr. Arnold and his young public relations/media rep. I viewed this as a perfect opportunity to present some promotional concepts to Arnold and receive an offer to do some public relations/media consulting for his company. I pitched the idea of having sponsorship purchase tickets as giveaways for Arnold's upcoming event. Underprivileged children, families of firefighters, policemen, and members of the Armed Forces and their families would be among the recipients of the giveaway tickets. In addition, I explained the process for getting free advertising in exchange for donating tickets as giveaways to media affiliates to give to their readers, viewers or listeners.

Mr. Arnold appeared impressed with my expertise and knowledge of how to advertise venues at significantly lower costs and said to his assistant, "Now see, I like that. She really knows what she's doing and how to best save me money. Why the fuck had you not thought of or done something like this? What the fuck am I paying you for?" In typical entertainment industry language, he began his effort to make me feel special—or rather, softening me up for something—but I didn't like that the young man had to be debased in the interim. Well, before this young associate had a chance to answer, the vice president of one of Philadelphia's major banking chains, an acquaintance of mine, walked into the restaurant. I introduced him to Arnold, conveyed the ideas I had just presented, and asked him to commit to a future sponsorship relationship with Mr. Arnold Productions. The VP confirmed his interest in the project. A few minutes later Jim Cassell, executive editor for the *Philadelphia Tribune*, also entered the restaurant, at which time I repeated the spiel. Jim agreed to engage in some type of promotional exchange with Mr. Arnold Productions, as well.

Mr. Arnold was elated to have made dependable contacts and I was happy to help in that way. He boasted on about how smart I was and how he looked forward to working with me, and the others. Suddenly, and I might add, rudely, his blandishment was interrupted by the South African businessman asking me if I'd ever been to South Africa. "No, I have not," I replied, hesitant. After all, Mr. Arnold was just speaking to me. "Well, you are hereby invited to come to my country. We could use someone as smart and able as you in our business endeavors there. You would love it and you'll be treated like royalty," the man said.

Mr. Arnold interrupted the man. "What are you doing? You have no right extending such an invitation! You don't know her personally and you don't know what man at this table she just might be in a relationship with!" Then he turned his attention to me, saying, "And you should have already declined the invite! What are you even listening to him for? Don't you know that you would receive a temporary white status as an African-American while visiting South Africa"....

Cutting in, I said to Mr. Arnold, "Had you not interrupted the conversation, I would have declined the invitation. Being fully aware of South Africa's racist policies, there is no way I would even consider going to such a place." See, from my perspective it would've been a betrayal to my own people and my heritage to be accepted while other people of color were not treated with equal status.

I wasn't necessarily bothered by Mr. Arnold's insertion; it indicated respect for me as a black woman and his motive to protect me, in spite of his crude delivery. James's watchful eye over me during the temporary upset at our table was evident, even comforting. Knowing he had my back made all the difference; it empowered me further. Admittedly, I was feeling pretty good, perhaps even a bit cocky because of the prospective move to secure freelance contract work with Mr. Arnold Productions. After all, I was in my town basically hosting Mr. Arnold and he was witnessing my influence with movers and shakers in Philadelphia.

During the process of clearing the table of our lunch plates, the waiter asked if anyone cared for some dessert. Immediately, dessert bids rounded the table stopping only at those of us who declined. "Okay, four desserts coming right out," the waiter said as the rest of us sat too full to eat another bite. Assuming that my attention was averted by conversation, the man seated directly across from me leaned over and whispered to an associate next to him and said, "She don't know it but she's the dessert." The two men burst into laughter. I was appalled but remained calm so as not to let on that I'd heard them, then said, "Excuse me, were you speaking to me? What's so funny? I didn't get it." Not surprising, I got no response from either of them.

* * *

Fully confident that I had Mr. Arnold's attention and what appeared to be the probability of working on some venues with him, I didn't hesitate to continue the conversation in Mr. Arnold's hospitality suite at the Bellevue Hotel. However, I had not anticipated Mr. Arnold's repeated phone interruptions. I distinctly recall one phone call in particular from a woman who had a beauty salon in downtown Philadelphia. Based on Mr. Arnold's conversation with her, they were friends and she wanted him to know about it. He asked her how the salon was going, and vowed to visit her establishment while in Philly. James interjected, "Sister Rita has a beauty salon, too. I've been there before. It's really plush; not only is hair done there, it has a hot tub and a massage room."

"Really? We'll have to stop by there, too. I love to see my people progressing in business," he added.

A few hours later, Mr. Arnold said that he was hungry again but wanted some soul food this time. "Sister Rita, where do you recommend we go?" he asked. I told him about Tobin's Inn in Germantown. So off we went to enjoy some of the best soul food to impress our guests.

When we arrived back at the Bellevue Hotel, everyone had dispersed from in front of the hotel, leaving Mr. Arnold, his young assistant, and another man. I, too, was about to leave when Mr. Arnold said to me, "If you're not in a rush, I'd like to hear more of your promotional ideas." Feeling sure this was a great opportunity to receive some contracts to work with Mr. Arnold, I returned to his suite. Now I would have the undivided attention of Mr. Arnold and his assistant. "*Great!*" I thought.

We had just sat down to engage in more promotional talks when Mr. Arnold interrupted the conversation and said, "So, you know about massages, right?" Surprised, I paused for what had to be about ten seconds. "Uh, yes, I'm knowledgeable of them but I don't do them. It's a specialty performed by the masseurs that work for me," I said. I refused to let myself think that he was hinting for a massage, so I gave him an answer that would quickly dispel that idea!

"Oh no, I was just wondering what you would recommend for the stiffness in my neck," he continued as he rubbed the left side of his neck. Before I could respond, he asked, "If I give you some money, would you go downstairs and see if there's something that I can use to relieve some of the soreness?"

Letting out a sigh I acquiesced. "Sure, Mr. Arnold," I said, leaving before he could give me any money. I wanted to ingratiate myself to him. Of course there was nothing in the lobby, so I walked to a nearby drugstore and purchased some anti-inflammatory muscle rub for him.

Still somewhat skeptical about what may have been Mr. Arnold's intention, I had already concluded that when I returned to the room, if the young assistant wasn't there and Mr. Arnold was alone, I was leaving. The more I thought of the lewd possibilities, the tighter I got. *"Just chill,"* I told myself. *"Mr. Arnold couldn't possibly be thinking of anything out of the way, particularly nothing of a sexual nature because he is old enough to be my father, perhaps my damn grandfather!"* I convinced myself.

Relieved to see the assistant and another man still there, I felt comfortable and determined that nothing was up. Momentarily, I sat on the sofa in the parlor until I heard him call me. "Is that you, Rita?"

"Yes, she's back," the assistant yelled back.

"Bring her back," insisted Mr. Arnold.

"Okay, this way," the assistant said, leading me through an open door, then closing it behind me. The shutting door literally reminded me of a huge metal door that closes off a large chamber of helpless captives. I could almost feel a harsh gust of wind as it shut closed behind me. I didn't know why I felt that way.

Once inside of the bedroom there was no denying what Mr. Arnold wanted. He was in bed covered to the top of his chest. His shoulders were bare, which indicated that the rest of him was nude — possibly. Immediately, I felt vulnerable. *"Damn! Okay, so*

*there are two men on the other side of that door. Here I am in a room with
another man who is most likely totally undressed under those covers."*
Were the two men outside the door there to keep me inside, or was
the plot for them to join in on sexually assaulting me? I wondered.
My God. What had I gotten myself into? *"Seriously?!"* Was I so
desperate for a contract? *"Damn!"* I thought. I began to seriously
question myself. I had to deal with the situation and my chances of
walking away unchallenged, or sexually assaulted. Which would
it be?

Mr. Arnold jolted me out of my frozen tracks and racing
thoughts. "Don't worry," he said. "I just want you to put some
ointment on my shoulder before you leave. Please."

"I don't feel comfortable with that, Mr. Arnold," I said with a
wavering voice.

"Girl, that's all I want. Ain't nobody trying to do nothing to you.
Can't you tell I'm in so much pain that I can't even reach the area to
put on the cream?" he said, putting on a convincing performance.

Confused between having compassion and plain old common
sense, I sure hoped he was telling the truth. So, as I stood there,
thawing just a bit, I squeezed some ointment into my hands and
walked over to him. He turned onto his stomach. I tried to stay at
arm's length as I leaned in slightly and applied the cream to his
shoulder. Still unnerved, my intention was to rub a little cream on
him and get the heck out — fast! Literally, after less than two seconds
of my applying the ointment, Mr. Arnold started squirming like a
serpent, moaning and groaning. Immediately, I stopped rubbing.
"Aw, that feels so good; don't stop," he said. "Please, keep going!"
He raised his body up into doggy style to reveal his total nudity.
On his hands and knees he was grinding and thrusting in midair.
"Ah, come on, baby, just do anything you want to do!"

I swear, time stood still. For a few seconds I didn't know if this
was real or an animated nightmare. A feeling of being a victim
locked in a chamber came over me. Utter disbelief held my feet
to the floor. My eyes were widened by fright, I couldn't close my
mouth, either, as I was staggered by what I saw. At that moment

I became rigid as a suppressed childhood memory of being attacked by two neighborhood boys became real again.

A DREADFUL FLASHBACK IN TIME

When I was very young, still living at home with my parents, I was on my way home from Belfield Recreation Center, after participating in an interpretive dance class. I was walking home and was about four blocks from my house. The class finished at 9 PM, and as usual I walked down 21st Street because two of the other girls in the dance class generally walked part of the way with me. However, they both went in opposite directions on Nedro Avenue, which was one of the streets crossing 21st Street. An older boy and his friend, Chubs, were walking behind me after my girl companions veered off.

The fact that boys were still behind me was not disturbing because it was normal for groups of kids to walk in the same direction after leaving the center. Besides that, even though he was considerably older than I was, Chubs was no stranger to me. However, he was considered a delinquent by many. I had no need to fear as he'd always been nice to me. This neighborhood was home. It had always been a safe haven for us kids. At least that's what I thought.

By the time I was approaching Church Lane and 21st Street, Chubs and the other guy were walking with me. We exchanged a few words with each other, nothing of relevance. Then Chubs and his coconspirator grabbed me and pulled me into an abandoned lot. Debris and rubble from a demolished house filled the area. The heap was directly behind another house on the corner across from the 21st street bar. I was stunned. What was happening?

Twisting my arm, causing me excruciating pain, and shoving me down to the ground, the demented duo savagely attempted to rip my clothes off. Terrified and unable to push Chubs off of me, while his friend held me down, I pleaded with them to stop. "SHUT THE FUCK UP OR I'LL KILL YOU!" I was devastated and feared the worst. I couldn't comprehend why Chubs was doing this to me because I had always been kind to him. He'd always given me the impression that he appreciated my kindness since he was shunned by other girls in the neighborhood. He was considered a fat slob, toothless at sixteen and missing half a finger on one hand, so the kids called him, Nub. Regardless, I had still befriended him. What changed? Why was he attacking me, now? While I found his Muppet-like shape repulsive, I had always felt sorry for him in spite of his dirty clothes and horrific body odor. Not so sorry that I wanted to be close to him, though. I had only exchanged minimal conversation, greetings and salutations. But, none of that mattered in my struggle to survive their sexual attack. I tried with all my might to push Chubs off of me. The harder I pushed the deeper my hands sank into his mushy body. While still struggling to get away, the thought came to me to somehow appease them. I didn't know if it'd work, but I had to try. I was fighting a losing battle for my innocence and I was desperate. Grasping for air, panting, I uttered, "Please, don't hurt me. I'll do anything you want, and I promise I won't tell anybody!" They ignored me and kept accosting me, still tearing away at my clothes. "Stop!" I shouted with little breath left. "Wait, don't rip off my clothes! I can't go home like that. Please!"

Chubs' companion didn't want to hear it and was still holding me down. He said to Chubs, "No, man! Fuck that shit! She's lying, she's just trying to get away!"

Sobbing, my face soaked in tears, I promised Chubs that I was not lying. "Look, Chubs, you know me, I'm not lying. You know I like you. I just don't want you to tell anybody that I did it. If you promise me you won't tell and just let me take my shorts off, I'll do it," I cried out to Chubs.

Believing my pledge, Chubs commanded his partner in crime to let me go. "She's cool, man. Let her up."

Once he helped me to my feet and took his grimy hands off me, I took off running and screaming as fast as I could. One of them reached for me and snatched my blouse, but I ran with such tremendous speed that my blouse slipped out of his hand. Since the unlit lot was only a few feet away from well-lit intersecting streets, with a constant flow of traffic, it increased my opportunity to escape. I felt confident that once I made it to the street where the attackers were exposed to the light, they would fear being caught and run off. Seeing them running in the opposite direction didn't stop me from hightailing it all the way home. My mother and younger sister were in the living room when I ran through the door panting like a dog. "Why are you out of breath?" my mother asked, as I flopped onto the sofa next to my sister.

"No reason. It was cold so I ran to keep warm," I answered. Not knowing me to be a liar, my trusting mother accepted my explanation. Believe me, I wanted to tell my sweet and caring mother the truth, but couldn't bring myself to do so. In the moment my predominant thought was to shower and wash away the physical and spiritual filth of Chubs and the entire experience.

As for the Mr. Arnold experience, it reeked of the flashback I just painted with Chubs. But the picture of Mr. Arnold on all fours, that was the worst sight I've ever seen in my life. It was a demeaning experience. Before my very eyes was Arnold's huge ashy black ass with his flabby skin jiggling and swinging as he humped the air. It closely resembled the rear end of an elderly elephant. A man I had admired, respected as an extremely successful promotional icon — and old enough to be my father — engaging in such filthy conduct. Angered at what was occurring, I found my voice and said, "It doesn't look like you need any help from me. It looks like you're enjoying yourself with whatever it is you think you're doing. I'm leaving!"

"Whew, wait, baby girl. I didn't mean anything by it. I never touched you, right? We're good, right? Come on, don't leave. I still want to hear more of your ideas and have you work on promotions for me," he said.

I ignored his ass and kept strutting. Aside from being angry and insulted, I was secretly worried about how I was going to get past the two men on the other side of the door. Thinking I might be sexually assaulted by all three men now, I hesitated to open the door. Regardless of my fears, I had to confront whatever waited for me in the next room. My mind began to race again. I imagined another Chubs experience and how I had to fight him and his friend off. I was way younger, stronger, and faster in those days. *"Oh, God, help me."* Trying to control racing images in my mind of being pinned down and raped, I felt my heart beating out of my chest; my palms were moist with nervous perspiration. Yet I found courage to open the door.

Words are inadequate to express my relief upon realizing that the two men I feared the most from were gone. The fool in the room behind me was still making lame excuses for why I needed to stay. I picked up the pace, left that hotel, and chucked the whole experience with the quickness! As I galloped along I kept looking back over my shoulder. By the time I got to the parking lot, a few blocks from the Bellevue Hotel, my heart was pounding so hard my chest hurt. I was out of breath from walking so fast to my car. Continuing to look over my shoulder the entire time, even once I got in my car, I feared that perhaps Mr. Arnold had me followed or even had sent some goons to bring me back. Who knows? After all he was a powerful individual, and with the vision still in my head of him on all fours like the dog he was, at that point I perceived him capable of anything.

I drove home in a state of shock. The entire trip was darkened with the image of his nude, grotesque body writhing like a snake and humping like a hippo in midair. I actually had to sit out in front of my house for a few minutes to collect myself before going in, just in case my kids were still up. God knows I didn't want them see me flushed with horror, as I was. Fortunately they were already asleep when I entered the house, which allowed me time to take the longest shower ever.

I just wanted to hug and kiss my children after that horrific scare. If things were just slightly worse, my kids might not have ever seen me again. After my shower I went into their rooms and embraced them. They were just youngsters in a deep sleep, unaware of my presence. But touching them was comforting to me because it finally convinced me that, at least for now, I was safe. Nonetheless, I realized things could have turned out far worse; I should have followed my instincts. Had I done so, I would not have been in that predicament where my life was at risk The possibility of my children being left motherless, was a real one.

Rita's Rule # 17

> Allah (SWT) gives his creatures instinct for a reason. Listening to your inner voice is a powerful source that can protect you from harmful situations.

BLACK GIRLS DON'T CRY

As usual, my favorite confidantes were the first ones I told about the Mr. Arnold incident. Who other than my best friend Flo Anthony and my sister, Zaynah? I'd felt incredibly guilty, stupid, and very unsure that anyone would have believed me if I'd reported the incident. I mean, it's not exactly the kind of discussion anyone wants to have with their spouse. From my perspective there were only two responses a man could have in matters of sexual assault against their wife: they could confront the perpetrator and inflict physical harm, which could result in someone losing their life or the spouse going to prison. Another option was for me to go straight to the police and convince them that Mr. Arnold had sexually harassed me and that I did not encourage the incident. Or, I could just keep my mouth shut, tell only a few trusted individuals, and avoid the backlash of an angry spouse and suffering humiliation because of my poor judgment. Furthermore, I knew that any legal prosecution befalling Mr. Arnold was highly unlikely. What was probable was that I'd be blamed, ridiculed, and perceived as a trouble-making menace in the promotion industry.

In all, I chose the cowardly position. Over all these years I'd never confronted the rich, famous and powerful Mr. Arnold, at least not until now. And, please understand that my willingness encompasses several reasons, none of which has anything to do with fifteen minutes of fame, monetary gain, or revenge. Actually, it was after witnessing woman after woman rise up and speak out against the likes of Harvey Weinstein, and even my cousin Bill Cosby, after years of painful silence. I related to their anguish, guilt, and shame because it happened to *me, too*. My guess is that I'm not the only woman my perpetrator acted this way with. Surprisingly this notion was confirmed during a conversation with a family friend, who I'll refer to as Derick. My kids and I considered him like an extended member of our family, and he called me Mom. He also knew Mr. Arnold quite well and worked with him for many years. Deliberately, I avoided revealing the name of my sexual assaulter to Derick when I described the incident to him. Abruptly, Derick broke into laughter, as I sat there in shock as to what he could possibly be finding so hilarious. Just as I was about to sharply demand an explanation for his outbursts, he said, "Aww! Hell, NO! Mom, don't tell me you fell for the old massage trick. Arnold's been using that shit on women for years!"

One thing was for sure and that was, as a black woman, I was intensely pressured by the same taboo as other black women. The taboo that says we should never turn our black men in to the legal authorities for any reason. Despite what they'd done to us, we could not be a part of bringing "our men" down, particularly one as accomplished and noted as Mr. Arnold. So, for years I lived with this, never wanting to be accused of intentionally bringing a "brother" down and knowing there would be individuals who'd despise me for not letting sleeping dogs lie. And, of course, there would always be those who chose not to believe my story like countless people choose to not believe all the women who have come out against other powerful men, and the like. I wish I'd done it sooner when it might have made a real difference.

⋆   ⋆   ⋆

I foolishly thought that the day would come when Mr. Arnold would have pulled me aside, showed some remorse, and apologized to me. That would have been affirmation of his remorse for his sexual deviant actions and that no woman should ever be victimized in that manner. Inevitably, cause and effect are a natural phenomenon of life though; for every action there is a reaction. The sexual predator is responsible for his own conduct, just as I am responsible for my response, or lack thereof. As a consequence, I shall forever regret not confronting the issue in real time. For decades I struggled with should-haves…would-haves…wish-I-hads. I came to realize that the extent of that trauma had run deeper within me than I had reckoned with; as a result, my professional and social lifestyle became stifled. The activities I once enjoyed became relegated to minimal engagements. I greatly reduced the number of boxing promotion and sporting events and political events I covered or attended. Yes, not accepting the negative impact and emotional scarring caused by his actions that evening at the Bellevue Stratford Hotel disturbed me more than I cared to admit, until now. My choice would have been to abstain from working on any sort of entertainment ventures. Had it not been for my husband's love of attending champion fight promotions, I would have never even been involved with any type of public relations. Because of my husband, Shamsud-Din, I was ultimately thrusted back into the political, sports, and entertainment arenas.

Realistically, that incident changed me, even though, with very few exceptions, I kept it mainly to myself. Basically, it nearly brought my public relationship career to a halt. I stopped interviewing male celebrities and meeting with men in private, and drastically reduced event planning. Obviously, this cost me financially, as well. Only after marrying Shamsud-Din did I feel more comfortable during fund-raising events which I confined to doing for SCMS.

Shamsud-Din loved attending boxing events. Naturally, I started going to fights with him, particularly Don King promotions. As I reentered the world of boxing, I mixed it up a bit this time. Along with interviewing and some scant promoting, I actually created boxing's first mascot, called DAK, which stood for Donald America King. The express purpose of DAK was to show a softer side of boxing. I'd even discussed it with Carl and Debbie King, Don King's children, upfront. DAK was of a feline persuasion. He was a cross between a cool cat and a cuddly lion designed to resemble Don King, who was the most famous promoter ever. DAK wore a sequined cummerbund as well as twelve-inch sequined cuffs, and a fake gold chain with the letters "DAK", as a pendant. Sequined spats covering from above his ankle to the instep of the foot were also part of DAK's attire. A large gold crown covered in fake jewels was attached to his head. Extra hair, sticking straight up from his head, was added to resemble Don King's trademark hair style. No additional clothing was added so as not to take away from the lion's body image. He was constructed of tan-colored furry material. On his pinky finger he wore a huge fake diamond ring the size of a golf ball.

I personally financed DAK. Sketching DAK was the easy part. Kiki had a bachelor's degree in fashion design, so I simply described my vision of DAK to her and she created a perfect sketch. The expense of paying to have DAK's costume fit and tailor made, and paying individuals to perform as DAK, cost me thousands. But it was worth every penny to experience the joy DAK brought to spectators, especially when entertaining youngsters confined in children's hospitals. They were paid to throw T-shirts out into the crowd from the ring at boxing matches and take pictures with fans too.

Though I had discussed the concept of DAK with Don King's son and daughter before putting the plan into action, it was their idea to reveal DAK during the Iron Mike Tyson vs. Evander Holyfield press conference. Nando, who worked to promote DKP (Don King Productions) fights, was the first to perform as DAK.

He knew just what to do; he circulated the room and gained the attention of everyone present, especially the press! What I didn't expect was that Nando—DAK—would go up on the stage while Mike and Evander were addressing the press. I was quite relieved when Iron Mike acknowledged DAK with a fist bump. Only Nando would have had the guts to do that.

Based on Don's facial expression, it looked as if he didn't take too kindly to the mascot. He had no idea where it came from, nor that the mascot was a surprise for him. Carl and Debbie appeared uneasy. Perhaps creating the mascot and allowing it to be presented at the press conference was a mistake? We weren't sure. So, Carl made the flippant remark, "Well, that didn't go over well with Don, so I guess DAK's ass is going back in the box." That was easy for him to say since it would not have been his financial loss. It would've been mine. By the time I'd paid to customize DAK and cases of T-shirts, and monetarily compensating person(s) posing as DAK, I was out no less than $9,000. At Carl's remark I thought, *"Oh, hell no. It's not going down like that."* I marched over to Don King as soon as he came off the stage and demanded his attention in the midst of my heated moment. Since I rarely ever said anything to him, outside of normal distant pleasantries, it was obvious he was caught off guard.

"Don, do you realize that the mascot is for you? It was a surprise. His name is DAK, which stands for Donald America King. It memorializes you the way Mickey Mouse does Walt Disney Corporation. You'll be the first boxing promoter ever to have a mascot," I explained. He appeared pleasantly surprised to find out that DAK was created in his image.

Letting out some robust laughter, Don replied, "Hell, I didn't know what in the hell that was or who was inside the costume." He gave approving nods and said, "Okay, cool. Thank ya," then disappeared into the crowd for a few. The press was a frenzy. Soon he managed to rejoin individuals on the stage, where he took questions from the press. A reporter yelled out, "Yo, Don! Who's the mascot? Where did it come from?" Don answered, "It's long overdue, and I'm the first boxing promoter to have one! The Pittsburgh Pirates and other sports teams have mascots, so why not boxing?"

In atypical, narcissistic fashion, Don took full credit for my invention of the mascot and didn't mention my contribution at all. His lack of consideration wasn't surprising nor did it bother me because I had accomplished my two main goals: one, was to bring a softer side of boxing to the public, and two, was to have DAK visit children's hospitals and make public appearances. Seeing the mascot bring smiles to children's faces and witnessing the joy that can still come, even when they're ill, was more than enough compensation for creating the mascot. To Don's credit, he did allow free range with the mascot being associated with the DKP productions, granted credentials for every event, and permitted DAK to enter the ring at live events to throw out T-shirts to the crowd.

RESCUING THE PROMOTION

Don requested my husband's help after running into problems with promoting a major fight. Political bureaucracy prevented DKP from promoting the Mike Tyson versus Bruce Seldon fight in Atlantic City, New Jersey. Don called my husband and asked if he could get the fight scheduled to be in Philadelphia. Added to the pressure was that the fight was due to take place in nine days. An impossible task for anybody other than someone as well connected as Shamsud-Din and the city of Philadelphia and throughout the state of Pennsylvania. In less than a few hours Shamsud-Din had put the wheel of productivity in motion, enabling a spectacular fight to take place in the City of Brotherly Love. The monetary gain for Don was impressive as well. Normally, individuals charge a substantial amount for finder's fees when negotiating events of such magnitude. But Shamsud-Din, he never asked Don for a cent, nor would he have taken any money had Don offered. That's just the kind of friend that Shamsud-Din is. As a matter fact, he often did favors for strangers as well, never expecting nor requesting anything in return.

Years of developing professional relationships and maintaining a flawless reputation and operating with dignity gave me the ability to deliver positive results for the promoter or fighters. And fortunately this placed me in a unique position. I was acquainted with many of the movers and shakers in the boxing world. Boxing promoters like Butch Lewis, Murad Muhammad, fighters like Eddie Mustafa Muhammad, Matthew Saad Muhammad, Larry Holmes, Michael Spinks, Trevor Berbick, David Bey, Smokin' Joe Frazier, along with boxing officials like Mariam Muhammad, Larry Hazard, Bob Lee, Rudy Battle, and James Binns, Esq. and journalists/commentators like Howard Cosell, Bert Sugar, and more who are worthy of being acknowledged. These individuals are legends in their own right, not just because of their contributions to the elevation of the sport of boxing. They are competent, respectful individuals who are regarded for their integrity. Not only were they major contributors to my climb up in the boxing industry, they were always willing to support charitable initiatives.

Undoubtedly, with the support of contacts like the aforementioned legends, I could've gone far in the boxing industry. I am confident that had I continued working diligently in the boxing promotion industry, I could have become a legend as well.

Throughout my tenure of working with boxing promoters on various venues, I've had the pleasure to be acquainted with many fighters, champions in fact. I'm attracted to fighters because of their gladiator spirit. Win or lose, it takes a lot of courage to go into a ring with an opponent, knowing that any moment you could be hit with a devastating blow that injures you or, worse, could be fatal. It takes dedication to become a champion and perseverance to maintain that status for over a period of time. There are many fighters who have accomplished this, and their contributions to the sport are noteworthy.

Bernard Hopkins, former middleweight champion who was undefeated for an unprecedented number of years, is such a warrior. I was elated when my husband ran into him during one of our visits to Philly. It had been more than twenty years since I'd been in Bernard's presence. Shamsud-Din and I have been involved with Bernard since he was a young man, long before he won his first championship. He was at our home nearly every day and we became very close. To see him looking so amazing was a pleasure. He looked as if he hadn't aged a bit and never stopped training for the next championship fight, which incidentally, he hasn't. Bernard still lives the life of an athlete in full training mode. He works out every day. Bernard has dedicated himself to improving the lives of convicted felons and those who are reentering society. He is using his celebrity to work with governors, law officials, and corporate entities to restore voting rights for ex-offenders and help them regain other rights after paying their debt to society. I could not be more proud of the young man who I have witnessed develop into an extraordinary man.

Out of all the aforementioned moguls associated with the sport of boxing, I've known Rudy Battle the longest. It's not just because of him being a longtime established figure in the professional fight promotion industry. Nor is it as a result of his years of formidable service as chairman of the Pennsylvania's Boxing Commission. Aside from these positions Rudy's respectful demeanor, particularly toward women, has always been evidence of his outstanding character. Unlike some of his male counterparts, who failed to regard women as equals and/or sexual harassed us, Rudy is always professional and a gentleman. If he can do anything to advance women's status in the fight game, he does. Rudy is also married to one of Philadelphia's most influential women, Maria Pajil Battle. Maria and I have been friends since our early high school days. In her position as senior vice president of marketing for a major nationally known insurance company, she approved substantial charitable contributions for the Sister Clara Muhammad School during my tenure as assistant director of education. We look forward to having dinner or attending some sort of social functioning together whenever I'm in Philadelphia.

CHARITABLE FUND-RAISER

It was the summer of 1989 when I decided to do a fund-raiser for the Sister Clara Muhammad School. I solicited the help of several of my friends in the boxing world along with Mayor W. Wilson Goode, who was mayor of the city of Philadelphia. My first choice was to have George Foreman participate in a mock boxing event: George Foreman vs. Mayor Goode.

After contacting the late Norman Henry to find out if George would be available, I learned that unfortunately he could not participate. So, now I needed a substitute. Promoter Murad Muhammad was gracious enough to offer Razor Ruddock, who was a contender to fight Mike Tyson at the time, to fill in.

Since I had been covering fights for several years, I had come in contact with Butch Lewis on numerous occasions. However, I did not develop a rapport with him until my good friend Flo Anthony introduced me to him. Flo was a competent professional with a plethora of contacts in the boxing industry, media, and entertainment world. Our collective professional talents and personal relationships with celebrities and business icons made us a powerful force.

I would be remiss not to acknowledge that it's because of my friendship with Flo that I became part of Butch's preferred group of friends. This positioned me to receive special privileges aside from press credentials for major championship fights. Perks of this sort are extremely empowering and provide recipients with a competitive edge over other media members.

I had become close friends with boxing promoter Butch Lewis and Michael Spinks, the light heavyweight champion who eventually won a heavyweight championship title after fighting Larry Holmes. Again, because of Flo, I worked on several of Butch Lewis's promotions. Also worthy of mention is that Flo Anthony was at the top of her game; she did voiceovers for *Sesame Street*, was a well-known gossip columnist, a best seller published author, founder of *Gladiator Magazine,* and knew the Who's Who across a broad spectrum of entertainers, journalists, sports icons, and the like. Moreover, Flo was an extremely generous, competent, and kind person. Unlike many individuals in the public relations business who guarded their contacts with their life, she readily shared hers. Always willing to give of herself without expecting anything in return, she exemplified the true meaning of friendship. Had it not been for her bringing me into Butch Lewis's circle, I may have had a good rapport with him but never would have developed the close platonic brother-and-sister relationship that we ultimately shared.

A SERIOUS OVERSIGHT

A few hours before the major fund-raising event was to occur, I received a phone call from Butch. Completely confident of Butch supporting the evening's gala affair, obviously, I was happy to hear from him. Wow, did I misconstrue the reason for Butch's call, but I was hit with a reality check after answering it.

"Hey, Butch," I pleasantly answered, to which he replied, "How the fuck are Michael and I supposed to be at your fund-raiser when I have an event in Atlantic City tonight? Why in the hell would you schedule something on the same night that you should be down here working with me?" Butch was yelling into the phone.

"I'm sorry, it was an oversight on my part. I didn't realize that we had an event on the same night," I replied, regretful.

"Don't do that shit no more," Butch insisted.

"Sorry, it won't happen again. I promise," I assured my friend.

"Look, just so you don't look bad, I'm sending Michael and Flo to Philly for the event," Butch told me.

"Thank you! Thank you!" I was never more relieved.

To give you an idea of how important this was, Michael Spinks was scheduled to do the color for a major Butch Lewis fight promotion. In other words, he was to be a commentator at ringside for the evening event. This meant that Butch had to replace Spinks with someone else at the last minute. Even though Butch cussed me out, he showed much love and consideration for me by sending Michael Spinks and Flo to help with the event. Besides that, to know Butch Lewis was to be aware that his bark was much worse than his bite. Wherein, if you were a friend of his, which I was privileged to be, there really was no bite.

Michael Spinks and Flo Anthony arrived in the limousine to the event where Michael filled in as a commentator for the fight. The marked fight card listed the fights that included: Razor Ruddock versus Wilson Goode, Smokin' Joe Frazier versus State Representative Dave Richardson Jr., and City Councilman Lucian Blackwell versus Leon Spinks. Of course, all bouts resulted in victories with the city officials.

In between rounds, while being spurred up by his corner men, Rep. Dave Richardson summoned me over to the boxing ring. As I stood close to him on the outside of the ring Dave whispered to me, "Hey, Rita, tell someone to tell Joe he's hitting too hard. I know for him it's light, but he's so strong I don't think he realizes how heavy-handed he is. I feel like I'm getting hit by a brick with each contact."

"No problem, Dave," I assured him as I proceeded to send a message to Smokin' Joe.

Catching up with Dave as he descended from the ring, I asked him if Joe's punches had gotten any lighter during the later rounds. He replied, "Yeah, at little. But through no fault of his own, Joe's just built like a brick wall." We both shared a good laugh about that, then focused our attention on the main bout between Mayor Goode and Razor Ruddock. It was hilarious to see Wilson Goode chase Razor around the ring and to knock him to the mat several times. For people familiar with the mayor, we knew him to be very serious and not much given to frolic. Such was not the case on this occasion. Mayor Goode certainly enjoyed his mock victory over one of boxing's most promising heavyweight champion contenders.

Like a real fight, the media rushed to the winner while still in the ring. Responding to a series of microphones and cameras in his face, Mayor Goode surprised everyone. His responses were consistent with that of real fighters who had just won a major championship belt. Describing his strategy and plans for defeating his opponent brought the crowd to its feet with applause. As the event planner, I was particularly pleased with the outcome of all the belts and specifically with the mayor's performance. Leading up to the event, naysayers had consistently warned me that the mayor would never, ever participate in such an exhibition. Proving them wrong is only trumped by the fact that the mayor enjoyed himself. After all, what man doesn't want to be heavyweight champ of the world, even if only for a night?

Jokingly, the fighters and their promoters argued that they were robbed, causing chaos in the boxing ring while the audience watched and laughed. Suddenly, without my knowledge or consent, several sheriffs from the Philadelphia Sheriff's Department descended into the ring, commanding everyone's attention. Sheriff John Green began to read off several offenses by his charge. Perhaps the most severe charges were coming to Philadelphia with the intent to cause bodily harm to city officials and fighting men over fifty!

As the crowd broke out into more laughter, the sheriffs handcuffed the fighters and took them from the ring. All but one of the celebrity guest fighters went along with the mock arrest. Later when I asked him why he refused to be handcuffed, he said it was because he may have had some traffic violations or something and wasn't sure that the sheriffs weren't using this as a ploy to address them. Of course he was joking. I didn't realize it at the time but that fund-raiser was the beginning of developing a relationship that led to my current marriage.

8

THE PERFECT MAN FOR ME

Like many women, I was always clear on the type of men I preferred. Being the romantic that I am, I knew someday he would come along. My criteria for the perfect man for me included him being intelligent, charismatic, courageous, honest, loyal, and within the right height.

Yes, being tall was important to me, because I don't do short. Being tall myself, I like my man to be tall enough so that I can wear high heels and not tower over him. While some might find that superficial or offensive, it's my personal taste.

I'm just not attracted to men shorter than I am. Now, don't go tripping; I'm not suggesting that a man has to be tall to be attractive. I just feel more feminine with a man taller than I am. Hey, in all fairness, there are many men who would not be attracted to a woman towering over them either. At least that's the lasting impression I have from childhood when I was taunted by some boys who referred to me as an Amazon or a giraffe. Anyway, Imam Shamsud-Din was that guy; he was definitely the man for me.

Though I had been in the imam's presence on countless occasions and always found him appealing, getting involved with him was not a consideration. At least it wasn't something the imam nor I had considered prior to three weeks before we tied the knot.

While I had converted to Islam in the late sixties, I had ceased my involvement in the Muslim community since 1976. Nonetheless, I had instilled Islamic values into my children since the day they were born.

They wanted to know more about Islam, and it was time for them to learn the religion of their birth. The same is true of my sister Zaynah's children, Asia and Sakina, who were like my own daughters, too. They were literally with my two children nearly every day. Likewise, Zaynah was like a mother to my children as we did pretty much everything together. Azim and Asia were only a few months apart in age. It was easy for us to babysit each other's kids because we were both nursing mothers for an overlapping period of time. I breast-fed her daughter when I watched the kids and she breast-fed my son when she watched them. This was so natural to us because she and I shared most of our developmental experiences together. We laughed, cried, and supported each other through every aspect of life.

Realizing that it was a mistake for me to have waited so long to teach them the more essential components of Islam, I decided to satisfy their interest in learning about our religion by sending them to Islamic classes. Of course, by them, I mean all of the kids — Azim, Asia, Kiki, and Sakina.

I solicited the help of my brothers in Islam, Nashid Elijah and Rafiq Naddar. They were both my *walis* (a trusted Muslim male friend who looks out for and protects non-married Muslim women). Brother Nashid picked up the children several times a week and took them to Islamic classes. His children had grown up in the community and were well-versed in Islam. My children and his children shared the same strong bond with each other as their father did with me and Zaynah. During the fund-raiser, I was informed that the imam (meaning Shamsud-Din) wanted to discuss the possibility of me doing more fund-raisers for the Sister Clara Muhammad School.

It was Memorial Day, May 1989, when Nashid informed me that the imam was going to attend a cookout at the home of a brother who lived in New Jersey. Nashid said the imam wanted me to come by the event to discuss doing more fund-raising for the school.

I arrived at the cookout accompanied with my sister Zaynah around 7 p.m. and joined the others in the yard until it got a little too cool for me. Retreating from the outdoor chill, I went into the living room and noticed that imam was seated in the dining room.

"Are you okay, sister?" he asked.

"Yes, I'm fine, it's just a little too chilly outside for me."

Next the imam did something that really shocked me. He got up from his chair, removed his jacket, walked toward me, and put his jacket around me.

"Is that better, sister?"

"Yes, much better, thank you," I replied, puzzled by his gesture.

To put his action in context, it's imperative to note the imam's reputation for being an honorable man, known for not playing with women despite the many attempts of women to seduce him. Fully aware of the imam's respectful regard for women, I knew providing his jacket to me was special. In the moment, it felt more like an expression of romantic intimacy.

Um, I think the imam likes me and not in a platonic way. My inclination would be confirmed the next day when the imam called my home.

Thinking he was looking for Brother Nashid, because he knew that I had been in the company of him and his wife Aisha earlier that evening, I said, "Brother Nashid is not here. He just left to take his kids home."

The imam's reply surprised me. "I'm not looking for Nashid. I called to speak to you," he said.

Initially, I didn't speak. Recovering from his statement, I managed to utter, "Me? Really?"

Countering my questioning tone, the imam convincingly answered, "Yes, you, sister. I called specifically to check on you. How are you doing? Are the children okay?"

After answering yes to both questions, I proceeded with my question by painting a picture: "If a Muslim woman had the opportunity to be the only wife of a man who cheated on her and was not practicing the values of Islam, or the opportunity to be one of the wives of a man who was practicing his religion and would treat her justly, which would be the better position for the Muslim woman?"

Without hesitation the imam interjected, "Sister, the answer is obvious; it's the latter."

Suddenly, without any hesitation I simply blurted out, "In that case, I'd like you to consider marrying me."

Admittedly, I wasn't sure what his answer would be, but what I was confident of was that it would be sincere. Naturally, I was delighted and relieved when the imam said with conviction, "Consider it done. Who is your wali?" He questioned. I replied, "Imam Adib Mahdi."

"Okay, I will speak with Mahdi and be in touch. Have a good night — As-Salamu-Alykium, sister."

I was fortunate in this matter because I actually had four brothers who could act in this capacity on my behalf. They included my biological brother Mikal, Adib Mahdi, Nashid Elijah, and Rafiq Nadar. Even though Adib was the name I mentioned, due to my close relationship with Rafiq and Nashid, it was a given that they would be included as my walis, as well. After Shamsud-Din spoke with Imam Mahdi, our less than three-week courtship began. Shamsud-Din and I were constantly chaperoned by Rafiq and Nashid.

I guess now is as good a time as any to mention that Shamsud-Din was already in a more than thirty-year marriage to another sister. I'm certain at this point some readers are outraged or in a quandary and have questions. You may be thinking, "How could I marry someone who was already married to another woman?" What a horrible person I must be is certainly the thought of some individuals. Well, before you get yourself all tied up in knots based on your values, relax, and have some respect for the fact that not everyone shares the same religious beliefs.

While I certainly respect and understand that some religions, particularly those practiced in America, do not practice polygyny, it is incumbent upon all of humanity to respect the rights and practices of others, particularly as it pertains to their religion. Muslims, like Mormons and other religious sects, do believe in men having the ordained right from Allah (SWT) God to have more than one wife. Granted, it's not widely practiced in America, but that does not make it any less virtuous. Like traditional Christian marriages, some can last till death-do-the-participants-part, while others end nearly as quickly as they began. I certainly don't make apologies for exercising my rights under the guidance of the religion of Islam to marry a man who has more than one wife. Nor am I suggesting that polygyny works in every case; each situation is based on the individuals who are partaking in the marriages. Perhaps putting it in layman's terms will provide readers with a better understanding of the practice and my reason for marrying the man of my dreams.

After a sixteen-year marriage that had long since run its course before ending in divorce, it was time to move on. Loyalty and commitment were important considerations for me to become involved in another serious relationship. Avoiding the mistakes of my first marriage was imperative. Consequently, I knew that any involvement with another man required sharing the same religious values. From my perspective, it didn't get any better than Imam Shamsud-Din Ali. After thirty years of marriage to him and being the recipient of his unwavering love, I know I made the right choice.

Being a novice to the religion of Islam, and I say novice because my earlier experience with Islam was not practicing the Sooner of Prophet Muhammad (SWS), meaning: *may the peace and blessing of God be upon him*. I vividly recall the exact moment that prompted me to get back into practicing my chosen religion. It occurred when Nashid and his wife, Aisha, paid me a visit. Taking pride in never being anything but an individual who on occasion would drink a glass of champagne, I also prided myself in having a bar fully stocked with alcoholic beverages. Because I didn't see any harm in taking an occasional drink at that time, in my ignorance I offered Nashid and Aisha something to drink. They both politely declined right before Nashid said, "No thanks, sister, but I would like to make prayer," as it was time for Maghrib, which is among the five prayers that comes in at sunset. "May I use your bathroom so that I can make *wudo*," a cleansing preparation performed before making any prayers, "and prepare for prayer?" Nashid asked.

"Sure," I replied. He proceeded to my living room facing east and called the Adan (the call to prayer). I had heard the call to prayer before but this time was different for me. I felt a chilling awakening overcome my entire existence as though this particular call to prayer was directed toward me personally. Obviously, it was a defining moment. But at the time I considered it a warning to take my religious obligations seriously, abstain from distractions, and become active in the Islamic community again. Certainly this included marrying a righteous Muslim man, which for me meant Imam Shamsud-Din Ali.

People often say it's the little things that count—a sentiment which I agree with—because little things can make big impressions. I could cite a number of such incidents wherein Shamsud-Din wowed me during our courtship and beyond...but I'll just highlight a few. It was around day three of our courtship. We were visiting one of the brothers in the Islamic community who had invited us to dinner. Since we were not married yet, and still being chaperoned, I had not been formally introduced to the Muslim community as a woman Shamsud-Din intended to marry. Consequently, most of our time together was spent with a group of brothers and me being the only woman except on occasion when another brother's wife would also be present.

Anyway, after indulging in a delectable meal of curried lamb, lemon herb and buttered fish, fried brown rice, and carrots sautéed in butter, brown sugar, and cinnamon, I was stuffed. "Sister, would you like some dessert?" asked the host. Feeling too full to eat what appeared to be a scrumptious chocolate layer cake, I politely declined.

About an hour later Shamsud-Din asked, "Are you sure you don't want any dessert?"

Speaking softly I replied, "Not anything heavy. However, I would like some of that ice cream with the orange sherbet swirl." I was referencing a Häagen-Dazs vanilla swirl ice cream which Shamsud-Din had introduced me to a few days earlier, but I wasn't sure of the brand name then.

Shamsud-Din turned and said, "Brothers, the sister said she'd like some ice cream."

"What kind of ice cream?" the brothers asked me.

I began to describe the flavor of ice cream before I was interrupted by another one of Shamsud-Din's never-cease-to-amaze-me moments. He told them, "Bring back every flavor they got." And that's exactly what they did! Now, just to be clear, I'm not talking about every flavor in the supermarket. I'm talking about every Häagen-Dazs flavor. Now, even the most non-romantic woman would have to admit that was pretty impressive. I know you women readers get my drift. While big things matter too, like I implied earlier, it's the small things that matter more sometimes. As women we look forward to our man showing us that he's attentive to our needs and desires through small gestures of showing his affection for us.

Other privileges of being Shamsud-Din's intended wife was the respect of having chaperones, never having to stand in line to wait for anything. For instance, brothers would always make advance ticket purchases for us. When we arrived at a theatre our tickets were ready so that we could just walk in and enjoy the show. However, the best benefit was having the brothers in Shamsud-Din's immediate circle with us at all times who could attest to the fact that we did everything by the book — the Holy Quran. This was of vital importance, particularly since I was about to enter into polygamy.

As I stated prior, we were entering the third week of our

courtship when we planned our ceremony for Tuesday of the following week. Looking back I vividly recall the sensational adrenaline rush of excitement I felt planning a wedding in two days. Then it suddenly hit me that I had not even told my parents. So I quickly drove by their home and prefaced the conversation with "Mom, I'm getting married on Tuesday in a private ceremony at my home, at 6 p.m. sharp. Make sure you tell Daddy!"

Mom was obviously befuddled. Her face said it all. The only word she uttered was "Ohhh-kay."

My late mother, Marie, was the kindest, most loving and understanding person I've ever known, but these virtues didn't keep her from being somewhat taken aback by her daughter entering into polygyny. So instead of just rushing off, as I had planned, I realized that it would be best to add some clarity for her.

"Don't worry, Mom, I know what I'm doing," I'd told her. "I'm marrying Imam Shamsud-Din Ali. Oh, by the way he's already married, but it's okay because it's permissible in Islam for him to marry more than one woman," I explained.

My mother's facial expression confirmed that she was still confused, but she managed to smile anyway and said, "Okay, sweetheart, as long as you know what you're doing."

"Trust me, Mom, this is the right thing for me and my children."

I knew this was difficult for my mother because she was a Christian, even though she was not a devout churchgoer. Nonetheless, there really wasn't time for extended dialogue, so I had to leave straight away. There was rarely a time that I entered my parents' home when she wasn't listening to gospel music or Sunday morning church services on WHAT or WDAS radio stations.

Literally, to know her was to love her. She was loved by virtually everyone who knew her. The vast majority of our friends called her Mom. Everybody in the neighborhood knew her as told by a group of kids always on our porch. No, I'm not talking about our peers because long after I left home kids continued adopting her as their other mom. Almost every time I stopped by to see my mother, there were bunches of little random neighborhood kids on the porch and on our steps who just loved Ms. Marie. She treated them like they were her grandchildren, providing them with juice, popsicles, candy, ice cream, cookies, and a variety of other snacks. Mostly, she showered them with love, affection, and needed mentoring, and it didn't matter if they were African-American or Caucasian; they were all her kids.

Being judgmental was never in my mother's nature. She always provided her children with morals, and insisted that we behave in accordance with the golden rule (*treat others as you want to be treated*), but she never demeaned us. So you can understand why I felt totally comfortable in informing my mother that I was about to exercise my religious right to participate in polygyny. I also knew that my mother was relieved when I told her who I was marrying because she had a fondness for Shamsud-Din, even though she had never personally met him. She had listened to him every day on the Georgie Woods radio show. Though he wasn't technically Georgie's co-host, he might as well have been for the amount of time he spent on the show each day, Monday through Friday.

Zaynah and Mikal were already practicing Muslims, so they were familiar with the criteria governing Islamic marriages. Though such was not the case for my other siblings, who were also nonjudgmental, I knew that they would respect my decision. Imam Adib Mahdi presided over the ceremony, witnessed by my family, two of my girlfriends, and of course my other walis, Nashid and Rafiq.

In retrospect, I guess I should have been prepared for some sort of adverse reaction to marrying the imam. Naïvely, I assumed the Islamic community under his leadership were fully accepting of all the tenets of Islam. What a big mistake that was. Total hysteria broke out among some members of the Philadelphia Masjid. Rumors and innuendoes and fabricated lies ran rampant throughout the community. Ironically, some of the self-proclaimed, most righteous Muslim women led the opposition against me. Keep in mind that some of them had sought to become the imam's second wife. For years a group of the same sisters had made repeated appointments to see the imam, claiming that there was some sort of problem that only he could resolve. And all the while they were after the imam, in secret, they placated the former wife by pretending their outrage was due to hurt they felt for her when in reality they envied me and had no particular affection for her at all. That marriage ended shortly after the imam married me. Since then I've been his only wife for thirty years now.

Membership for the Masjid and enrollment for the affiliated Sister Clara Muhammad School (SCMS) significantly declined. Student registration dropped from nearly six hundred to sixty students. Think I was disturbed by nearly half of the congregation jumping ship? Think again. I was relieved that the hypocrites left and took their hypocrisy and negative energy with them. The vast majority of them only occupied space and did little to no work to better the conditions in the school or the Muslim community at large. The absence of interference from such individuals provided an opportunity to foster new life into the Masjid and school. Financing the school became a major priority.

FUND-RAISING FOR SCMS

By utilizing the imam's contacts and my public relations and event planning skills, political and celebrity contacts, I executed an aggressive fund-raising campaign for Sister Clara Muhammad School and Philadelphia Masjid.

Though most of the teaching staff had left the school, a few individuals who declared themselves Muslims committed to the school stayed on. Needless to say, I was pleased to have some people who were familiar with the SCMS program, particularly since I had never run an educational institution before. My education consisted of earned college credits and a teaching certification in cosmetology. Being the proprietor of a business also equipped me with administrative leadership skills. Determined to continue providing quality education for SCMS students, I committed myself to long hours, seven days a week at the masjid and the school. Unbeknownst to me, a woman who had risen from the ranks of working in the daycare now ran the main office. Apparently, based on her woven web of deception, she was planning a coup to overthrow the imam's authority, oust me from the position of assistant director of education, and take over the school. Nevertheless, her wicked plan was averted after two other educators warned me about the plot.

It was late in the afternoon of the preceding day when they had planned to offer the imam an ultimatum threatening that either I be removed from my position or they would resign. Cleverly, they had locked all the doors to the classrooms in an effort to create chaos on the next morning. Had their plan worked, students would have been locked out of their classrooms, void of instructors and unable to receive any teaching.

Priceless best describes the crushed looks on their faces when I hit them with a devastating blow. Sarcastically thanking them for their generous offer to remain at the school, I declined their offer and accepted their resignation effective immediately. Nothing gave me greater pleasure than that moment knowing that they were completely baffled.

You see, what they failed to realize is a simple law of power.

Rita's Rule # 18

Never show your hand unless you know with certainty that you hold the trump.

In this case, the wannabe administrator/former preschool attendant, underestimated her targeted person. At the same time she overestimated her influence on members of the staff. Assuming that since she had put in many years in the community, she automatically had the loyalty of individuals she'd been associated with. Her shabbily executed plan failed miserably because she did not realize that she wasn't even a worthy opponent. I was much more skillful in terms of being a people person and in a short amount of time had gained the respect and loyalty of the majority of staff she tried to corrupt and coerce to work against me. Granted, without the support of the teachers who apprised me of the situation, I would have been ill-prepared. Empowered with the knowledge imparted by them, I expeditiously brought in my own staff to replace those who mistakenly perceived themselves as invincible.

* * *

Neither the staff nor I had ever worked so hard physically and mentally. Surely, the task of running the school entailed a tremendous amount of labor. Collectively, we worked every aspect of the institution—like preparing meals in the cafeteria, attending to all administrative activities, teaching classes, providing tutorial services for students needing extra help, and keeping the school clean. Our struggles with insufficient staffing would soon end as Sauda (Elma) Bey came through with an army for the help we needed.

Sister Sauda was a pioneer in the Muslim community and was highly respected by everyone who knew her. I always loved her and considered myself fortunate to know her. One of the first things I noticed about her, beyond her hard work and dedication to Islamic causes, was her swagger. That's right, the sister had style from her fabulous fur coats down to her stylish shoes. Beyond that, she was a people person with an extraordinary personality that captured the love of everyone she knew. Sauda and Brother Kenyatta raised their children as Muslims. Kenyatta Bey was also an influential and highly regarded brother in the Islamic community. It wouldn't be an exaggeration to express that the entire Bey family were revered throughout the Muslim community and throughout the city at large.

Remarkably, the involvement of three generations of the Bey family supporting the school was a game changer. Sauda and her eldest daughter, Latifah, took over the cafeteria. In true Bey tradition, they cooked such delectable meals that it brought customers from all over the city.

On an occasion when the weekly dinner menu featured roast turkey with cornbread stuffing, I had forgotten to purchase the premixed boxed cornbread stuffing. When I informed Sauda of my oversight she laughed and said, "Don't worry, I got it." Like magic she whipped up batter from scratch, cooked it on top of the stove, seasoned it, and produced the best stuffing I'd ever tasted. From then on I've used her recipe to wow guests every time I make stuffing. But, that's not all I learned from my beloved Sister Sauda. Like the members of her family, Sauda was dedicated to the Islamic community and worked tirelessly to improve the quality of community life for Muslims. I knew her from my early years of being in the Muslim community and always admired her. To my good fortune she took me under her wing, which became integral in my development as a young convert to the religion of Islam.

Between Sauda, her immediate family members, in conjunction with the extended Bey family and friends, the school had an abundance of volunteers. The south Philly crew of young Muslim brothers were a phenomenal asset to the school. They worked tirelessly to raise funds to keep the school up and running. Young men though they were, barely out of their teens, they were quite the organizers. Fridays and sometimes three days of dinner sales provided thousands of dollars to the masjid and Sister Clara Muhammad School (SCMS) and was a tremendous help. The efforts of these brothers helped to pay for utilities, the tuition assistance program, and other necessities. The late Rafi Ali, Shamsud-Din's only offspring, was also an essential supporter of the masjid and school. Though Rafi grew up in the Mt Airy section of Philadelphia, he was close friends with the aforementioned group. Their ties went back to parents who grew up together in south Philly. They were extremely devoted to the school. By the next year student enrollment had reached capacity, and the masjid was fully supported as well.

Rafi Ali, who I'd known and loved since he was about four years old, never wavered in support of his father's marriage to me. We had always been close throughout the years. When I opened my beauty salon on Germantown Avenue, it was close to where he grew up. Rafi often stopped by the salon to visit with me and my sister. He showed traits of leadership at an early age. Rafi always stood out among the crowd and his peers. Admiration for Rafi extended far beyond the Islamic community. Like his father he had lasting friendships with people of all walks of life.

Rafi was the only child from his father's first marriage. He had always wanted a brother and sister, growing up. While that never manifested during that union, Rafi was elated to gain a brother and sister when I married his father. He vehemently rejected the term stepbrother or stepsister and never permitted anyone to reference my children, Azim or Kiki, in that way. During his overnight stays and daily visits, there were always long discussions on a variety of subjects, primarily in regards to Islam.. It would not be an exaggeration to say that the Philadelphia Masjid and SCMS relationships resembled that of a close-knit family. Every individual was no different than that of family members. We were definitely close and willfully invested in the success of both institutions.

*   *   *

Running a school with an enrollment of upwards of 600 students ranging from six-month-old infants to twelfth graders obviously required more than the aforementioned volunteers. Thus, while I would love to recognize and mention each of them, it's not possible. However, there are specific staff members whose participation was vital to the functionality of the school. Faruq Ahmad, the chief of security, and Abdul Muquit Hadid, assistant chief of security, were essential to the overall operations of the institutions.

As overseers of staff, assigned to various departments of SCMS, these individuals did an amazing job. Aside from security their supervision included, but was not limited to, running the cafeteria, upkeep of the building, supply purchasing, and machinery maintenance. Zaynah Rasool, executive administrator, Sayeedah Quaye, principal, along with Shafeequah Muhammad and Initsar Shah were part of the administration and also taught classes. Collectively, we performed a superabundance of duties. Depending on the need, we taught classes, worked the lunchroom, mentored students, and so on. In short, no job was beneath us, as we were more than employees and/or volunteers. We were committed to a higher calling to empower students to achieve academic excellence, with a focus on moral development.

One major person on the scene and in my life who was influential in bringing this about was a jewel of a woman, Sister Habibah Abdus-Shahid. Our initial meeting got off to a rough start. In fact, whatever the disagreement was about must have been trivial because I don't even recall what the issue was. However, what I do know is that I was defensive and therefore reacted from a guarded position. Already under attack by many women in the Islamic community, I was overly sensitive. I was viewed as an outsider who captured the imam through some sort of unsavory seduction, a disgusting and ridiculous notion which I naturally resented. Consequently, with the exception of a handful of sisters who treated me kindly, I perceived the rest of them as enemies out to harm me. My adversarial demeanor was on full display the moment Sister Habibah began speaking to me; rightfully so she was incensed about it and didn't hesitate to tell me so. Our heated exchange grew so loud that it caused a couple of brothers to intervene. Though the incident would have never risen to a physical confrontation, from a distance it may have appeared worse than it was. Nonetheless, a few observers thought it best to separate us. What they didn't realize was that, though angry, I was just about to walk away, and Habibah was far too sophisticated to strike anyone over words. Moreover, she was the epitome of a true Muslim woman. A couple of days after our heated exchange of words, she saw me in the hallway and greeted me with the usual proper Muslim greeting: "As-Salamu-Alyikum, Sister Faridah," she'd said. I did not honor our Muslim tradition with the proper response to her. In fact, I said nothing back at all. With that she grabbed me by the arm and stopped me in my tracks. "Look, in Islam we only have three days to resolve an argument! I'm just as annoyed with you as you are with me! Inshallah (God willing) I'm not going to hell because of a grudge you won't let go of! Come on now, this is day two. Sisterhood is more important than this, Faridah!" Looking straight into her eyes, I was captured by her warm smile and instantly recognized the strength and humanity of a devout believer in Allah (SWT).

That was the beginning of a loving sisterhood and respect for Sister Habibah. She still remains, in my mind and heart as one of the strongest and most gracious women I ever had the pleasure of knowing. She mothered six children and registered all but one into our school; that's because her oldest daughter was already a high school graduate. Once she did, our entire community became increasingly unified. I'll always be grateful that she snatched me out of my stubborn emotions and forced me to see through more mature eyes. Our friendship was cemented after that.

Habibah was truly advanced in her knowledge of Islam, which she obtained from attending Islamic studies classes and reading hundreds of books which she had compiled for her personal library. We were fortunate to have her volunteer to teach the Islamic studies and Arabic classes to the SCMS students. She was a tremendous asset to the staff and students.

One morning after some time had passed, I saw Habibah scurrying across the street, apparently rushing to catch a trolley. She looked radiant on this bright sunny day. Her beautiful caramel complexion glowed from the rays of the sunlight gently shining on her, which complemented her attractive face. Attired in a soft, flowing Islamic overgarment with a floral print *khimar* (head covering for Muslim women), Habibah always stood out among the sisterhood. However, I noticed she was holding her stomach. "Habibah, where are you going in such a hurry?" I called out to her.

She responded, "I have to go. Girl, something is wrong with my stomach. I gotta see what's going on," she said.

Concerned, I said, "Do you think it is something you ate?"

"Nah. Trust me, it's not that. It's something going on that seems more serious than that," she said, holding her lower stomach. I offered to drive her home, but she declined the ride, insisting on taking public transportation.

"Okay, well, I'll see you later!" I said.

It wasn't too long—perhaps a day or so—before I'd gotten the news that she was hospitalized with a terminal condition. Immediately, I said, "No way. I don't believe that." I was completely in denial and just could not accept that she was that ill. But while I didn't want to accept it, and held out hope that she would recover, I needed to visit her anyway. So, I began plans to make my way to the hospital but was interrupted by a phone call informing me that she had passed away. I was immediately bereft. It felt like a gut shot. I'd lost a dear friend, sister, and mentor all at once. I could not believe my sister had slipped away that quickly. I grieved for family, friends, and particularly her children. She was such a caring and devoted mother, wife, and revered member of the Muslim community, I knew it would be a tremendous loss to all who knew her. Habibah's presence had become like a beacon that penetrated the fog that had descended on our school and community, and now that light was out. To this day my eyes tear when I think about her and the devastating loss to her family, the school, community, and me. My emotions are an admixture of sadness and joy for Allah (SWT) granting me the blessing of having Habibah in my life and benefiting from her humanity.

After the passing of Sister Habibah, the Iman and I immediately granted a full scholarship for all of her children to complete their studies through the twelfth grade at the Sister Clara Muhammad School. As a result of Habibah's contributions to the school and the Islamic community, we extended the scholarship program in her name to every student in need of a partial or full scholarship. Numerous families and students owe a note of gratitude to Sister

---

Habibah for receiving financial aid in her name. It simply is not true that time completely heals all hurt, but it does lessen that piercing pain which initially occurs from tragedy.

COMMUNITY INVOLVEMENT

Community outreach was always a priority for members of the Philadelphia Masjid and Sister Clara Muhammad School (SCMS). Like Christianity, Islam is a religion of inclusion. Extending a welcoming invitation to individuals of all backgrounds, ethnicities, and faiths to join in community activities sponsored by Muslims was readily practiced. Therefore, we were always open to advancing concepts that improved the quality of life for residents in the surrounding area of our religious compound and beyond.

My husband's rise to prominence throughout the city of Philadelphia and the state of Pennsylvania had extreme influence on the lives of our citizens for many years. Peoples of all faiths, professions, and social status relied on him during election time—because of his political influence, too—and admired him for his humanity. While we were not born into the religion of Islam, and are of African-American descent, we held significant positions in the Philadelphia Masjid and we were highly regarded in the secular community. We ran a large school that was inclusive of all students from diverse backgrounds; we enrolled them all. After I became assistant director of education for the school, with the help of others, we increased the enrollment and monetary contributions which came from corporations, unions, and private individuals. This enabled us to operate the school and take in hundreds of students whose parents otherwise lacked the ability to pay for private school. Even with that support, there was never enough money to run the school. Shamsud-Din and I contributed a considerable amount of our personal funds to keep the school going. More than 90 percent of our graduates went on to receive scholarships from some of the most prestigious schools in the world. The school was adjacent to the masjid and offered a variety of community programs for Muslims as well as non-Muslims.

Fund-raising for the school was in full effect and generated from broader community support. The community college classes at the school were going well. Shamsud-Din and I were a power couple among the political sector and Philadelphia's social elites. Things couldn't have been better. Or at least that's what I perceived at the time. It's not that there were no signs or warnings of better or worse things to come. As an influential force in the city, and beyond, I was riding the wave of success and completely naïve of the powerful forces of evil that lurked within my surroundings.

WORDS OF CAUTION IGNORED

Reflecting back on a conversation I'd had with the late Dr. Samuel L. Evans, who always referred to me as his goddaughter, I realized the wisdom and warning he was trying to convey back then. During a car ride to drop him off at his home, he had said to me from the front passenger seat, as I sat in the back, "You know, Faridah, you and Shamsud-Din are very visible and being viewed as awfully powerful people in this town. You're doing a lot of good things and helping a lot of people. The forces-that-be have their eyes on you all."

Coming from Dr. Evans—known for being someone who tells it like it is and who rarely compliments anyone—I felt flattered by his comment. While basking in Sam's praise, and perceiving that he had concluded his statement, I joyfully responded, "Thanks, godfather. I really appreciate you saying that. Coming from you, that means a lot!"

Turning his head over his left shoulder, and giving me a stern look in the eyes, he said, "That's not necessarily a good thing. That's when the governments and other political opponents come after you. You people just don't get it. The more you help black folk and the more influence you have on people in general, the greater threat you are perceived to be. You and Shams need to be careful, particularly since you're Muslims, and this ain't no good time to be a Muslim in America after 9/11!"

Somewhat perplexed by the harsh tone of his comment, I opted to ignore the warning without any verbal response. I really had to bite my tongue because in the moment I didn't get what Sam meant. It appeared to me to be an imprecise call on his part, which I attributed to a great man, though he was, being out of touch with the current political climate. How naïve and wrong I was. Sam's words would come to mind many times in my solitude, once the federal plot to take down my family and me began to take shape.

Factually, America has an appalling record when it comes to mass incarceration, particularly of minorities. Certainly this is a situation I have a wealth of knowledge and interest in. Therefore, I could elaborate on it, but there's extensive research on this topic. In this regard, I'll simply direct your attention to three segments from a recent article featured in OpenInvest, submitted 2/21/2018:

The U.S. is the world leader in incarceration, but not all Americans are incarcerated equally. Here are some staggering statistics about who's in prison in America: A staggering 2.3 million people are incarcerated in the U.S. — a 500 percent increase over the last forty years.[1] The boom doesn't come from rising crime but rather changes in law and policy. As the number of incarcerations soared, prison industrialists saw an opportunity to capitalize and started bidding for the right to incarcerate Americans, leading to a "profit before welfare" attitude to inmate populations that often include the mentally ill and vulnerable. The prison industrial complex, which is in part operated and funded by public companies (and the public), could very well keep growing under the auspices of a pro-incarceration and pro-private prisons administration.

Here are some fast facts about incarcerated Americans:

1) Many people should not be in prison.
A rapid increase in inmates has resulted in overcrowding in prisons, fiscal burdens on U.S. states, and the rise of private prisons where abuse and neglect are shockingly prevalent. Yet

growing evidence suggests mass incarceration does not prevent crime. Indeed, a 2016 report by the Brennan Center for Justice at NYU School of Law concluded that 40 percent of the U.S. prison population — 576,000 people — are behind bars with no compelling public safety reason.

2) Race plays a huge part.

People of color account for 37 percent of the U.S. population, yet they represent 67 percent of the prison population. Black men are nearly six times as likely to be incarcerated as white men, and federal courts imposed prison sentences on black men that were 19 percent longer than those imposed on similarly situated white men between 2011 and 2016.[2] Meanwhile Hispanic men are more than twice as likely to be incarcerated as non-Hispanic white men and face sentences 5 percent longer than white counterparts according to the same report.

These racial disparities are also prevalent in youth facilities. As of October 2015, there were 48,043 youths being held in juvenile facilities, and 44 percent of these were African-American. Work to cut the number of teenagers sent to juvenile facilities in favor of intervention and rehabilitation has resulted in a successful 50 percent drop in the last decade, with no negative impact on public safety.

3) Most felony convictions happen without a trial.

Many serious convictions don't get heard in court because proceedings stop when the accused agrees to make a guilty plea, usually in return for a reduced sentence. Plea bargains make up 94 percent of state felony convictions and some 97 percent of federal ones, according to a report by The Atlantic. Estimates for misdemeanor convictions are even higher, prompting widespread concerns that too often the accused are coerced into pleading guilty or not told their full options. OpenInvest (2018) https://www.openinvest.co/blog/statistics-prison-america/.

Reading the aforementioned statistics not only validates the imperfections of the U.S. justice system; it confirms that racism is a major contributing factor in determining who will become victims of incarceration.

Dr. Ali's 2 time great grandparents, Zack Cosby, his wife Louisa and one of their 18 children.

My grandparents Zack & Emma Allen.

My parents, Mr. & Mrs. Samuel and Marie Williams, who married young and honored their union until my father's death.

My brothers, twins, Mitchell and Michael.

Here I am at approximately 4 1/2 years old.

Me and my baby sister, Shirley, (AKA) Zaynah. Mother used strips of brown paper bags in place of rollers to set our hair. With that accomplished, we were all set to attend Easter Sunday service.

This photo would be my last one taken with my sisters, Zaynah and Delores, prior to their deaths.

Descendants of the Cosby Clan gathered on the sad occasion of a memorial service for my oldest sister, Delores.

Cosby family descendants gathered for a happy occasion, a surprise dinner for my brother, Mikal. He's seated next to me in the center on the bottom row.

Dr. Rita Ali reunited with her nephew Kareem Barksdale after more than 20 years. FYI, Kareem played, and was a local star, on the Lower Merion High School Basketball Team with Kobe Bryant; they won the Pennsylvania State Championship in 1996.

This photo of me and Muhammad Ali captures the very moment he elevated my professional career by bringing attention to my professional credentials.

Muhammad Ali featured with sculptured bust of himself, commissioned by Dr. Rita Ali and donated to the African American Cultural Museum in Philadelphia, PA where it still remains.

Muhammad Ali posing with sculptured bust in his image.

My baby girl, Kiki, age 4, preparing to present flowers to Muhammad Ali's wife, Veronica Ali, during Muhammad Ali Day tribute.

The incomparable
Gene Kilroy and me.
I expressed gratitude
to him earlier in this
book for defending
my honor against a
slanderous lie.

Me, Andrea and Jeremiah
Shabazz at the opening of
Resorts, Atlantic City's first
casino, on May 26, 1978. We
had resumed our friendship,
after the conflict over my
relationship with Muhammad,
and were back to enjoying each
other's company.

Rita Ali with
Boxing Promoter
Murad Muhammad
who received a
proclamation from the
City of Philadelphia
for promoting the first
championship fight in
Philadelphia in over
thirty two years, which
Dr. Ali convinced
him to do.

I'm here with Lana Shabazz and Muhammad Ali during an appearance by The Champ at a Philadelphia Center City department store.

Lana Shabazz (author of Cooking for the Champ), myself, and WBA light heavyweight champion, Mathew Saad Muhammad, during an award ceremony in New York, N.Y. honoring me with the Woman of Excellence Award for my contributions to the sport of boxing. The late Congresswoman, Shirley Chisholm, was also honored on that occasion for her contributions to society, as a member of the U.S. House of Representatives.

My dear friend, the late Smokin' Joe Frazier, during one of his many visits to my home, posing with my daughter Kiki, niece Sakina, son Azim and niece Asia.

Me with Smokin'
Joe Frazier.

DAK, Boxing's first Mascot,
created by Dr. Rita Ali, in the
image of Don King.

Me, with promoter
Don King, after I
had just pitched
a promotional
strategy to him. I
perceived it as a
golden opportunity
to discuss my vision
with the king of
boxing promotions.

My interview with heavy weight champion, Larry Holmes. It was a major accomplishment which increased my recognition as a serious columnist.

Don King, Mike Tyson, husband Shamsud-Din, daughter Kiki, and me, dining at a local Philadelphia eatery affiliated with United Muslim Masjid.

Dr. Ali joined by her childhood friend the late State Representative Dave Richardson, and longtime friend, the former General Manager of WDAS Radio Station, Cody Anderson, at her 40th birthday celebration.

I'm at the control panel here, preparing to provide health and beauty tips for WDAS radio listeners.

Me, with the late Ed Bradley, host of 60 Minutes, posing in Philadelphia city hall after Bradley was a guest on the Georgie Woods radio broadcast, which I was the producer of.

Dr. Rita Ali's swearing in ceremony to serve a nine-year commission on the Pennsylvania State Board of Cosmetology.

Here I am being honored in city hall, by Mayor W. Wilson Goode, for my outstanding accomplishments as a media personality, commissioner, entrepreneur, affiliations with sports, music, and global icons.

Me posing with my niece Asia, Mayor Goode, niece Sakina, son Azim and daughter Lakiha.

Co-founder of Philadelphia International Records, Kenny Gamble, (AKA) Luqman Abdul Haqq, and his wife Fatimah, on their wedding day, Dr. Rita Ali and Shamsud-Din Ali.

President Bill Clinton and me. I consider myself fortunate to have met such an icon, who I greatly admire.

Legendary founder of original R&B group, "The Temptations," my daughter, Jahaira and me. As an admirer of extraordinary musical artistry, I wanted Jahaira to experience the joy of a phenomenal performance and the privilege of meeting Otis Williams.

My lifetime friend, Ron Tyson, member of the Temptations, with my Granddaughter, Mikey Tyson.

My brother, Mikal, with official boxing Judge, Lynn Carter (recent inductee to the PA Boxing Hall of Fame), renown R&B recording artist, Kathy Sledge, along with me and my husband, Shamsud-Din Ali.

Flashback of me and my 6 months old Saint Bernard puppy, Penelope.

Fast forward to the current family pet Mars, a one-year- old Golden Doodle who thinks he's human.

My husband and me with our son Azim.

The wedding of my granddaughter, Dr. Saeedah Ali Charles, and Dr. Jaytron Charles, here posing with the bride's family: her sister Laila, father Brahiem, sister Ruqayyah, niece Aleenah, mother Kiesha, bride & groom, grandfather who presided over the ceremony, Shamsud-Din Ali, and brother Zaki.

Accomplished business women, Maria Battle, Fatima Abdul-Haqq, and me, having a girl's night out in Philadelphia.

Dr. Arby White, and me, in Bermuda during a surprise birthday party for Arby, coordinated by her husband, Ronald White, Esq.

My brother, Mikal Williams, my close friend, Frances Jones, (a prominent Philadelphia Business Woman) and myself, along with my husband, Shamsud-Din at the Style & Grace Fashion Show fundraiser in Philadelphia.

Me and my lifelong friend, Sonny Hill, former basketball player, announcer, a member of the Philadelphia Sports Hall of Fame, sports radio personality, executive advisor for the Philadelphia 76ers, known as Mr. Basketball and "The Mayor of Basketball," founder of the eponymous Sonny Hill League and for his many contributions to the game.

Me and Vivian Crawford, Esq. at a gathering in Philadelphia. We've been best friends since high school days at Germantown High School.

Family members attending my doctoral commencement: Azim, Morocco, Antonio in the next row between, (Morocco and Kiki) and Mike.

OH, HAPPY DAY when Dr. Rita Ali walked to receive her Doctorate in Business Administration!

The late congressman, Lucien Blackwell, Dr. Rita Ali and her Husband Imam Shamsud-Din Ali. Photo taken during Dr. Ali's tenure as chief of staff for Blackwell's campaign headquarters.

Philadelphia city councilwoman, Janie Blackwell, presenting a proclamation to my husband, Shamsud-Din Ali, at an appreciation celebration in his honor.

Reconnecting with close friends, during a major fight promotion weekend, in Las Vegas. Brenda Spinks (Leon Spinks' wife) Flo Anthony, me, boxing champions Leon Spinks and Michael Spinks.

Phenomenal Boxing icon Bernard Hopkins, dining with me, Philadelphia's Register of Wills, Ronald Donatucci, Esq., Shamsud-Din and Ronald Donatucci, Jr.

Me, posing with criminal justice reform advocates, Jamila T. Davis and Dawud Bey, CEO of Do 4 Self nonprofit organization.
They are making a difference in the lives of many incarcerated persons and those reentering society upon their release from prison.

Me, posing with a phenomenal group of advocates for criminal justice reform and supporters of WE 2 MATTER, a nonprofit organization founded by me. These individuals are committed to helping the incarcerated, as well as, persons reentering to society post prison, to restore a dignified life. Standing: Tommy Kurdy, Danny Lansdale, Amanda Levale, Dr. Rita Ali, Tyler Hauser, Toni Welch, seated: Vincent Braggs, Jennifer and Felicia Lieberman.

Me, with CNN's Van Jones, Esq., who was instrumental in getting the *Criminal Justice Reform Bill* passed, resulting in the early release for thousands of nonviolent offenders.

Me with my grandson, Miquel Tyson, sharing a few minutes together before his next day departure to Haiti on a humanitarian mission trip.

Rita spending time with her bonus son, global entertainment promoter, Fred Madzimba (AKA) Frenchy.

I was elated to meet Akon on his visit to Tyson Ranch. It's common for various celebrities to stop by to just chat with Mike Tyson, or be a guest on his podcast. However, Akon's global status far exceeds his success as an entertainer. His humanitarian efforts in Senegal are socially and economically empowering the lives of countless residents of that country.

Private family celebration of my birthday, January 10, 2019. Standing: Jahaira Spicer, Milan Tyson, Rafi Spicer, Mike Tyson, Kiki Tyson, Azim Spicer, Sitting: Shamsud-Din Ali, me, and Morocco Tyson.

Celebration of my grandson Amir Tyson's graduation from American University in Washington DC, where he earned a bachelor's degree in communications. Standing: Mike, Rana, Gina, Mikey, Milan and Amir, Seated: Shamsud-Din, me, Morocco, Kiki, and Monica.

Former National Republican Chairman and current MSNBC contributor the incomparable, Michael Steele, Esq., his wife Angela, with me and my husband. I've long admired Michael as among the most honorable true conservative voices and influencer for positive social change.

Actor, Chuck Zito, Me, hip-hop rapper, Flavor Flav and Nico Ali Walsh (*Muhammad Ali's Grandson*), at Tyson Ranch during a promo endorsement of "Triple Jeopardy." Notice, Chuck is holding a copy of my book.

Dr. Ali with Khalilah Muhammad, *Muhammad Ali's former wife and mother of their four children*. The longtime friends were reunited and interviewed for the filming of a documentary on Muhammad Ali.

A fun day for Dr. Ali meeting iconic rapper and record producer, Too Short.

9

TIME TO ADDRESS THE ELEPHANT IN THE BOOK

Being under federal indictment feels exactly like not one but a herd of unstoppable elephants charging at you all at the same time, experiencing the attack of multiple forces, including the two most powerful forces in modern day culture: the media and the federal government (the FBI). Providing the context that preceded me being indicted by the federal government necessitates understanding the specifics of what occurred prior. Pay attention to details because it's imperative that I explain the story as it happened. It starts with consenting to meet with an administrator of the Community College of Philadelphia (CCP) adult education program, who I shall refer to as Doretha Wagner.

Doretha called and asked me to meet with her in my office at the Sister Clara Muhammad School (SCMS), where she inquired if the school would be interested in conducting adult basic education (ABE) classes in our facility. She expressed an anxiousness to expand the program into our school because of its diversity and the specific area of West Philadelphia. Unbeknownst to me, Ms. Wagner was a highly regarded African-American woman in the Pennsylvania Republican Party. I had never met, heard of, nor had any affiliation with her prior.

Doretha inquired if the administration would consider renting classroom space to CCP for conducting ABE classes at our facility at $450 per classroom per semester, based on the same timeframe as the regularly scheduled CCP classes. It included fall, spring, and two summer sessions. Again, it is important to emphasize that this was only $450 per semester per class, not per month.

All aspects of running the community college were at the discretion of CCP. They set up an office in the school that was equipped with a phone. Applicants were hired directly by CCP, paid and assigned by CCP staff. Doretha spent countless hours at the school perfecting the program, working the staff, and overseeing student progress, as well as employment applications.

With only a few weeks for enrollment, Doretha indicated that, at maximum, if enough students to fill two classes would sign up, it would be great. English as a second language, Arabic as a second language, computer science, GED, job readiness skills, and citizenship classes were among the courses offered. A flyer listing the classes was distributed at Jumah (Friday prayer/religious service). Dissemination of information on the CCP program generated a profusion of interest. Much to Doretha's surprise and sheer delight, enrollment far exceeded her expectations. There were exceedingly more than enough students for fifteen, the required number of students needed to pre-register classes for CCP to approve it. As a result of such a large number of applicants registering for the classes, CCP needed to hire more instructors.

Rapturous and determined to get the classes up and running, Doretha asked to speak with SCMS staff to determine if any of them would be interested in instructing classes for CCP. She had total access to the SCMS staff, conducted interviews, and hired more individuals who met her employment criteria or rejected applicants at her discretion.

Not everyone Doretha hired for the school taught classes. Some individuals performed other tasks such as processing recruitment applications, or traveling to and from SCMS to CCP with paperwork as instructed by Wagner.

A few members of the SCMS administration, hired by Doretha, eagerly assisted with processing applications and scheduling students into various classes. I had nothing to do with enrollment or operating any aspect of the CCP program. In fact, my office was down the hall from the office used by CCP, which I never visited. So I wasn't present when Doretha met with or interviewed any of the SCMS staff pursuant to the (CCP) adult education program.

Consistent with programs of this nature throughout the U.S., enrolling students does not necessarily guarantee student retention throughout the duration of the semester. Generally, classes of this sort require a minimum enrollment of fifteen students for a course to be approved. However, as noted by CCP representatives and Doretha, the dropout rate is high. According to some instructors, they are lucky to have more than a few students complete the course.

Such was not the case at SCMS, perhaps because of the type of classes offered and where they were being held. Our facility was also regarded as a beacon of progress in a low-income, heavily populated area of West Philadelphia. Additionally, the building was open twenty-four hours a day, seven days a week. This is because the school was adjacent to the masjid (the worship area of the building), where members of the Islamic community came to make prayers.

Muslims, particularly women, were elated to be able to attend classes in a Muslim institution where the option to attend classes for women only was offered. Non-Muslim community residents were equally pleased to attend a safe, wholesome environment that welcomed everyone's participation.

The cafeteria remained open throughout the duration of class time. This allowed students to purchase snacks and/or meals in conjunction with having a place to congregate during breaks.

Many of the daytime classes included senior citizens from the neighborhood. They loved interacting with the younger students in the school.

Classes were scheduled from:

8 a.m. to 12 p.m.
12 to 4 p.m. and
5:30 to 9:30 - Monday through Friday, and on weekends.

Instructors were afforded the opportunity of having flexible schedules. Doretha permitted instructors to switch classes with each other and cover classes on a fluctuating schedule as long as the classes were covered. To her credit, she stayed on top of things concerning staff, and monitored whether or not classes were being attended by students, and instructors. She also went over student applications with a fine-tooth comb.

At times some of the instructors complained about how forceful Doretha was and voiced their dislike for the condescending manner she addressed them. Issues of this sort did not involve me, so I stayed out of it.

Again, it is important to stress that at no time was running the Adult Education Program my responsibility. My only commitment, pursuant to the contract that I signed as an administrator of the school, was to ensure classroom availability. I never received one dime from the college, but that did not stop me from being supportive. I took pride in the relationship between the Muslim community and the thought of the community college providing beneficial classes for applicants. Whenever Doretha suggested anything that would make the program better, if it was in my power, I did it.

My background in public relations came in handy, as I was fully knowledgeable of how to promote venues, charitable events, and so on. Getting the word out consisted of distributing flyers, announcements after daily prayers, public service announcements on radio shows, and word of mouth. Simply stated, considerable efforts went into promoting what I still perceived was a worthy program. For that reason, and only for that reason, I took time out of my pressing schedule to increase participation in the CCP ABA program.

Offering classes and ensuring a safe and wholesome environment was the easy part. There were always plenty of eligible applicants at the start of each semester. However—as is typical in adult education classes in our country—maintaining student participation was always problematic. All of the classes started off with fifteen or more enthusiastic students, but as time progressed attendance dropped in some classes. As noted by educators, in these type of programs, it is typical to have less students by the end of the semester.

The situation at our facility was no exception. Instructors would show up earnestly anxious to teach. To their dismay, near the end of the semester, just a few students attended certain classes. This was more so in the GED classes than other courses. Such was never the case in the computer science courses or English as a second language. These classes were always well-attended.

Even as of today I have the fondest memories of witnessing numerous individuals who were helped by the CCP program. Particularly moving was seeing the interaction of senior citizens in the same classroom as elementary school children. Some of the senior citizens were actually enrolled in morning and afternoon classes.

Words are inadequate to describe how much pleasure, comfort, and nurturing the elderly participants put into the SCMS students. It was a fair exchange because the senior citizens derived just as much fulfillment from being with the youngsters. All things considered, anyone taking part in such a successful and rewarding program would feel good about it. What was shocking and devastating in many respects was the plot in the making. While innocent, well-meaning, law-abiding, and unsuspecting individuals were devoted to improving community life for others and worked hard for such causes, we were under attack. Yes, under attack!

Long before CCP classes were scheduled at the Muslim facility, there were satellite basic adult education programs throughout the city of Philadelphia.

According to official FBI testimony, which would later come out in the trial against me, several other sites were under surveillance in conjunction with SCMS. That seemed fair enough, that they felt there was a reason to investigate these locations because of suspicions of fraudulent behavior. To that point, I have no problem. What is problematic is when the federal government engages in selective prosecution.

In spite of the prosecution's vehement denial, and pretense of posturing of being insulted that anyone could accuse them of bias, the facts tell a distinctively different story. Only individuals associated with SCMS, and I, were charged with a ghost employee scam. Federal agents' testimony, under oath, disputed the charge. When cross-examined by lawyers for the defense, agents revealed that federal undercover agents had visited the SCMS facility on more than one occasion. Subsequently, they noted that there was activity specifically related to CCP classes being held at the Muslim facility.

Remember, Doretha was a highly regarded member of the Republican Party, and now she was also the lead defendant in the case. Formerly, she held a prominent position with U.S. Senator Arlen Specter and according to her she was influential in developing the basic adult education program for the Pennsylvania Commonwealth, which operated out of the Philadelphia Community College.

According to Doretha, she had a personal relationship with the Bush family. I vividly recall attending the Republican convention, at her invitation, held in Philadelphia from July 31 through August 3, 2000. Doretha spoke of partnering with a woman whose name I don't recall. I met this woman, who resided in a mansion located in the Chestnut Hill area of Philadelphia. The two of them had designed commemorative scarfs to sell at the convention. They were planning to sell the scarfs for $250.00 each. Doretha expressed to me that she was disturbed that the items were not selling and that they were going to lose their investment.

Whether Doretha initiated the phone call or her phone rang,

I don't recall. However, I do vividly remember the conversation. Doretha explained that she was extremely upset about what she perceived to be a foreseeable loss of her investment. I was close enough to the phone to hear that it was a woman's voice coming through Doretha's cell phone. "Don't worry, Doretha, we'll just have the Republican Party buy all of the scarfs and give them out as souvenirs."

Instantaneously, Doretha's frantic demeanor was elevated to utter joy as she thanked the woman profusely. Afterward Doretha turned to me and informed me that the woman on the other end of the phone was no other than Barbara Bush. Whether or not it was truly Barbara Bush, I cannot say for certain, but I had no reason to believe otherwise.

As a matter of fact, Doretha consistently expressed her devotion and love for the Republican Party, particularly the Bush family. Additionally, with unwavering passion, she voiced her only frustration with the Republican Party pertaining to what she described as their disloyalty to President George H. Bush during his pursuit for a second term. According to Doretha, high-ranking Republican officials and other integral members of the party avoided contact with the former president when he campaigned in Pennsylvania. Apparently, they perceived being seen with the former president as a kiss of death to their own political career aspirations.

Proudly, Doretha confirmed proof of her devotion to the former president by displaying a picture of her and her son meeting with President Bush in front of a jet at the airport during his visit to Pennsylvania. Vibrantly I recall the rage in Doretha's voice when she spoke of the day the former president came to Philadelphia in his quest for reelection. She also expressed contempt for members of the Republican Party who deserted President Bush due to fears of being associated with him because of his low poll numbers. Not her, though. She stood on conviction and unilaterally made her commitment known by meeting the president at the plane and traveling with him throughout the day.

Confirmation of Doretha's status in the Republican Party was in plain sight when I accompanied her to the RNC (Republican National Convention). Everything about her demeanor conveyed a woman confident in her abilities: her slightly above average height, her medium brown complexion and minimal gray hair that glimmered beneath her natural black hair, her extensive vocabulary and commanding tone of voice were all indicative of her distinguished demeanor. I believe she also had a master's degree from the University of Pennsylvania. That with her unique standing in the Republican Party further contributed to her memorable first impression. However, my admiration for Doretha went far beyond our professional relationship. I truly admired her compassion for advancing social causes, particularly in the field of education. We were similar in that regard and from our mutual interests developed a friendship.

Doretha was as committed as I was to ensure that the CCP program at SCMS continued to do well. She frequently visited our location and met with instructors and individuals she had hired to work with her on the CCP project. As a courtesy, SCMS provided a small office for CCP where Doretha and other CCP staff maintained files, records, and installed their own telephone system separate from SCMS. I know for a fact that Doretha insisted on the staff complying with their responsibilities to the CCP program despite staff complaining about Doretha micromanaging them. To them she was once again cracking that whip. It wasn't that Doretha was complaining about the performance of the CCP staff; she had often expressed delight with how things were going. Actually, it had more to do with her authoritarian style of leadership than any complaints about attendance or tardiness. Without a doubt the worst of it was when Doretha was overly assertive; she would show up unannounced in their classrooms to monitor their teaching methods. This got on their nerves in real time. To the credit of the teaching staff, it's not that they were slacking in any area. They just didn't like what they perceived to be intrusiveness on the part of their boss.

SCMS's principal, Syeeda Quaye, and Zaynah Rasool, chief academic administrator (who just happened to be my sister), spent countless hours of their own time to ensure the success of the CCP program.

LEARNING OF THE INDICTMENT

General consensus implies that FBI investigations are conducted, or at least should be done, in a covert manner. Sharing incriminating suspicions or information about potential defendants is not supposed to be provided to the press. Nor should members of the media work in conjunction with the FBI as if they are honorary agents. Certainly media has every right to cover newsworthy stories. What they don't have a right to do is work with law enforcement to distort truths and use their position to convict defendants in the media.

Just like the FBI and U.S. attorneys put forth an image of seeking only the truth, and being above distorting evidence, some members of the press are guilty of the same conduct. Exculpatory evidence is also supposed to be a part of any investigation. For whatever reason(s) none of these principles applied in our situation.

Since SCMS did actually have a CCP program operating on our premise, it disputes any claim of a ghost employee scram. Being vilified all day every day for over a year by the press in essence taints any potential jury pool. To use a common analysis, once people repeatedly hear, absorb, and believe media distortions, receiving a fair trial becomes null and void. Without exaggerations, my family members and I were written about nearly every day in the *Philadelphia Daily News*, and nearly as often in the *Philadelphia Inquirer*. Network news media featured some uncomplimentary headline about us throughout each day. They preempted each segment with specialized music created just for the lead-in to segments about us.

COVERT FED SURVEILLANCE

Here's what was shocking: When cross-examined by defense attorneys, FBI agents and other government witnesses were forced to admit that surveillance of the SCMS showed classroom activity consistent with CCP classes being held at the school. Such was not the case at several other sites where CCP rented classroom space. Unlike some of CCP's community sites that weren't even a commercial dwelling, SCMS was an actual school building. The agent also had to admit that there were different sites, unaffiliated with SCMS, that showed no activity.

One of the dwellings that was supposed to be conducting CCP classes wasn't even in a commercial building. It was a residential house. With emphasis, I repeat-a residential house without lights, locked doors, and no signs of CCP classes being held there at any time. Compare that, and keep in mind that this is just one example of other sites of SCMS that always showed classes in operation.

AND THE PLOT THICKENS

Why was the federal government spending taxpayers' money to spy on a small adult education program in the first place? That's the operative question. Giving them the benefit of doubt, let's say they perceived it as a horrible crime, detrimental to society, and therefore brought the whole force of the FBI to investigate the situation. Then one must assume that the objective of the FBI would be to bring about just results. If it is to be believed that that was their reasoning, then why would they not bring charges against anyone they thought to be guilty? That's not what they did. They only brought indictments against persons affiliated with SCMS, specifically me and my children.

Perhaps the feds neglected to bring charges against anyone affiliated with the CCP site held in a residential row house because the program was affiliated with one of the members of the Philadelphia City Council. Perhaps they failed to bring charges against other CCP satellite sites, that showed no evidence of classes being held, for political reasons or personal biases against Muslims. In any event, targeting only SCMS associates is evidence enough of selective prosecution. Other possible contributors to an Islamic facility and members of its community being singled out could have a direct correlation to the horrific events that took place on 9/11.

THE 9/11 CLIMATE

Prior to and beyond the horrors of 9/11, Christians, Catholics, Jews, and Muslims in Philadelphia and throughout the U.S. shared meaningful relationships. It was not unheard of for ministers, rabbis, and imams to welcome representatives of different denominations into their places of worship. I always enjoyed accompanying my husband when he was invited to speak at parishes, churches, and synagogues. He was always well received, appreciated, and invited to return. Philadelphia's religious, secular, political, and social community ties were extremely strong. The bond we shared was not shattered. We held to a small-town family-like atmosphere in spite of Philly being a large city. In this regard, the reference to Philadelphia being acclaimed as *The City of Brotherly Love* — and I would add to that, *And Sisterly Affection* — is absolutely true. I can personally attest to what a unified city it is. This is not to suggest that the citizens of Philadelphia are void of any problems. I'm merely emphasizing the benefits of being exposed to culturally diverse communities that share a common bond of humanity. With or without a crisis Philadelphians were always there for each other.

As I stated prior, not even the cowardly act of terrorism, by demented individuals claiming to be Muslims, divided Philadelphia. However, such was not the case for all Americans. The post-9/11 climate engendered hostile attitudes toward Muslims. Some uninformed and misguided U.S. citizens perceived all Muslims as terrorists or that we were empathetic to radical Islamic groups.

The fed's announcement of their investigation, shortly after

9/11, suggested that they perceived this as the perfect opportunity to indict us. Seeking to sever my husband's longstanding relationship with political forces, surely the timing was great for the federal government to indict two of Philadelphia's most prominent members of the Islamic community.

THE BUILDUP TO INDICTMENTS

After relentless months of being under publicized federal investigation, I went from being a subject of the investigation to being the target. Of course, I learned this from newspaper articles. Nearly all the stories included negative distortions about Shamsud-Din and the CCP program even though he had nothing to do with the program. When I say nothing I mean precisely that—NOTHING. In conjunction with depicting him as part of a scam to defraud the CCP of finances unearned, there were constant mentions of him in a pay-to-play political conspiracy.

LEGAL CONSULTATION

After continuous taunting and threats of being the target of the federal probe, I was indicted. I met with an attorney who badgered me to testify against my husband, who too was under investigation, though not yet indicted. Shamsud-Din had recommended him and considered him an outstanding lawyer and a good friend. However, the gentle spoken man made it clear that, if retained, his job would be to represent me as my attorney, not as Shamsud-Din's friend. After going over the charges and estimating his fee, I felt comfortable with him. However, what he said next shocked me to my core.

"Listen, I know you're concerned about the federal investigation of your husband. The U.S. attorneys are not interested in prosecuting you; they really want you to cooperate and bring down your husband, the mayor, Ron White, and some of their affiliates."

Confused by his comment, I replied, "I don't understand. What more do they want from me? I've already spoken with them and told them everything I know about this business."

That's when the attorney leaned in close to me and said, "You don't get it, do you? They don't want you to tell the truth. They want to get a conviction against your husband. They've already perceived you as someone who thinks you're tough. If you don't cooperate with them, they're going to keep digging and digging until they find something to put you in prison for." And even though I had never had any prior legal hurdles to clear, that is exactly what the feds did.

Still unclear about what the attorney meant, I asked him to elaborate on the matter. He went on to explain that he had formerly been a U.S. attorney. In addition, he stressed that they succeed in getting a conviction more than 93 percent of the time. Think about it, an indictment reading *the U.S. Government vs. whomever the defendant is* puts anyone at a distinct disadvantage from the outset.

Don't just take my word for it; there are countless confirmations of this premise cited in books, journals, and scholarly articles.

To quote Yant, 1991: *The American judicial system is far too often a source of injustice for the innocent rather than justice for the guilty. Despite all the alleged protections built into the trial process, a person facing criminal charges is virtually presumed guilty until proven innocent — not the reverse.*

STRANGE OCCURRENCES

Latham Park, located in Cheltenham Township, a suburb of Philadelphia, is where my husband and I resided. It was a prestigious gated community consisting of about thirty mansions, perfectly, elaborately landscaped, and rarely visited by random passersby. For the most part, only residents, invited guests, or persons making deliveries entered the park. Based on this type of atmosphere, it is understandable why I was so surprised at what occurred on that quiet afternoon that I just happened to be home, which was infrequent.

The rare sound of my doorbell ringing with simultaneous knocking on my front door immediately caught my attention. Opening the interior door, but leaving the outer glass/metal security door closed, I was surprised to see two women. One of them was actually scary-looking. A visual of a disheveled but ugly version of Roseanne Barr came to mind. Honestly, she had heavy, black, puffy circles around the eyes and manly dark facial hair. And she was built like Miss Piggy; she could've been a human Muppet—a sloppily dressed one. Even her hair was grimy, as if it hadn't been shampooed in months. Her expression was that of a wild animal that had come to devour me.

Standing beside her was a younger woman of average height, average size, and normal attire. She had a large professional camera in her hand with the lens pointed right at my face. I tried to collect my thoughts or inquire if I could be of some help to these strangers I thought were obviously at the wrong house. Then the crazy-looking woman aggressively shouted, "Faridah Ali, why did you steal six million dollars from the Philadelphia Community College?"

The question made no sense, nor had any validity. It became clear that this overzealous Miss Piggy woman was a member of some type of media affiliate. Extremely aggravated with her disrespectful declaration, I reacted by slamming the door in her face. That seemed to aggravate her more as she persisted in shouting through the closed door for at least five more minutes: "That's all right! You don't have to answer my question now! But you're going to wish you had, because you're going to jail, Miss High and Mighty!"

I would find out later that her name, which I shall refer to as, was Katie Chappelle. Please note her name change is not out of retaliation or legal concerns. Again, like other unethical persons I have discussed, the thought of promoting her name is unacceptable. She'll gain no fame from readers of this book. To date I don't know what she hated more, the fact that I lived in an upper class neighborhood and would not dare reduce myself to a black underling and succumb to her authority and crude questioning, or was it because I was a Muslim? Surely, I thought, it had to be something other than just trying to ascertain information about an alleged story. Time would prove that she was far more invested than I even imagined from that initial encounter. Her actions appeared more in line with someone performing as an ordained disciple of the feds to disseminate lies about me personally, my role in the school, my position in the community, my family, and the Muslim community at large.

A day or so after her visit to my home, the story broke and was plastered in the papers and on the local news. Think about it, how is that Katie knew about the feds' investigation, which was supposed to be conducted in secret? Logically, there's only one sensible conclusion. Katie was working with the feds as added assurance to take down the Ali family. And just like a premier butcher takes a mallet to a piece of meat, beating it repetitively until it's tenderized, Katie butchered us in her articles until she shattered our good names in the press. Claims of me embezzling $6 million from the Philadelphia Community College persisted from that day forward. All day, every day for months, my husband, son, daughter and I were taunted and harassed by members of the press. They were stationed outside our home, my husband's office, and the school. Harrowing lies regarding us certainly contributed to the revitalization of the waning sales of the *Philadelphia Daily News* and *Philadelphia Inquirer*.

Undoubtedly, we've all seen movies or TV shows wherein the press hounds persons of interest in such a manner. However, we know it's basically exaggerated for the sake of a Hollywood portrayal. It couldn't possibly be that way in real life. I just didn't believe it to be so, and neither did my husband. We thought it was just over dramatized for purposes of capturing or holding the attention of viewers. Ironically, upon watching a Lifetime movie together which consisted of the press acting in such a manner, I turned to my husband and said laughingly, "Come on, no press acts like that; knocking people over, surrounding them with microphones in their faces, shouting at them, and following them everywhere, right?"

He simply smiled and said, "I doubt it. That's a bit ridiculous."

Well, time and time again members of the media proved us wrong. The movie depiction couldn't have been more accurate because, in fact, that's exactly how the media interacted with us.

Learning I was a so-called object of the investigation came as a result of the news media. That was then followed up by one phone call from an FBI agent claiming he wanted me to know first that I had been elevated from a mere subject to a full-on target of the investigation. Before I could even get a call into my lawyer, reporters were all over it. I contacted family friend and member of the Islamic community Tariq El Shabazz, Esq. and he stopped everything and told me to come directly to his office. He was so gracious and accommodating that I felt a sense of comfort knowing he sincerely cared about our family. After leaving the office of one of Philadelphia's most prominent attorneys involved in the case, I was literally pinned against the wall outside of his building. Members of the media were like sharks in a state of frenzy after smelling blood in the water. I began to be seriously concerned for my safety, especially when Azim had to push a male reporter, who had nearly knocked me to the ground. At that point, the reporter and my son exchanged a few hostile words with each other until my husband interceded: "Don't engage with them like that, son. That's exactly what they want. They want to depict us as bad people, hoodlums, and terrorist Muslims."

Nodding, Azim said, "Okay, Dad, I got it."

Katie, who appeared to harbor pure hatred, also appeared to be part of a campaign to taint any potential jurors. She went far beyond what I believe was her assignment with the feds to help them obtain a guilty verdict. Showing up at a license and inspection hearing I attended on behalf of the school to secure a permit for operating our day care, she followed me through the halls yelling and foaming at the mouth while spraying spit with every foul word. I'm not ashamed to admit that I really felt like slapping her in the moment, but of course I didn't. Instead of giving in to emotion, I remained composed. It wasn't easy though because I was certain that her bullying tactics would not have been presented under different circumstances. Seriously, in my heart, I believed she was nothing more than a coward propagated by the feds. Like the feds Katie apparently knew the takedown game of collaboration she played as an extension of government. Saturating the community with overt lies and distorting the image of persons facing a federal trial is an unjust tactic against those charged with a crime. I wasn't just a defendant being versed by the U.S. government. I was the victim of outright persecution. Under the advice of my attorney, my husband and I were told to never, ever respond to the press, not even to defend ourselves.

"Extremely difficult" understates the level of helplessness we felt while under attack. We were void of the ability to fight back even minimally. We knew that the mistruths and lies that were repeatedly disseminated into the public domain would be accepted as truth by some, and etched in stone like gospel by others. In essence, as a defendant, you are confronted with surrendering your defense strategy to your attorney and hoping for the best.

＊　　＊　　＊

In spite of the fact that I was not the big fish the feds were ultimately after, I remained the focal interest for media pillory. I was slandered and defamed with every accusation. There were even innuendos that linked me to drug dealers. Overall, they depicted me as an unscrupulous, greedy, and generally lowlife person. Two outlandish articles come to mind. The first one was a front-page spread in the *Philadelphia Daily News* that featured a full-frontal picture of me from my shoulders up, with a caption that read: "Iman Married a RAT." Never a subscriber or fan of the *Philadelphia Daily News*, nor the *Inquirer*, I wasn't actually aware of the article until it was brought to my attention by others who were concerned about my safety. After reading it, there was no doubt in my mind that the collaborators of the article intended to cause me harm.

I had actually gotten a surprising call while consulting with another attorney who I was considering for representation for what was an obvious indictment to come. Shamsud-Din and I were in the lawyer's office when he got an urgent phone call, which he took of course. Upon hanging up the phone, the attorney had a perplexed look on his face and said to us, "You'll never guess who that was."

Neither my husband nor I had any idea who it could have been. Before we had a chance to respond to him, however, he blurted out, looking at me only, "That was Jessie Coleman. He wanted to know if you were fearful for your safety as a result of the article. If so, you can speak with him about it." Jessie Colman was one of the lead FBI agents on the case the feds were crafting against us. As I was still processing the attorney's words, even considering the offer, the lawyer interjected and said, "No! You don't need to talk to them! They're not out to help or protect you!"

Although that article was quite alarming and I would have been inclined to speak with Jesse Coleman about it, due to the nature of it and the deadly possibilities as a result, I sat quiet after the attorney's impassioned interjection. The article wasn't just an attempt to destroy my pubic image. The writer quite likely intended to provoke someone into harming me, perhaps even assassinating me. I realize that my discernment may come off a bit dramatic, and providing further context is necessary. You see, the writer didn't simply suggest that I was a rat — implying I was some sort of informant — the suggestion was that I was also responsible for the arrest and conviction of the so-called Junior Black Mafia (JBM) member and leader, Aaron Jones, who the feds charged with murder, illegal distribution of drugs, and other horrific crimes. Nevertheless, I kissed my husband good-bye and proceeded to the Sister Clara Muhammad School with the intent to put in another long day at work.

* * *

No sooner had I'd settled in behind my desk and gotten to work than I was distracted by an incoming call from the main office, wherein the receptionist informed me of a visitor. "Who is it?" I asked, a little bit flustered. Unfamiliar with the name of the person requesting to meet with me, I asked the reason for the visit. The receptionist stated that it was a woman who said I did not know her but it was urgent that she speak with me. Puzzled, I agreed to meet the stranger. "Bring her in," I told the receptionist.

Looking up from my work-bestrewn desk, I took keen notice of the woman entering my office. She was a petite, well-dressed African-American woman with a smooth, light brown complexion, and black well-groomed short hair. Most concerning was the frantic look on her face as she took a seat across from me, on the other side of my desk.

"How can I help you?" I inquired.

"Actually, I'm here to help you," replied the woman.

In the moment, I took her statement to be condescending, or perhaps even sarcastic. Instinctively, I felt like lashing out at her and demanding that she explain her comment immediately. However, something in her demeanor seemed sincere and, instead, I felt a sense of calm. But that feeling immediately changed when she reached into her large tote bag. Already somewhat jittery about the article depicting me as a rat, and having a stranger in my office now pulling some unknown something from her bag, I began to feel extremely vulnerable. Was she reaching for a gun? My heart was racing, and my chest felt tight as a flash of heat overcame my entire body. With no time to react or protect myself, I was relieved when she pulled out a copy of the daily news. "Did you see this?" she asked, pointing to the front page. I simply nodded, yes. I wanted to ask why she had the paper, and why she was showing it to me.

"I don't know whether or not you realize it, but the feds just put a hit out on you. They're dirty like that," she said. "This is nothing more than the feds' attempt to provoke someone into killing you. More than anyone, they know how dangerous calling you a rat is. They know that there are gang members who would automatically take it upon themselves to get rid of a snitch, or a person they perceived to be a possible witness against them or their leadership," she stressed.

Speechless, but not totally shocked by her comment, I suddenly realized the impact of how threatening the article was as my eyes began to well up with tears.

"It's not true," I said.

She replied, "I know. As a matter of fact we know that you had nothing to do with the Junior Black Mafia. You couldn't possibly have been a snitch because none of us know you," she continued. "It was also confirmed by Aaron Jones, who called my husband, and other so-called members of the JBM, to tell them that the article was a lie. He said he knew you and your husband, Imam Shamsud-Din, from the Muslim community. Aaron was really upset about what they wrote about you. He said that you were a good sister and wanted everyone to know that and hoped no harm will come to you."

Aaron's comment meant a lot to me even though it didn't entirely remove the concerns I had for my safety. *What if someone didn't get the message, or still decided to go rogue and harm me, or my family?*, I pondered. It was a horrible position to be in, and totally uncalled for. As if the feds had not already beaten my family and me down enough, now they wanted me dead? I felt so angry and disheartened with everyone involved with persecuting us. Surely, the feds knew better than that; therefore, the only objective for their conduct was to either frighten me into cooperating or simply get rid of me, and for what? I thought. *Who does this over an alleged white-collar crime, which I strongly believe the feds know did not occur?*

As for Aaron Jones, my brief acquaintance with him occurred as a result of him becoming a member of the Islamic community. He started coming out to the Philadelphia Masjid a few months before he was arrested, tried, and convicted for crimes that resulted in him being on death row until today. For him to have such regard for a woman he barely knew speaks volumes about his humanity and makes it difficult to believe that he's who the feds depicted him to be. Call me cynical, but after the way they treated my family and me, I'm hard-pressed to believe everything that comes from them. In any event, I'm grateful to Aaron for his efforts to ensure my safety by denouncing the lies reported in the paper that day.

In addition, I also appreciated the woman for going out of her way to console me on that dreadful morning. Thank goodness, she'd had further detailed conversations with others who were affiliated with the JBM. She'd told me that she'd been besieged with calls all morning from girlfriends, family members, and friends of Aaron Jones and others who the feds had described as members of the so-called JBM. Collectively, their consensus was that I was never knowledgeable of any JBM activity and therefore could not have snitched on anyone. Honestly, I can't even confirm the existence of the JBM. My only knowledge of it was from media accounts alleging Aaron as the leader and others as members. For all I know the JBM legend could have been as fraudulent as the charges against me. Of course, that didn't stop the feds or their media minions from continuing to pounce on my family and me. Before the young lady left I thanked her profusely as she embraced me with a warm, sincere hug.

Perception is definitely reality for individuals lost in emotional reasoning as opposed to thought. Lies repeated often, and over a period of time, find a nesting place inside the minds of those who are susceptible to gossip and are always looking for the worst in others. Perhaps the distortions about me being involved with drug dealers were perceived by some to have merit. That might explain the extremely frightening experience I encountered at my home about eighteen months before I even married my husband. I believe it was all connected and started way back then. It was during my time as a single divorced mother. Only myself, my son Azim, who was fourteen at the time, my daughter Kiki, who was twelve, and my two nieces Asia, who was 14 and Sakina, who was 10, occupied the large home.

One night, back then, before all the federal investigations began, I was abruptly jolted out of a sound sleep by loud pounding on my front door and the non-stop ringing of my doorbell. Barefoot, I headed toward the disruptive sounds, which drew me to the top of my wrought-iron winding staircase. Alarmed, I followed the curve toward the steps. Normally I would have hit the foyer lights from upstairs before going to the door. However, the voice in my head told me to quietly approach in the dark. I crept down the stairs as the banging and ringing continued. Standing on the cold marble floor, I leaned forward and looked through the peephole. The full moon illuminated the front yard. The bright outdoor lights right above the front door were on and the security lights at both corners of the yard were bright, also, affording me a clear view of the culprits.

I was very frightened to see a dark-skinned African-American man wearing a hoody which covered all but a small area of his face as he continued knocking on my door and ringing the bell. Startled by the stranger who had no reason to be at my door, I remained silent and walked toward the library to the right of me, positioning myself far enough from the window that I could see out of it, but go unseen from the outside. Then I saw another individual. Crouched down alongside the bushes below the window was another African-American man holding a gun.

Similar to his partner in crime, he too was wearing a hoodie, which hid most of his face as well. Suppressing the urge to scream, I remained focused even though my heart was pounding hard and fast. Necessity for survival and protecting my family enabled me to think instead of panicking. Taking in a deep breath, I sank my voice into a deep, manly bass tone and yelled out, "You two niggers! You've got one second to get away from my door before I blow you both the fuck away! Starting with the nigger in the bushes, I will shoot your ass right through this window!"

Like jackrabbits the two cowardly would-be intruders ran for their lives. I had pulled off the bluff of a lifetime.

Rita's Rule # 19

Panic accelerates stressful situations. Keep your emotions under self-management and apply sound reasoning when confronted with the possibility of danger or harm. The ability to think in times of crisis provides the best chance of survival.

To further ensure the safety of our family, I called the police, who came immediately. The officers conducted a thorough search of my exterior property and the neighborhood but were unable to apprehend the two suspects. Since my home was located in Cheltenham Township, but only a few blocks from the Philadelphia dividing line, I assume their escape plan included departing the suburbs and entering Philadelphia immediately.

Never before had I encountered any sort of attempted invasion. Wondering who or what could possibly be the reason for such a threatening occurrence. My thoughts were perhaps it had something to do with a man I had met earlier that year.

* * *

The day he came into our beauty salon, Zaynah took an instant disliking to him. I presumed it was because of who he had come with; we were introduced to him by a brother named Shakur. I'd barely known Shakur other than for being a male groupie who had hung around Muhammad Ali. Though never taken seriously by anyone I knew, I found him amusing. Similar to a king's court gesture, Shakur had a gift for making people laugh. He had never been to my salon before, and I was puzzled how he even knew where it was. Somehow people like him seemed to have a way of slithering their way into the company of prominent individuals. Upon Shakur introducing, a man I'll refer to as Gerald to my sister and me, we learned that he was the brother of a friend of ours. Moreover, Gerald was a sibling within a respected African-American pedigree family. Impressions of Gerald differed vastly between Zaynah and me; she considered him scum while I saw him as a mannerly gentleman.

Assurance of who I believed Gerald really was occurred when I was working with Butch Lewis during the championship fight between Michael Spinks and Mike Tyson. First I ran into Gerald while leaving the weigh-in. As we walked together toward the lobby, we ran into Muhammad Ali and Norman Henry. They wrongly assumed Gerald and I had come to the fight together and sanctioned him as a good Muslim brother.

Norman Henry had been involved with boxing greats for years and was loved by everyone who was acquainted with him. So when two men who I trusted, loved, and admired implied what a good guy Gerald was, I believed them. Over a span of several months Gerald visited me at my home. Why would this be important? Because of what was later revealed. I had not seen him in years when it was revealed in the newspapers that he was an alleged drug dealer. Supposedly, he was the major player in supplying drugs to the so-called Junior Black Mafia. Whether Gerald was or wasn't, I myself was never involved in any drug trafficking. Since he frequently visited my home, it wasn't farfetched to think that perhaps those men who sought to invade my home presumed that Gerald hid money or drugs there. Of course, I never knew this for sure; it's just the most likely scenario. Certainly it provides the best theory for why those two intruders might've been at my door with a gun drawn.

THE HATEFUL RHETORIC BEAT GOES ON

Around the time I learned of the feds' pursuit of me, my husband and other prominent Philadelphians, primarily affluent African-Americans, were also named as persons of interest in a federal probe.

Words matter. False accusations are powerful enough to impact one's health. I recall seeing one of the men indicted in the pay-to-play case against Ronald White, Esquire, Shamsud-Din, John Johnson, and a city official. Poor John. It was heartbreaking to see this kind, meek man reduced to a frightened nervous wreck over the course of his trial and the accusations against him.

Encountering John a block away from city hall one cold windy day, I thought he looked fragile. Concerned for his well-being I asked him if he was okay. John admitted to being overwhelmed with the indictment, which he considered an unjust attack based on racism. John was already in his late fifties and was the sole caregiver for his elderly mother, who he lived with. He couldn't afford to carry the weight that'd been put on him. Unfortunately, the stress of the indictment ultimately caused John to suffer a fatal heart attack, a major loss to friends and family, especially his helpless mother. Ronald White, Esquire, who was a major subject of the investigation, also passed away before the trial took place. There's no way the legacy of Philadelphia's most prominent African-American men could be complete without mentioning him, also. He was one of the most powerful attorneys and political brokers in America. He was very close with the late Sam Staten, Sr., who was the business manager for local 332, one of Philadelphia's largest and most influential unions. Its diversified membership included hardworking men from every ethnic group in the city. Ron White, Sam Staten, Sr., Shamsud-Din, and Kenny Gamble were all a force as individuals as it was. However, collectively, they were an unstoppable social and political force of reckoning in the city of Philadelphia and throughout the Pennsylvania Commonwealth. Their influence strengthened relationships among peoples of all ethnic and religious denominations. Primarily, they were admired for helping to improve the lives of countless individuals.

Ron was from the Richard Alan projects, and affectionately known as Billy Boy; he worked his way up from the streets to prominence. In the political arena he was a phenomenal fund-raiser. Republicans and Democrats catered to him for his ability to raise enormous amounts of capital to support their campaign initiatives.

But, politics was not his only interest; in fact, his passion for educating youths exceeded his commitment to helping qualitative politicians get elected. He and his wife, Dr. Arby Odom White, one of my dearest friends, founded a nonprofit organization that provided scholarships for academically inclined students. Lavish annual events featured an array of promising young individuals who received acclamations and acknowledgment for their earnest efforts. Ron and Arby were also among the largest personal contributors to the Sister Clara Muhammad School. Beyond that, Ron took time out of his busy schedule to chair our Tribute to Education Banquet ever year. He put the full force of his staff behind the event and raised hundreds of thousands of dollars for our school.

Obviously, none of these accomplishments and/or his service to the community meant anything to the federal prosecutors who sought to destroy him. They treated Ron with the kind of contempt and disrespect that appeared to be based on jealousy, hatred, and racism more than the alleged crimes. Statements issued by the feds after Ron's death confirmed their contempt and their inhumane, unprofessional, and disrespectful conduct toward this man. The expressed grief of thousands who attended Ron's funeral and mourned his death was also completely disregarded by the feds.

According to an article in a Philadelphia newspaper, the feds couldn't resist stating that they regretted Ron's death too because they were looking forward to convicting him and sending him to prison. Note how the feds could stoop so low as to continue to demonize a dead man who was no longer present to defend himself. So much for "innocent until proven guilty." Not surprising though because historically, prosecutors have discounted that perception in addition to their blatant, deliberate willingness to disregard exculpatory evidence. Think about it; can you recall any time when a prosecutor presented exculpatory evidence on behalf of the accused? No, it just doesn't happen. Such behavior from so-called officers of the court, who should conduct themselves respectfully, is actually deplorable. Worst of all, what they believed to be a crime on Ron's part was never proven, nor was he proven to have been guilty of any other crime. Therefore he deserved the presumption of innocence until proven guilty. NEWSFLASH – to all those committed to tarnishing Attorney Ronald White and his family's good name, Ron's legacy remains that of an innocent man.

Before concluding the comments about Ron and his wife, I feel compelled to emphasize what an extraordinary friend Arby has been to me. There are numerous incidents that I could cite regarding her kindness, love, emotional support, and generosity toward me, but that would necessitate writing a whole book on that subject alone. So, I'll simply describe two occurrences that are etched in my heart and mind forever. I had already been convicted of a felony when I received an invitation to attend a private dinner for Arby's birthday along with some of her closest friends. By now, after paying to retain the services of several lawyers to defend family members and myself, we were economically challenged. I still managed to get Arby a nice gift, not because she expected anything, that's not who she is, but I couldn't imagine giving someone so special to me anything cheap. That was just me. Just as the gathering was about to end, Arby slipped something in my hand. Realizing it was money, I insisted on giving it back. But Arby wasn't having it. She hugged me and insisted that I take what amounted to be several hundred-dollar bills. As if that wasn't enough, a few days before I was to self-surrender to Danbury Federal Prison Camp, Arby hosted an event for me at her lavish Mt. Airy mansion. The guest consisted of a small group of Philadelphia's most prominent women. They were there to show their support and wish me well. But in spite of their attempts to maintain an upbeat atmosphere, I could feel their pain at the inevitable fate which awaited me. To fully comprehend this situation, it's important to note that we were not familiar with or exposed to our friends being incarcerated. Nonetheless, everyone did their best to stay positive.

Cheryl Steward was among the women at Arby's home on that emotional evening. She and I became close friends during her employment as Ron White's office manager. She also worked hard ensuring that every detail of the fund-raising events for the religious school I ran was attended to. Together with Ron, who chaired our annual education banquet, Cheryl helped us raise thousands of dollars. Upon my release from Danbury, Cheryl hosted a coming home celebration for me at her home. At the end of the evening she handed me an envelope about an inch thick containing over six thousand dollars. Arby was not in attendance that night, but Cheryl informed me that Arby had contributed a large amount to the collection. Prior to the feds indicting me, six thousand dollars seemed like a small sum of money. After all, I spent more than that on my American Express credit card bill alone; and that was a mere fraction of my monthly expenses. Seriously, serving prison time and losing my financial wealth really put things into perspective. Honestly, after being relegated to a state of economic despair, that money seemed like a million dollars. It also humbled me and made me even more grateful for friends like Arby and Cheryl as well as all those who continue to support me.

Vivian Crawford, Esq. is also among my longtime friends that exceeded the typical benefits of friendship. Vivian grew up privileged in the same area of Philadelphia as did I. We also attended Germantown high school together. Her parents owned a boutique Hotel where famous African-Americans stayed when performing in Philadelphia. Her position as an attorney provided the opportunity for her to visit me at the halfway house and obtain passes for me to leave the building for meetings in her office. She always treated me to a great meal, which was a welcomed change from eating halfway house food. On more than one occasion Vivian also put a few hundred dollars in my purse. Aside from that she attended to any of my legal concerns pro bono whenever I required the discernment of an attorney. Surly there were other supporters that also contributed to my wellbeing in one way or another. I'm appreciative of everyone for their prayers, encouragement, and everyone that attended my trials and/or sentencing hearings.

10

FEDERAL GOVERNMENT PURSUIT

Obviously, the federal government has enormous resources that exceed that of the average person, even the vast majority of wealthy persons. But misuse of their resourcefulness remains pervasive as they prey like fixated beasts on one defenseless gazelle; federal agents zoom in on the individual(s) of interest and forsake other forms of dangerous criminals to bring down the innocent object of their focus. Like a lion that seeks to feast on an animal that appears to be among the weakest of the herd, in spite of the fact that many other members of the herd are much bigger, meatier, and slower, the lion's predatory instincts are to simply ignore all other more suitable prospects. A prime example of how this relates to federal indictments, convictions, and incarcerations is evident in numerous arrest patterns. The FBI will collaborate with murderers, thieves, drug dealers, and various types of hardened criminals who wreak havoc on society to bring down a white-collar crime target. Certainly, this is not to suggest that white-collar crimes should be void of prosecution—to the contrary. They should definitely be brought to justice. Justice is the operative concept; punishment should fit the crime. But such is not the case with many federal prosecutions. It is at the discretion of the FBI agent and U.S. attorney to determine whom they will prosecute, and for what crime or whether they actually committed any illegal act. They will basically befriend and pay whom they please to act in the capacity of a federal informant, and vigorously go after their subject (the one or few they've forced into their control) of choice and put them in jail, regardless of the crime.

In many incidents, their prosecution, better described as persecution, is motivated by personal disdain of individuals and in the case of my family, I believe politically motivated agendas, hatred for the religion of Islam, as well as racism, all major factors on the part of the federal government charging me and my family members with numerous felonies.

* * *

IT'S A FAMILY AFFAIR CONVICTONS

At this time, it is important to revert to the convictions of my family members, as well as what happened to the LEAD defendants, Doretha Wagner and her son, in our case. While we served time via house arrest, and or a combination of house arrest and incarceration, the lead defendant and her son never served a day in prison. And, all the while, my family was vilified in the daily papers, on the local news, and on some national media outlets, every single day. We were advised by our attorneys not to speak out in the press. We obeyed. By the time we got the trial, we were so defamed and ill-spoken of that there was no way a jury could *not* convict us.

CONTEMPT FOR ISLAMIC LEADER – IMAM SHAMSUDID-DIN ALI

Although the feds, and certain members of its seemingly controlled media, made a big to-do over the imam knowing many guys from the streets, they were fully aware of his positive influence on them, too. Some of these individuals were proclaimed as criminals by the federal government. Whether or not this assessment was in fact true mattered not to the imam because he was in the business of redemption. Countless men with criminal backgrounds, who wanted it bad enough, have changed their lives and embraced positive citizenship as a result of the imam's influence. Surely, the FBI knows this to be accurate; after all they'd been spying on us and gathering so-called evidence to forge a case against the imam and the Muslim community. Why not notice the positive, as well, and allow for implementation of morality? Their vicious intentions only manifested in their selective prosecution of him, our children, and me.

Midway between the time that the feds started their attack on us and the time my trial began, Sam Evans summoned me to his office. Sitting directly across from Sam, on the other side of his desk, I listened intently as he unveiled what he described as a chilling plot orchestrated by the federal government against us. According to Sam the scheme to take us down went far beyond the U.S. attorney's office in Philadelphia. Orchestration of the government's subversion tactics came directly from top White House officials. The concept was carried over from the Republican Party's plans to not only obtain the presidency but to ensure that there would never be another Democratic president for the next hundred years. Promoting an image of moral white knights riding in on white horses to save America worked for the Republicans, and they had a successful takeover as they depicted President Bill Clinton as immoral because of his involvement with Monica Lewinsky, years before.

Void of proof I can't state with certainty that Sam's discernment was accurate. Sam was considered a powerful political force by presidents over several decades. Given that fact, I considered his comments valid. Besides the attack on us, affluent African-Americans and elected officials in other cities were under attack as well. Personally, I'd always felt that since Shamsud-Din had supported so many politicians during their campaigns, it would have been good if the support could have been reciprocated. Joining forces could have prevented the feds from having full reign to convict us; the support for us could've had a positive long-term impact. Unfortunately, instead, several elected officials were convicted of state and federal crimes themselves.

Running from truth and not defending individuals they knew were innocent weakened the Democratic Party throughout Philadelphia and the Pennsylvania Commonwealth. Consequently, this left what was once a solid group of people, committed to public service, vulnerable to be picked off one by one. Since convicting my husband and me, several black elected officials were convicted of crimes; they consisted of, but were not limited to, a judge, state senators, congressmen, and more. These were all good persons we knew personally and had been helpful in some capacity. Sadly, I noticed that individuals who practice evil fight harder for their cause than people who fight for good.

Rita's Rule # 20

Evil people are not stronger than good people, they simply fight harder. Good people must fully commit to defeating evil forces by fighting against them on every level.

DRAMATIC RAID

Prior to anyone in my family or me being indicted, the feds launched a raid on several locations associated with me and my husband. As if we weren't already subjected to far too much negative press, I learned that our family residence was under siege by a slew of federal agents. I wasn't at home when the feds initiated the raid upon our house. I was actually at SCMS working when I received a call from an individual whom I will refer to as Nedi. (I will also detail much more about his lack of moral character in later chapters.)

Little did I know at the time that Nedi was actually an informant for the federal government who was aware that our phone lines were being wiretapped and we were under surveillance. At the time both my husband and I perceived Nedi to be just another member of the Philadelphia Masjid. Naïvely we thought Nedi was committed to the same principles of integrity and Islamic values as we were. In actuality he was being paid by the federal government to spy on us, obtain dirt on us, and/or lie on Shamsud-Din.

Pretending to be concerned about me, he called me acting as if he was shocked about the raid that was taking place at our residence. In a frantic voice he stated, "Ummi," (Arabic term for mother) "the feds are raiding your house right now. Turn on the news, it's being filmed. Listen, did you need help getting out of town? Because I'll help you." Completely unaware that he was recording our conversation, I took his statement to be one of panic derived from concern, but nevertheless bizarre. Annoyed, with such a ridiculous suggestion, expeditiously I rebutted: "No! No! Hell, no I don't want you to get me out of town. Are you crazy, why the hell would I leave town because the feds are raiding my house? If FBI agents are at my house right now, I'm going to my house." With that I hung up the phone, turned on the news, and saw a split screen in four sections. The screen showed four separate raids, three other locations along with our home. Simultaneous raids of my husband's office, our home, Mayor John Street's office, and prominent attorney Ronald White's office were on full display on every local news channel. Helicopters hovered above our home, and vans and cars displaying FBI symbols lined our street, along with a slew of TV cameras.

Expeditiously, I rushed home and had to park several houses away from our residence because the street was blocked off with FBI agents and cars, news media vans, and reporters. From the moment I got out of my automobile, members of the press were all over me taking pictures and shouting out questions, all of which I ignored. The front door of my home was wide open. As I entered the foyer, I was stopped by an FBI agent who already knew who I was. "Ms. Ali, you can come in but once you do, you'll have to stay in here," he said, pointing to the library, which was right off of the foyer entrance of the home. "Okay," I answered.

Entering the library, I joined my husband and grandsons Rafi and Antonio, who were already confined to that area of the house. Several hours went by as the federal agents went through every inch of our home. They even turned the pockets of our clothing inside out, examined every piece of mail, leafed through and shook open pages of books in our library, searched our cars, garage, pool house, trash cans, cabinets, and the exterior grounds.

Ironically, they never said what the hell they were looking for; surely it wasn't drugs as they always tried to depict my husband as having unsavory ties with drug dealers who they claim attended the Philadelphia Masjid. They asked me to open up our safe, which contained important papers, such as checking account statements, mortgage payments, deeds to our properties, titles to our cars and jewelry. There was also a substantial amount of fine jewelry, which included cuff links, diamond necklaces, diamond tennis bracelet, Rolex watches, Cartier watches/earrings, and a six-carat solitaire diamond platinum engagement ring, I pleaded with the agent to at least leave me my engagement ring. It was the item I was most attached to because of sentimental value. Astonished best describes my feelings when the agent informed me that he was not going to take any of the jewelry or money. He was just going to take photos of it and that I could put it all back. However, they did leave with some of our paperwork that we never received back. Immediately upon their departure, I discussed their actions with my husband and pondered as to what they could possibly have been looking for. And why out of everything that they went through the jewelry, the money, that they only took a few letters, a proposal for the charter school application I had been working on and seemingly nothing else? At first glance that's how it appeared until going through the house we noticed the FBI agents had searched a small file cabinet containing my husband's papers. One missing item in particular stood out.

Suddenly, like a bolt of lightning carrying a surge of knowledge, we knew exactly what the raid was all about. My husband and I both concluded that obviously they were only concerned about the paperwork they took out of his office. But why? And then it became clear. All of that work, the helicopters flying overhead, media attention, and a slew of agents in and out of our home was for one sole purpose. The only thing of substance that they took from the paperwork was a letter from the current U.S. attorney Pat Meehan, who was supposedly on friendly terms with my husband. The letter was from when Meehan was the district attorney in Delaware County Pennsylvania. It was praise for Shamsud-Din's outstanding contributions during a youth development conference at a Catholic high school in Delaware County. Meehan was duly impressed with how this Muslim cleric was able to connect with an audience of high school students. Shamsud-Din had been requested to address the students on the topic of drug and alcohol abuse, which had been an escalated concern for the school's faculty members. Ostensibly, he did such an exceptional job on explaining the potentially evil and/or debilitating woes of alcohol and drugs that it had a positive impact on the students as well as Meehan. It's also apparent that's what the FBI agents were looking for because *THAT LETTER WAS MISSING.*

Now it all made sense why the FBI raided our house, we thought. The feds had spent hard-earned taxpayers' money just to retrieve a letter from the head U.S. attorney bestowing accolades on my husband. There was no way that they wanted that letter to show up in a trial or sentencing procedure. After all, how could they justify wiretapping a family and paying a criminal informant to lie on an innocent man so that they could build a fraudulent case against my husband? It is more than reasonable to assume that the FBI, U.S. attorneys, and the head U.S. attorney Pat Meehan did not want that letter to surface during my husband's trial or at any sentencing hearing.

At the very least it would make people question why he was being charged with a pay-to-play scheme, to get Democrats elected on a local, state, and national level. Why after all of the deceptive articles about him being some mob figure there was never any such evidence pertaining to such crimes, nor was he ever charged with anything of that sort?

The letter that mysteriously went missing on the day of the raid would only add to the premise that Shamsud-Din, our children, and I were simply victims of an elaborate plot to weaken the Democratic Party. It is common knowledge that the government will start with individuals low on the totem pole of the defendants they will then put the squeeze on them to catch the bigger fish. In the case of my family they started with me, and when I would not lie on my husband and other elected officials and prominent African-American businessmen, they went after my children to pressure them to turn on me, so that I would be pressured to turn on my husband. They underestimated our strengths as individuals who valued truth. Therefore, we all paid a heavy cost for standing on our convictions. My husband paid the most as he was eventually found guilty and sentenced to eighty-seven months of incarceration.

Confirmation of more unscrupulous tactics appeared in an article of an interview with a popular local rapper, Tommy Hilfiger. Tommy disclosed that FBI agents had visited him while he was incarcerated and offered him a *get out of jail free* pass. The offer was contingent on Tommy providing dirt on Shamsud-Din. This was consistent with the same kind of deal the feds made with Nedi. But Tommy outright refused to take part in any plot against Shamsud-Din. In no uncertain terms Tommy insisted that he didn't know Shamsud-Din on a personal level. Hilfiger further explained that he knew Azim socially and that he would never lie on Shamsud-Din because he admired him as a holy man. Tommy's actions are worthy of praise because no one wants to be incarcerated. Given the opportunity to get out of prison, let alone be paid by the feds as an undercover traitor, is something that weak individuals would jump at. Such is not the case for standup people like Tommy, my husband, children, and me.

If you're thinking it sounds like some elaborate plot coming from the highest levels of the U.S. political powers, you're not alone. Consistent with the discernment of many individuals in touch with government officials, I'm convinced that it was part of an elaborate scheme. A high-ranking elected official and a law enforcement agent who happened to be friends of ours confirmed the extent of the federal probe. According to him and others in the know, there was a plan to change Pennsylvania's electoral college from generally trending blue to permanently being red in any future presidential elections. Obtaining Pennsylvania's twenty electors, along with Ohio's eighteen and Florida's twenty-nine, is crucial to get candidates closer to securing the 270 needed to win the Presidency in a general election. To achieve such a mission Republicans needed to dismantle the Democratic machine and weaken the union's support for Democratic candidates in Philadelphia. If you take Philadelphia, you take Pennsylvania. It's that simple.

THE ARREST

Initially, and throughout the entire ordeal, not only was I treated with hostility and contempt, so too was anyone close to me. A prime example occurred on the day I was indicted; my sister Zaynah was also dragged into the prosecution. Zaynah had stated before the grand jury that my only role in the community college was as a facilitator of a lease agreement. Telling the truth, and in spite of no evidence to the contrary, Zaynah was charged with perjury. Kiki, Zaynah, and I were ordered to surrender the next morning at eight to the U.S. attorney's office. When we arrived we were immediately separated. After a few more minutes we were handcuffed with our hands behind our backs and then led into an uncomfortable cell for seven hours to wait for the arraignment. At least they'd relieved us of the handcuffs. Once the word spread of our arrests, it wasn't long before protestors realized we were in a cell. An eruption of male voices reverberated from somewhere close by. I could hear them. Recalling one voice that rose above the others I clearly heard, "Oh hell no! You're going too far now arresting good Muslim women and treating them like that!"

"Shut up! Keep it down!" yelled the federal officers who led us to the cell.

Zaynah, Kiki, and I simply looked at each other and smiled at what was a jovial moment, even though we were in a horrific situation.

The cell was disgusting as it reeked of urine from the lidless metal toilet. Two benches, also constructed of steel, were mounted to the floor on opposite sides of the cell. Bars across the front of it allowed anyone to see inside. The situation forced me to hold my full bladder until I couldn't take it anymore. So, right there in the presence of male agents parading back and forth, I had no choice but to use the common toilet but not without making some attempt toward privacy. "Zaynah, please stand in front of me," I asked my sister, which she did while I squatted high over the smelly toilet. After wiping myself I quickly discovered that there was no running water in the metal sink mounted to the wall. Gross. Next, Zaynah also had to use the toilet, so I covered her as she had done for me. It was a truly demeaning experience, which only got worse as time went on.

Another woman was placed in the cell with us about an hour into our detention. Doretha Wagner passed our cell hours later — about fifteen minutes before it was time to be taken downstairs to the courtroom for our arraignment. It was undeniable that the feds handled Doretha with favorable bias; she was even taken to a cell by herself even though there was never any perceived threat to her being locked up with us. The feds simply handled her more humanely. Knowing that we had to wait several hours before the arraignment, while Doretha waited only a few minutes confirmed that there was an act of courtesy to her. We were also ordered to surrender our passports, but to my knowledge Doretha was not subjected to the same stripping.

Handcuffed behind our backs in a courtroom filled with spectators and media, we sat uncomfortable for what seemed like an eternity. Was I feeling sorry for my sister, my daughter, and myself? Not likely. Was I resentful of Doretha and the treatment she received versus our obvious abusive treatment? Perhaps. Moreover I was keenly observant of it and couldn't understand it.

See, little things matter. Granted, it's true we were all under arrest, but while Zaynah, Kiki, and I sat there with our hands and fingers going numb, with sharp pains shooting up and down our arms and through our backs as a result of being handcuffed behind our back for such a long period of time, Doretha was far more comfortable. Her handcuffs were not tight at all. There was a long chain that connected the cuffs around her wrists that gave her extended mobility wherein she could dangle her arms alongside her hips. Our handcuffs pinned our hands together without the slightest room for adjustment.

CONTINUED LIES & DISTORTIONS

After days and weeks of total fabrications, innuendos, and continued lead stories in the newspapers, media, and television, the trial began. By then my attorney and I had listened to over 38,000 taped conversations of my husband, children, and myself. It's important to point out that none of the tapes revealed any criminal activities on our part. But that didn't stop the feds from twisting the conversations and telling an already biased jury that we didn't mean what we said. It had to mean what the feds interpreted our words to mean. My naturally mild-mannered, soft-spoken husband never once used any profane language, nor did he raise his voice. Admittedly, not all of my communications were as gentle as his; I used a few choice words but stayed within legal perimeters.

More disturbing than the government's efforts to relegate my family to a position of despair was their covert actions to fracture the Islamic community. No one or nothing will ever convince me that their all-out attacks on my son, daughter, husband and me was solely derived from a contrived ghost employee scam. Senseless best defines spending millions of dollars on false charges. Wherein even if the allegations were true, the effort, time and money wasted by the FBI and the abundance of media attention on a nonviolent offense would be the real crime. It's even worse when you consider that no crime actually occurred. Regretfully, I'll always dread that the Islamic community, comprised of countless Muslims devoted to righteousness, was negatively impacted by LIES about my family and me.

STRATEGIES AND TRICKS LEADING TO MY TRIAL

Doretha Wagner had her trial separate from mine obviously because she was the primary defendant with greater liability exposure, and I was the secondary defendant because I was brought in and accused on a theory with no proof at all. On the morning of the trial the *Daily News* played another dirty trick. This time, instead of my face covering the front page, they featured my daughter. The caption read *The Woman Who Broke Up Mike Tyson's Marriage*. This was another lie obviously meant to turn prospective jurors against me, Kiki and Azim, who by now had been indicted along with me and were on trial simply for being my son and daughter. And secondly, this had nothing to do with the trial. Just for the record, Mike had long been divorced when this despicable fabrication was presented. One juror requested to be dismissed immediately from the jury pool, claiming that he could not be fair to anyone affiliated with Mike Tyson. Thankfully, the judge granted his request. Certainly, no defendant wants an admitted biased juror judging them.

Prior to the jury selection my attorney suggested that I peruse the section containing potential jurors to see if anyone visually stood out as someone to reject. When I did so, instantly I noticed a scruffy-looking Caucasian man wearing a black and red plaid lumberjack type shirt. He was unkempt from hair to shoes; everything about him needed to be washed and shampooed. If that weren't bad enough, his piercing, hateful look sent a chilling feeling through my being. "Let's reject this one," I said to my attorney.

Based on intensive media coverage, all the jurors were obviously aware of the negative press about me. Somehow, the plaid-shirted man was among the jurors selected. The prosecution's case proceeded with one distortion after another. They claimed that I had run a ghost employee scam, wherein I defrauded the Philadelphia Community College (CCP) of hundreds of thousands of dollars.

Proceeding with CCP administrators as their first witnesses to take the stand, the U.S. attorney attempted to establish its premise. They also used FBI agents, CCP administrators, and an individual from Sister Clara Muhammad School to solidify their case.

Sitting at the defendant's table with Azim and Kiki, accompanied by our lawyers, listening to lies and distortions about my alleged input in the program was difficult. Nonetheless, I maintained my emotionless posture. In spite of witness after witness there was no testimony wherein anyone could confirm the government's case even though they tried. When cross-examined by the defense attorneys, FBI agents had to admit that during their undercover observation of the school there was activity consistent with the adult education program occurring.

The CCP administrator also concurred that upon his unannounced visits to the school, classes were being conducted. It was also revealed that the CCP's human resource department was responsible for processing applications and hiring applicants to work in the program at the Sister Clara Muhammad School. CCP also paid their workers directly. At no time did I interview or hire anyone, nor did I receive any monetary compensation from CCP. My only affiliation with the program was signing a lease agreement to rent classroom space in the amount of $450 per course, per semester. Considering that fall and spring semesters were sixteen weeks long and the two summer semesters were six weeks each, that was a small amount of money to rent commercial space.

A big deal was made about flyers and other recruitment information to promote the CCP program being distributed by the Sister Clara Muhammad School (SCMS). Prosecutors also claimed that resumes were falsified, instructors didn't instruct classes, students did not show up for classes, and they blamed it all on me. Strangely, the prosecution alleged that the program consisting of about twenty-two instructors didn't exist, but with the exception of my son and daughter, the feds didn't charge any instructor with a crime. More important is the fact that individuals hired by Doretha Wagner were not restricted to instructing classes. Some of them, like Azim and Kiki, taught classes and performed other tasks for the CCP, as directed by Doretha. Similar to others hired by Wager, Azim and Kiki performed tasks beyond teaching classes. And in fact put in more than the required hours. A continuing theme suggests selective prosecution remains. *Why them and not others hired by CCP?*

THE U.S. GOVERNMENT VS. RITA ALI & FAMILY

By the time the trial began I had already decided against using the first lawyer who'd suggested that I consider a plea bargain. Implicit in the deal he suggested would necessitate cooperating with the government, lying on others, six months of incarceration, and a $60,000 retainer for the lawyer. By now the only option for Azim, Kiki, and me was to go to trial. The first order of business consisted of motions made before the court under the jurisdiction of John P. Fullam, the presiding judge. Zaynah's attorney, Gil Scutti, was amazing and put forth a brilliant argument against her being charged with perjury. Judge Fullam concurred with his argument and dropped the perjury charge against Zaynah. Gil had been a former U.S. attorney himself and knew the ins and outs of how the system operated. He didn't represent me but offered support and free advice throughout the entire ordeal. Gil continued to advise me legally, and we are still friends today; in fact he's like a brother to me. Every time I see him, it is genuinely heartwarming. His help to us during those injurious times will never be forgotten. I have no doubt he'd still avail himself to me, even now!

Proceeding to the opening arguments, the U.S. attorney put forth their claims of an elaborate ghost employee scam consisting of bank fraud, wire fraud, and just about any other crime they could throw in. Charges of bank fraud against me were based on every time any employee from the community college received a check, even though I did not write the checks nor hire any of the employees. Wire fraud included any phone calls made in reference to the agreement between the college and the lessor. A combination of separate accounts, each of which carries a sentence of a ridiculous number of years [of incarceration]. As if that wasn't enough to terrorize any defendant, I was facing hundreds of thousands of dollars in restitution. Nevertheless, I stood on my principles; never to plead guilty for something I did not do even if it meant spending the rest of my life in prison.

In presenting their case the government had already distorted the meaning of a wiretapped conversation between Kiki and me. My attorney, Garland Giles, whose father was also a federal judge, made a compelling opening argument in an attempt to clarify my comment. I was quite pleased. Garland explained the true content of it. Garland began by making a comparison of when someone's favorite football team loses the game and the fans express their disappointment by sneering things like, "Those guys didn't do nothing on the field!" Of course the fans are not suggesting that their favorite sport icons didn't show up for the game, or merely sat on the bench and did nothing. It's a way of expressing an opinion that their team lost because not enough effort was put in by the players. That is exactly what I meant in a conversation with Kiki when I said she made more money working for the college, doing nothing, than she did laboring on unrelated projects, wherein she was not being properly compensated. I was referring to Kiki's frustration about putting in an enormous amount of labor, time, and effort on a project which paid far less than she desired. Great comparison scenario, right? At least my supporters and I felt really good about it. I just knew that the jurors got it because it was so simple to understand, especially since people use statements like that on a consistent basis. With no actual evidence of what we were charged with, the government had twisted our words to use them against us.

Remember, the prosecution presented no witnesses or proof that the basic education program had not existed. Yet the defendants called witness, after witness, all of whom provided undisputable evidence that they had either taught classes, been a student in the program, and/or witnessed the classes and programs taking place.

During every recess I stood to my feet and headed for the exit sign atop of the double doors that led into the hallway, where I could just breathe for a few. Without fail, I was followed by an overflow of supporters and well-wishers who stood with me right beyond those doors. They happily expressed their consensus that the defendant's attorneys had won every round.

When court was back in session, supporters of the Islamic community, family, and friends poured back into the courtroom. Only one or two rows seated the prosecutors, IRS agents, FBI agents, and media personnel. Otherwise the room was filled beyond capacity with my supporters. Vigorous efforts on the part of the prosecutors to eliminate my support fell on deaf ears. But that didn't stop the U.S. attorneys from consistently describing me as a thief, and otherwise unsavory character. During the closing argument one of the prosecutors actually turned toward the spectators. Red-faced and all, foaming at the mouth, he yelled at the top of his lungs, "Faridah Ali is no saint! She's like a Dr. Jekyll and Mrs. Hyde and she's no Clara Muhammad!"

He was referring to the late Sister Clara Muhammad, who the school was named after. In an unprecedented rebuttal the entire courtroom of my supporters responded, "Yes, she is!"

Judge Fullam admonished the prosecutor to turn from the audience and face the court, meaning the judge's bench. At that time Fullam jokingly said, "Well, I guess you heard that as far as her community is concerned, she represents Sister Clara Muhammad."

Near the end of the trial, but before the closing arguments, Judge Fullam summoned the defense and the prosecutor to a sidebar. According to the defense attorneys representing my daughter, son, and me, Fullam strongly urged the prosecution to reach some type of agreement with the defense. He further expressed his perception that we were good people and didn't want to see us hurt. The prosecutors offered six months probation to Azim and Kiki. Overly confident of obtaining a guilty verdict in my case, the prosecutors refused to offer me any compromise. They so desperately wanted their pound of flesh that they denied any consideration for any sort of reduced charges on my behalf. It mattered not because neither my kids, nor I, were ever going to confess guilt for something we did not do—besides, we would be naïve to be so confident that we'd be acquitted. Thus, Kiki and Azim rejected the prosecution's offer. At that point there wasn't much to do but proceed to the closing arguments, which were pretty consistent with the opening arguments.

CHARGING THE JURORS

In what was an exceptional action by Judge Fullam, he charged the jurors. He turned directly to them and proceeded to voice his opinion:

To paraphrase Judge Fullam, his comments made it crystal clear that in all his years on the bench, he'd never seen a case where the prosecution provided less evidence than in this trial. "I want you to know that all these people you see sitting on the prosecution's side, the U.S. attorneys, the FBI agents, and the IRS agents do not walk on water nor wear cloaks. The evidence presented by the prosecution in this case has nothing to do with a ghost employee scam. Faridah Ali was not responsible for registering students, hiring instructors, or ensuring that students attended the classes. As most who have attended college will attest, there is an unwritten rule; it's the fifteen-minute rule. If students are in the classroom for fifteen minutes or more, and the instructor does not show up, they can leave without any consequences. Students will not be considered absent if the instructor shows up after that point and they have left the classroom. The same applies to instructors who enter the classroom and wait for the same amount of time, wherein no students show up. The instructor may also leave without penalty. The instructor will still be paid for conducting the class, regardless of students not attending.

"It is also common knowledge that in most adult education classes, students will sign up for classes, but many will fail to complete the course. Instructors are lucky if they have a few students, if any, left by the end of the semester. Again, that was not the responsibility of Faridah Ali, whether or not she participated in promoting the program, recommended instructors to the community college, or supported initiatives of the program. Faridah Ali simply signed a lease agreement with the college.

"The facts are simple, either the program existed or it did not. You have heard the government's own witnesses testify that the program existed and that when undercover agents observed the school on various occasions, there was activity consistent with the program being in operation. You are the fact-finders in this case, therefore, it is your decision. However, if you concur with me that the program existed, you must acquit Faridah Ali and these defendants."

Wow! What a powerful declaration by the judge, who was eighty-two years old at the time and had been on the bench for decades. Surely, the jurors would respect the judge's discernment, and rely on the fact that there was no evidence of illegal activity on the part of the defendants. Lawyers and supporters for the defendants, as well as the defendants (us) themselves, felt a sense of confidence that an acquittal was imminent. We were, however, prepared to wait at least several hours for the jurors to review the testimonies. With that in mind, most people left the courtroom and relied on receiving notice when the jurors had reached a decision.

Incidentally, prior to the jurors departing the courtroom for deliberation, the judge stressed that no one was to enter the area where the jurors would be. All but two people left the courtroom; Azim and his wife remained. What they witnessed was alarming. They saw several FBI agents go back in the area where the jurors were. This disturbing action caused them to convey what had taken place to the defense attorneys. For whatever reason, the lawyers made no inquiry to the judge about it.

Generally, a quick verdict favors the defense, so we were elated when the jurors came back in forty-five minutes. Oh, how enthused they were to announce that they'd found me guilty of twenty-three counts. I was facing a ridiculous amount of prison time. Still facing the jurors, as defendants are always instructed to do by the court, I braced myself for the big dramatic verdict reveal. I stood before a group of twelve, none of whom related to us, nor were any of the jurors my peers. In the chilling silence of the courtroom, filled with onlookers suppressing their emotions, I couldn't help but notice the cold, heartless expressions on the jurors' faces. Remember the juror with the red and black checkered lumberjack shirt? I'll never forget his look of sheer pleasure. When we made eye contact, he stuck out his head and chest, and with all the joy of a lottery winner he looked at me with a smirk that suggested, *Yeah, we got you all.* Immediately, I was distracted by thoughts of a prior incident, which prompted me to smile as I looked upward toward the ceiling.

Recalling a few weeks before all of the mess with the FBI probe was revealed, I had set aside enough money to go to a health spa, which I referred to as a fat camp. Envisioning that I would lose some weight, I had chosen a place in Hunter, New York. I was just about ready to wire my deposit when I received a phone call. On the other line was Brother Faruq Ahmad, chief of operations for the Sister Clara Muhammad School. After informing me that the boiler for the furnace at the school was inoperable, I knew what that meant. There went my spa/vacation/weight loss retreat. I instructed the brother to meet me at my house to pick up the money, as soon as I had time to go to the bank and withdraw the money. Keep in mind this was from my personal account. Frustration overcame me and I went into a childish tantrum. Tears running down my face, crying aloud and with nose running, I angrily cried out:

> "Oh, Allah (SWT): I know I'm not the best Muslim and wasn't the best Christian before, either. But I'm a good person. All I wanted to do was take my fat butt to a place where my food proportions would be controlled, I could use the workout room, and walk mountain trails to get back my girlish figure. It's just not fair!"

It was precisely the thought of that meltdown that caused me to smile because I knew what was to come. I was going to be sentenced to Danbury Federal Correctional Institute, a prison that often housed high-profile inmates who committed white collar crimes. I didn't fit either category, but I was going. Regardless, the irony of it is that in my mean-spirited words to Allah (SWT), the Almighty was answering an actual prayer. Think about it. While incarcerated an inmate's food proportions are controlled. Danbury Federal was located a few miles from the resort I wanted to go to in Hunter, New York. There'd also be beautiful hillsides, with trails that I could walk and lose weight. There'd be a gym, as well.

Rita's Rule 19

The power of prayer should never be taken lightly. Therefore, be careful what you wish/pray for and be specific.

Our heavenly father does not take prayer lightly. In that precise moment, I knew the spiritual backlash I had brought on myself. With such intense emotions attached to my own desires, I foolishly questioned Allah (SWT) in a condescending manner. So what could I do but accept my plight. I exactly got what I'd asked for. Moving forward I would make sure any plea to my Lord would be very specific. Moreover, I was committed to never question Allah (SWT) in such an aggressive manner again. That was a major mistake on my part, which I would never repeat.

Rita's Rule # 21

Ownership of one's mistakes requires taking responsibility for putting yourself in an undesirable position. Embrace your blunder with objective truth in the spirit of learning and growing from an error will enable you to avoid a repeated episode.

It seemed to aggravate some people that I would receive the verdict with a smile. How could anyone facing an enormous amount of incarceration time be so, unperturbed? Oh, how it aggravated certain onlookers, mainly the jurors. Well, only I knew of my tantrum before Allah (SWT). Only I knew what such a sentence was really all about; it was my revelation, not theirs.

*   *   *

Back to that day in the courtroom, Judge Fullam did not hesitate to voice his disdain for the verdict. It became even more evident when the prosecutors wanted to put the question before the jurors about my properties and overall financial worth. Judge Fullam was furious. "With that jury? Absolutely not!," he'd scowled. "They are dismissed! In fact I'm considering invoking rule 29," (meaning to overturn the jury verdict) the judge stated right before selecting the sentencing date and allowing all defendants to remain out on our own recognizance.

PREPARING FOR TRIAL

My attorney, Garland Giles, and I listened to every tape then passed on the information to Tariq Shabazz, Kiki's attorney, and other defense lawyers, too. Recalling the 38,000 surveillance tapes the feds used as their excuse to prosecute me, they along with the media, made a big deal out of a few of them. The first so-called bombshell tape consisted of a conversation between Kiki and me. At the request of Doretha Wagner, Kiki had accepted a position to work in the CCP program. Not only did Kiki conduct weekend classes, she also did an enormous amount of paperwork and typing for Doretha, but she wasn't the only one to perform duties beyond her original assignment. Azim and a few others assisted Doretha with tasks for the CCP program unrelated to teaching courses. No one found it unusual or inconsistent with their original employment position. Typically, subordinates adhere to the commands of their leadership. Like others in the program, Kiki did whatever Doretha required of her.

On the surveillance tapes, Kiki was complaining about some freelance work, outside of the scope of CCP that she had done, which she had not been properly paid for. I recall asking her how much she had made from the project and/or projects that she gave reference to. She had indicated an amount that in my opinion wasn't worth the aggravation. So, in a flippant reply I'd said, "Wow, that's not even worth your time. You make more than that working for the college doing nothing. Why bother? It's not worth it and it's gonna cost you more in the expenses you have to put out than the contracts are worth."

Needless to say, that was just trope speech on my part; you know, a figure of speech. I was not trying to suggest that working for the community college did not exist.

Another call I received was from an instructor whose classes had not been scheduled. Regarding that concern, I assured the person that the matter would be taken care of and not to worry about it. I then transferred his call to the main office and considered the matter resolved. Considering that I told the instructor that the matter would be addressed, I safely assumed that once I informed the individual handling the CCP's scheduling, the instructor would begin teaching classes. I also believed he would have to make up any missed classes.

There was also a recording of me on a phone call with a woman named Miss Wilson. She called my home asking to speak with Azim Spicer. When I informed her that he was not at home, she asked if I knew when he might be available to speak with her regarding a business matter. I informed her that he was not currently available because he was working. Furthermore, I explained that he was working for the community college that particular evening and that his schedule varied because he would also sometimes work for the college during weekdays. Finally, I suggested that she contact him on weekends because he did not generally work then. I also agreed to pass on her information to Azim so that he could return her call.

Inasmuch as this conversation took place without me having any knowledge of a wiretap on our home phone, clearly I was responding truthfully. The instant that I conveyed that he was working for the community college, should have solidified that the program was indeed operational. So much for exculpatory evidence as it meant absolutely nothing to the FBI or U.S. attorneys.

In search for the truth, prosecutors are supposed to look for exculpatory evidence as well. They should reveal any facts that point to the innocence of potential defendants and abstain from charging them with crimes when they know there is factual evidence to the contrary. Let's not kid ourselves or be naïve to the fact that that is not what most prosecutors do. They are more so out to get convictions and boost their careers. That's how many of them receive notoriety, go on to become elected officials, and/or advance to other lofty positions and lifestyles.

Not only was there plenty of evidence pertaining to our innocence, the FBI and the prosecution were definitely aware of it. Even worse, they tried, and were successful, in their efforts to prevent exculpatory evidence from being presented at the trial. Undoubtedly, they all heard the same 38,000 tapes that I and our attorneys listened to.

THE WIRETAPS ARE BACK

The next tape the U.S. attorney used to intimidate me was played for the judge. In this recording I'm speaking to my husband minutes after Doretha Wagner had called me to inform me of the 9/11 attack on our country. As I recalled, I believe Doretha speculated that it had something to do with the Palestinian and Jewish conflict. My husband also expressed similar thought in his recall, which also took place directly after I had spoken to Doretha. Distinctively, I remember telling him I had to go because my only concern was about our daughter's well-being. Kiki lived two blocks from the World Trade Center, where the two planes had crashed into the buildings. Franticly, I tried to reach her on her cell phone with no success. Finally, I remembered she had a landline by which I was finally able to reach her and learned that she was okay.

Like all Americans and/or persons with any humanity, I was devastated by what had occurred. Cell phones were immediately blocked, limiting communications. Public transportation was also brought to a halt throughout Manhattan, making it difficult to impossible for people to vacate the city. Yet, my daughter needed to vacate her building as per the instruction of the authorities. When she attempted to do so, smoke, dust, and debris were so thick that she couldn't see and had difficulty breathing. This prompted her to return to her apartment and call me. I instructed her to wet a towel, place it over her mouth, put some sunglasses on, and just start walking as far as she could until she was out of the area. Doretha, who had lived in New York, called me to inform me of the only route out of the city. Using Doretha's suggestion my daughter was able to get out of the city, catch a bus, and make her way to the Philadelphia suburbs where we resided at the time.

One might wonder what that account has to do with this overall story. Well, it's imperative to mention it because it demonstrates how callously and inhumanely the U.S. attorney treated me. They would stop at nothing to destroy my image. Not even the conversation of a distressed mother frantic to help her daughter, in a life-threatening situation, made them have even the slightest bit of compassion or humanity.

The U.S. attorney also played what they perceived to be a potentially damning tape of me yelling at, and threatening bodily harm, to a former student. I had received a call from the school about an irate student who had threatened to attack one of the administrators. This administrator was very petite and was seven months' pregnant at the time. Need I say she also happened to be my daughter-in-law? I'd said to the student, "I'll beat your ass if you lay a hand on her!" Of course I never intended to physically touch the student. However, I certainly wanted her to think so. The student was the victim of a broken home, and both parents were incarcerated. She and her siblings were recipients of a full paid tuition grant, sponsored by my husband and me. In other words, we paid for their private education throughout all the years they attended our school.

Evidently the prosecutors perceived this tape as the smoking gun to prove I was a horrible person. An argument ensued between the defense and the U.S. attorney. My lawyer objected to the tape being played insisting it was prejudicial and irrelevant to the case. Judge Kauffman ordered me and the other two parties to his chambers. After hearing the tapes, and both sides of the argument, he denied the prosecutors motion. He further added it was obvious that I was using a tough love bluff as a deterrent to having the student arrested. My attorney also informed the judge that the student in question was in the courtroom as a character witness for me, and would testify that she would never had graduated from high school if not for me. With that, the prosecutors threw in the towel on that round.

GOVERNMENT'S CLOSING ARGUMENT

For now, I will take the liberty of summing up the prosecution's case against us. Keep in mind that, as stated prior, in spite of a lot of yelling, screaming, and conjecture, the U.S. attorneys never provided any evidence that I was a beneficiary of illegal funds from the Philadelphia Community College Program. Nor did they provide evidence that a ghost employee scam took place, or that Azim and Kiki did not teach classes, or do other work for the college. In a fair proceeding, wherein the jurors were not predisposed to lies, or prompted to hate Muslims by the rhetoric of some media and politicians after 9/11, we should have, and most likely would have been found innocent. At least that's what Judge Fullam obviously thought and so did all fair-minded individuals.

SENTENCE # 1

Irrespective of our innocence we were mandated to serving time under the confines of home, under house arrest. By we, I'm referring only to Azim, Kiki, and me. It strikes me odd, that Doretha's son, who was on trial with us, was not sentenced along with us. Unlike his mother, who strategically had her trial severed from ours, her son was found guilty along with my son, daughter and me. No big deal some might say. The assumption about house arrest is, it's not real prison; if you're still in your home, as opposed to a prison, facility, what's the hardship in that? Make no mistake about it; while less burdensome than being locked down in a facility, house arrest is no picnic. Individuals are still stripped of their liberties; we were restricted from leaving our home or stepping outside of our door, beyond a few feet. Wearing an ankle bracelet was mandatory. And, being subjected to random visits from federal officers, presiding over us during the duration of our house arrest, was pretty imposing, too. Don't get me wrong, in no way am I suggesting that imprisonment would have been better. I'm just making the point that the restrictions of house arrest are indeed a form of judicial punishment.

Azim and Kiki had completed their six-months house arrest while I was desperately looking forward to my twelve-month sentence coming to an end. However, like a poorly written plot in an R-rated movie, the feds were not done with me, yet. Creatively, they charged me with a superseding indictment. Except for including me in the case against my husband, attorney Ron White, and members of Mayor John Street's staff, the feds charged me with virtually the same articles listed in their first indictment against me. How is that possible? Legally and technically there was no justification for it.

By this time our finances had substantially decreased and the feds knew it. FBI agents and U.S. attorneys are quite aware of how expensive it is to put up a defense. Irrespective of how much economic resources individuals may be privy to, their monetary leverage is no match for the millions of dollars the government has access to. It doesn't come out of their personal income, so there's no disadvantage for U.S. attorneys who have unlimited money to spend on getting convictions. And they do exactly that.

In preparation for providing relevant details of the government's trumped-up case against me and my children, I reread some of the charges listed in one of the indictments. I discovered that the extent of charges was beyond what I recalled. To the government's credit, they are masters at exaggeration and propaganda. They actually brought me up on RICO charges, which stands for Racketeer Influenced and Corrupt Organization Act. *"How utterly ridiculous and vicious,"* I thought to myself. But then again, nothing the feds did to take me or my family down shocked me at this point. RICO, by all accounts, immediately paints an image of a mob boss figure. People automatically associate underworld figures like Al Capone and Nicky Scarfo with the RICO Act. These type individuals were accused of the most heinous crimes stemming from extortion, drug trafficking, murder, and so on. As I was reading the indictment I noticed where the feds included that my family and I used the ghost employee scam and other scams to gain property and income we were not entitled to.

The feds had to know that that was an outright lie. I have always worked hard and was a successful businesswoman who owned properties. They were fully aware that, of my own volition and ability, I had legally accrued wealth long before I was ever married to Shamsud-Din or before I ever signed a lease agreement for the CCP program. So, their assertion about me using a scam to attain real estate was totally unfounded. Besides that, they never even mentioned what property I was supposed to have gained from the alleged scam. They just kept throwing anything into the indictment to see what would eventually stick.

Reading count after count, written out in legalese on white paper, in seemingly endless logging, can be quite convincing. Couple that with the fact that most law-abiding citizens have confidence in our judicial system, so a juror becomes convinced of what is presented to them. Most perceive federal agents to be honorable people. I know, once upon a time, I perceived them to be the highest level of law enforcement and trusted them to have integrity. By no means do I believe that all of them are dishonest. However, some of them are definitely driven to lies and deceptive practices. Thus, U.S. attorneys achieve guilty verdicts that often exceed the level of crime committed, and too often their victory comes at the expense of innocent people.

A SMALL VICTORY FOR ONE DEFENDANT

The 3rd Circuit Court of Appeals made a substantial ruling in Doretha Wagner's favor. The court ruled that a conversation, which the government alleged proved conspiracy, was vague. Furthermore, the conversation did not specify any act of conspiracy between Doretha and myself to operate a ghost employee scam. Nor did the conversation provide evidence of any conspiracy as alleged by U.S. attorneys. Apparently, the government was able to successfully overturn the 3rd Circuit's decision by appealing to the next highest court. The only thing this proves it that with unlimited resources, unmatched finances, and no personal consequences, U.S. attorneys can file and/or re-file appeals until they get the results they seek. However, it's beyond peculiar that the feds never charged Zaynah with conspiracy even though they claimed she conspired along with Doretha and me to defraud the CCP. They only charged her with perjury. It resulted from her testimony before the grand jury. Zaynah insisted that, to the best of her knowledge, no illegal conduct occurred in the CCP program. So, angered by the truth not conforming to the feds' distorted version of the facts, they retaliated against Zaynah. Perjury is the feds' trump card that they frequently use against anyone they choose. The truth matters not because they get to decide if a statement is a lie, if they deem it to be so. Actually, they can charge someone with perjury even when they know the individual told the truth. Certainly, they weren't about to cut me or my family members any breaks, but their conduct toward Doretha and her son indicated the opposite.

FINALLY DORETHA'S TRIAL

I had already been sentenced, not once, not twice, but three times on primarily the same charges, while Doretha still hadn't even gone to trial yet. I will provide further details on being sentenced multiple times in later chapters. Doretha was eventually brought to trial and found guilty and sentenced to serve prison time. I very much wanted to be there, but I was still incarcerated at the time; however, some of my supporters were in the courtroom for her trial and would relay information to me about it. I learned from them that her defense was to blame everything on me. I wasn't bothered or surprised by it. I'd always viewed Doretha to be the consummate self-preservationist no matter who or what else had to be sacrificed. What baffled me was how I was deserving of blame when I was never in the position of power. Common sense defies me being the orchestrator of any scam when I had no insight into how the CCP program worked, nor had the capability to manipulate their system; only Doretha sat at the helm of the CCP. She made that crystal clear to everyone.

Doretha used her position and influence to do as she pleased; she made decisions that turned out to be unethical too. One such decision was to put her son on the community college payroll. I actually found this out as it became a part of the indictment. I hadn't known this prior. I couldn't have known because I never once saw her son on the premises. You see, the school was located in the Philadelphia area and her son lived in another part of the country—on the West Coast, in fact. Obviously, he could not physically conduct classes!

Initially, when I learned that he was indicted, along with my children, I gave Doretha the benefit of the doubt. I thought perhaps she hired her son as a legal consultant since he had been to law school. This would have been consistent with the way she had other staff members doing a variety of tasks. That thought was completely shattered when it was revealed, during the trial, that her son knew nothing about being on the payroll for the community college.

I had only met Doretha's son on one occasion, and he'd struck me as an outstanding, honorable young man. He was just about to embark on a career as an attorney when he was dragged into an unfortunate situation that could have tarnished his professional reputation. My heart broke for him every time I looked across the room and saw him sitting with his defense attorney. If he was put on the payroll without his knowledge, there was no way he should have been charged. I prayed for him just as I'd prayed that my kids would be vindicated from crimes they did not commit. If my memory serves correct, ultimately he was able to get on with his life and practice law after all was said and done. I don't know if that means the feds expunged his record, or if the situation—that being he's now a convicted felon—had no effect on him practicing law.

I had a real problem with the media's constant attack on my children and me, while they rarely had anything to say about Doretha and her son, guilty or not. How could the primary defendant who controlled the hiring, assigned positions, and acted as dictator of all who worked under her, not be held to a higher standard than I? And let's just say, if her son knowingly participated in a ghost employee scam, as charged by the federal government, why would he not be held to a higher standard than Azim and Kiki? Granted, not one witness testified on behalf of Doretha's son to say that he actually participated in classes. To the contrary; there was substantial evidence, and witness testimony, confirming that Azim and Kiki conducted classes and performed other tasks as directed by Doretha Wagner.

MORE FAVORABLE TREATMENT FOR DORETHA

The most compelling confirmation of preferential treatment for Doretha and her son, by the federal government, was revealed during one of the mandatory visits to my probation officer, long after her trial and sentencing. "By the way, where is Doretha serving time?" I asked my probation officer. He looked away from me and shook his head then said, "Faridah, I didn't even want to tell you this but since you asked I'm not going to lie. Doretha isn't serving any time in prison. She has never served one day, in fact," he told me.

While I had no way to verify whether or not Doretha went to prison, I just took my probation officer at his word, in the moment. However, later on, I just had to do my own investigation and research. And there it was; confirmed that she'd obviously never served a minute of time, unlike what I'd been subjected to twice. Lack of records was all the confirmation I needed. There were no records at all. It just further proved that my probation officer told me the truth. It didn't shock me at all that Doretha managed to avoid serving prison time. Besides, based on how the feds came after my family and me, and how they desecrated us in the media, it was us they wanted in the first place. They were never out to get Doretha. It's unimaginable to me why she would not have gotten at the very least equal punishment. As someone who has served prison time, I know that you have to be nearly dead to avoid incarceration. I know this now as I witnessed the blind, the mentally ill, amputees, and seriously ill women being forced to serve out their sentences in prison. To my knowledge, Doretha Wagner doesn't fit any of these criteria.

Honestly, I have to applaud Doretha for her "great escape" because she managed manipulate the system to keep herself and her son out of prison. The fact that they did not serve any prison time does not disturb me. I don't think they deserved to go to prison. But, neither did I, or my children! With no uncertainty, it can be concluded that the differential treatment against my family and me is evidence of selected persecution, not justice.

11

HEADED TO PRISON

WOW! The reality of being a convicted felon was weighty enough. On the other hand, actually being confined in a prison was a reality I could barely conceptualize. Although I dreaded the thought of it, I was determined to face my unavoidable plight with courage and dignity. As a reminder, the twenty-four-month sentence was my second go-round in prison due to the feds imposing a superseding indictment. However, remember, Judge Fullam had already remanded me to house arrest on the first indictment. This time it was Judge Bruce Kauffman who sentenced me to two years of incarceration. Based on his own words at the beginning of the sentencing hearing, I felt he didn't want me to serve prison time because he'd said to the prosecution, "I know what we're here to do today and I know what the prosecution seeks to have done today. However, I just have to ask the prosecution if it is fundamentally fair to sentence this woman, Faridah Ali, again for something she's already been sentenced for?"

Prior to proceeding with the hearing, the bailiff informed the judge that there was an overflow of supporters in the hallway who wanted to come into the courtroom. The bailiff explained that he had informed them that there was not enough room to accommodate the rest of them. Within seconds, surprisingly, from out of nowhere a deep, robust voice called out, "Your Honor, may I say something?"

Of course this caused a bit of a stir as absolutely everyone in the courtroom now focused attention on the person behind the great voice. As it turned out, it was one of the brothers from the Muslim community. *Oh no*, I thought. *The judge is going to be aggravated and may perceive the interruption as a disrespectful act of aggression.* In that very instant I was concerned about possible repercussions. I prayed that Judge Kauffman didn't think the 6'2" man with a warm brown complexion and meticulously trimmed beard was engaged in any sort of protest on behalf of the Islamic community, in support of me. There was no mistaking that he was a Muslim because he wore a throb (a floor-length robe-like garment worn by Muslim men), and a kufi (a small type of hat also worn by Muslim men). Nonetheless, I didn't want the judge to assume that I was behind the man's action and take it out on me.

Gazing down from his lofty position, Judge Kaufman replied, "Yes, what is it, sir?"

A courtroom filled with shocked, now anxious, spectators on the edge of their seats, waited for the Muslim brother's response.

"Well, Your Honor, we are Muslims and are used to sitting on the floor for Jumah, (the Islamic prayer and religious service), so if you let the rest of the supporters in, the brothers will gladly sit on the floor and let the sisters sit on the benches," the brother pled humbly.

Apparently, touched by the brother's assertion, Judge Kaufman smiled. "Yes, okay, I'll permit it. Bailiff, let the rest of the people enter the courtroom," he said. Now, I had a smile on my face. What a sigh of relief it was for everyone supporting me, as well as myself, that the judge exhibited such humanity. Not everyone was happy about it though; the U.S. attorneys, members of the media, even the bailiff also sighed. Of course theirs were not out of compassion or relief. They sighed with contempt for the judge's decision because of the overflow of persons that were there to support me.

Moving forward, hearing proceedings were typical. The U.S. attorneys put forth their reasons why I should be receiving a lengthy jail sentence. Naturally, my attorney argued for the opposite. Here's what was different. The U.S. attorney desperately wanted me to testify and repeatedly insisted that I do so. It was obvious that they viewed this as an opportunity to discredit my character on the witness stand. Surely, by now they believed their projection of me and perceived me to be stupid, arrogant, and an out-of-control heathen. Provoking me to lash out on the stand would validate their premise. They wanted nothing less than me being mandated to prison. For them it was imperative to tarnish my reputation and turn my supporters against me.

The prosecution continued to insist that I testify. When the judge inquired as to why this was so important, they claimed it was because I had pled nolo contendere. They further claimed that by not admitting guilt, I could hold a press conference and profess that I only pled nolo contendere because I was innocent and couldn't afford to pay anymore legal expenses. *What nerve they have*, I thought as I sat there listening to their arguments. After all, it was the feds who continued to overtly make distorted statements about me to the press and dispensed lies about me to the media. Now they're concerned about me speaking with the press. *What hypocrites*, I thought. I didn't think the judge was going to grant their request, but he surprised me.

Judge Kaufman said he would like to hear directly from me, but it was my choice. Garland Giles did not argue this sentencing hearing. Gail Weilheimer, a brilliant attorney, who was an affiliate of the prestigious Allen Frank Law Firm and currently a judge, represented me. Gail called for a brief recess to discuss the matter with me. As we huddled close together, she strongly insisted that I not take the stand because she was fully aware of how brutal the U.S. attorneys had been from their initial action against me. She said, "I'm strongly opposed to you being cross-examined by any of the three U.S. attorneys who are trying you."

Yes, there were three U.S. attorneys who collaborated prosecuting me like a wrestling tag team, each of them seeking to place me in a virtual choke hold. Unlike my attorney, I couldn't care less about the prosecution's attempt to bully me on the witness stand. There was no way to trick me into incriminating myself because I was innocent of the charges. Taking charge of the situation, I expressed my disagreement with the attorney and explained why. Hearing the judge state that he was confused and would prefer that I take the stand, even though he could not force me, meant that I should accommodate his wish. For me, this was a no-brainer. When a judge requests something of a defendant, it's actually a demand. You see, Judge Kauffman was under the impression that I was taking responsibility for my actions, but the U.S. attorney was disputing that. They argued that my silence was equivalent to me not taking responsibility. This is because the prosecution deliberately misrepresented what taking responsibility meant in my case. This is a big deal because it's important to understand the federal government's process for sentencing. Mandatory guidelines are used to calculate the level of punishment that convicted felons are subjected to. Considerations of certain factors, such as character letters, if it's an individual's first offense, if they take responsibility for committing a crime, and so on, can benefit defendants. Judges have the discretion to deviate from the guidelines and reduce any imposed punishment. It can mean the difference between receiving probation, less prison time, or even impact how one serves a prison sentence. There's a big difference between going to a prison camp and a maximum security federal facility, and the judge decides which one of these the defendant will serve out their sentence in. Since the prosecution sought the worst possible punishment for me, they did not want the judge to reduce my sentence by accepting that I had taken responsibility for my actions.

Completely aware of the possible consequences for not taking the stand, I instructed my attorney to inform the judge that I would comply with taking the stand. My decision pulled bright smiles up on the prosecution's faces. They could hardly hold back their enthusiasm for the opportunity to get me on the stand. Now it was the prosecution's turn to huddle and discuss their strategy for cross-examining me. As I walked toward the witness stand to be sworn in, I could feel the tension in the room; it wasn't just from the anticipation of the prosecution and their media disciples. My supporters appeared to be on edge as well. Obviously, the two opposing sides had different reasons to be anxious.

After being sworn in, my attorney asked if I was taking responsibility for my actions. I affirmed that I was. When it was time for the U.S. attorney to cross-examine me, he rushed to the front of the courtroom and stood as close to me as possible.

"So," he said smugly, "You claim you are taking responsibility for your actions. Is that correct?"

For sure this was his Perry Mason moment where he was going to, once and for all, solve the big mystery. Anyway, I answered simply, "Yes."

"SSSOOO," the U.S. attorney said emphatically, looking more confident than ever, "you're admitting guilt for the charges in the indictment?"

"No, I'm not admitting guilt to anything," I responded. He looked completely startled and the prosecutor just shook his head.

Judge Kauffman quickly interjected, "Now, Mrs. Ali, you expressed in a letter from you to me that you were remorseful for what had occurred. I'm confused."

"It's exactly as I stated, Your Honor. This woman isn't taking responsibility or showing remorse for anything!" said the prosecutor.

"Yeah, I'm confused," the judge said again.

Feeling compelled to speak, I asked the judge if I could explain my answer, which he permitted me to do.

"To be clear, Your Honor, I meant what I said in the letter, but it should not be mistaken for confession of a crime I did not commit. What I meant was, I regret not being more involved in my oversight of the community college program, even though it was not my responsibility to manage the operation. As assistant director of the Sister Clara Muhammad School, I regret not being more knowledgeable of what was going on and protecting the fine reputation of the school. That's what I take responsibility for, that's what I regret."

Angrily, the prosecutor blurted out, "Didn't you say that you felt like you were being persecuted by the federal government regarding this indictment?"

"Yes, I did," I shot back.

I could tell the prosecutor was stunned by my honest answer. Apparently he expected me to lie. My recourse was to turn toward the judge and ask if I could explain my sentiment. Again, Judge Kaufman allowed me to proceed with my explanation. Staring the prosecutor right in his eyes, I stated the following:

"Yes, to me it feels like persecution. Day after day countless media stories have painted me as a horrible person and so have the U.S. attorneys. And as for the media, wherein you state that I can go out and hold a press conference, that is not my intention. Before Allah (SWT) and all of these witnesses in this courtroom I can state unequivocally I will not do any such thing. You have repeatedly accused me of being a liar, but now because it serves your purpose you want me to lie on myself and say I did something that I did not do. Well, that's something I'm never, ever going to do; never will I say I did something I did not do!"

The prosecutor replied, "I'm not trying to get you to lie, I'm simply laboring to get to the truth." His tone was much more subdued than at any time throughout the trial.

Obviously recognizing that his verbal assault was not rendering the results he desired, he declared, "No further questions." With that, the judge imposed a twenty-four-month sentence and recommended that my time be served in a federal prison camp.

The thirty days granted me to get my affairs in order went by fast. I just wanted to get it over with. My brother Mikal, sister Zaynah, along with Muslim sisters, Intisar Shah and Shafeeqah Muhammad, escorted me to the Danbury Federal Prison. The mood was somewhat solemn in my brother's SUV during the approximately two-hour drive in pouring down rain. I wasn't sad. In fact, I was upbeat and made every effort to comfort everyone in the car.

When we arrived at the prison camp, it was still pouring outside, so we all made a mad dash for the building. We shook ourselves and brushed off as much rain from our soaked clothing as possible then walked toward the counter, assuming it was the place to check in. "May I help you?" said an intake officer.

"Yes. I'm here to self-surrender," I answered.

"Okay," she said matter-of-fact. Then politely she said to those accompanying me that they could have a seat in the area across the room and that I could sit with them for a few more minutes. I could tell my family and friends wanted to stay with me until the very last moment. But I wanted to spare them that ordeal because I knew it would be more painful for them to see me escorted off in handcuffs like a common criminal.

As gently as possible I explained to them that I wanted them to leave now because it would be too difficult for everyone if they stayed any longer. Tearfully and reluctantly they honored my request. They showered me with love, affection, and words of encouragement before saying our final farewell. With a heavy heart I watched them run toward the car and slowly drive away. Shortly after their departure, the correction officer summoned me to the counter, asked to see my identification, and proceeded to process me into the system. Although I dreaded being handcuffed again, fortunately I was not. I was simply taken into another area of the building, provided prison attire to change into, and given a pillowcase full of items. It contained a pillow, dingy sheets, and a nasty-looking army green blanket. That was disturbing enough to me; however, having to strip naked and submit to vaginal and rectal probes by a nonmedical professional was truly the most demeaning experience during the process. I was also ordered to open my mouth while the correction officer put her fingers all around my gums and teeth to make sure I didn't have any contraband. She also removed the band from my ponytail and thoroughly went through my hair looking for contraband as well.

Once that was over I was walked to the door, was shown the path leading up the hill to another building, and instructed to take the prison-issued items with me and report to the case manager. By the time I reached the other building, the sun was shining bright. Upon opening one of the double doors, I noticed about six steps leading up to a platform. Next, I heard someone say, "As-Salamu-Alykum Sister Faridah Ali." Instinctively, I returned the greeting and asked, "Do you know me?" even though I could not make out who I was speaking to. From my position I could only see a blurred image of a tall person who was standing in front of a window. The glare of the sun encased the person. As I got closer, I saw a tall woman with dreadlocks below her waist, dressed in Khaki pants, a T- shirt and Timberland style boots. Her face was pleasant and her demeanor was warm.

Holding my pillow knapsack over my left shoulder, I climbed the stairs. Remaining at the top of the stairs, the sister, who I will refer to as Jazz, said, "I don't know you personally, but everyone knows who you are."

"How's that?" I asked.

"News travels fast, especially about a high-profile person like you," she said with a smile.

Surprised by her comment, I remained focused on the task before me. "So, where am I supposed to go now?" I asked her. Pointing down the hall she directed me to the caseworker's office on the left side of the building. As I walked forward, I noticed several offices on one side as well as large dormitory rooms, each of which contained three bunk beds. Some inmates were moving about the hall, and some of them were seated on their bunks, reading and knitting. A novice to prison life, I was trying to absorb as much as possible. This was quite new to me. I had expected the inmates to be more contained as opposed to freely moving about.

By now I had reached a line of about seventeen inmates standing in the front of two offices. I got in the line with the inmates who were also waiting to see the case manager. The other line was for those waiting to see the counselor. I could tell that the women in line were dressed different from the majority of inmates. Later I learned that new arrivals like me had different attire because we had yet to be issued regular prison clothing and shoes. We would wear pullover V-neck tops with elastic waistband pants until we were provided with button-down blouses and zipper front khaki pants.

Finally after standing in line for over an hour, it was my turn to meet with the case manager. Emotionless and without any eye contact, the man on the other side of the desk remained silent as he continued writing on the paper forms before him. His office resembled more of a closet than a room. The lighting was rather dull against the puke greenish-gray walls. It reminded me more of an interrogation room than an intake room. Suddenly, I heard, "Do you know of any reason why you could not be housed among the general population?"

I was totally perplexed. "Excuse me. What do you mean?" I asked. *Is he talking to me?*

From there he finally looked up at me straight on and provided an explanation. "Do you feel you'd be in physical jeopardy among the inmate community? Or do you feel the need to be placed in the Segregated Housing Unit?" he continued.

I said, "No."

Next, he asked if I knew of any codefendants in my case currently incarcerated at Danbury Federal Prison Camp. After responding no again, the case manager gave me my bed and dorm assignment, and I left the room to figure the rest out on my own—my dormitory bunk and all. It was the coldest and most unconcerned encounter I'd ever had. *Oh well,* I thought, *I'd better get used to it because I'm likely to receive the same treatment from other Federal Bureau of Prison's personnel.*

Getting processed into Danbury's system included getting at the end of yet another line, this time, to see the counselor. Again, there was a man with office décor matching the caseworker's office. Aside from that, there's not much more to describe, as the entire ordeal mimicked the first intake meeting. This time, though, the counselor introduced me to an inmate who would give me a brief tour of the facility. It was an oblong building about the length of an inner-city block and the width of a quarter of the average city block.

Puke greenish gray was the color throughout the entire building. At the entrance of the building there was a large cafeteria to the left. At the other end of the building, toward the right, was a computer lab, and across the hall were classrooms.

Once the tour was over, I went directly to my dorm and began the process of settling in, whatever that really meant. Making the bed was the first task, but before placing sheets on it, I asked for some plastic trash bags. The mattress had multiple stains on it, which could have been from sweat, saliva, or other disgusting bodily fluids. The thought of having only a dingy previously shared sheet between my flesh and that repulsive mattress gave me the creeps. So, I got the two large trash bags, cut them open, and tucked them around the mattress to create a makeshift mattress cover. That still wasn't a sufficient enough separation between the sheets and me having to lie directly on them. As a result, I decided to just lie on top of the thick green army style blanket. At least it provided a few layers of separation between my body and the mattress.

Second, I organized the few items I had and placed them in my small 3x4.5 size locker. Just as I was about to complete what would be my final task for the day, I sat on the edge of my bed and let out a sigh of relief. It was the lower bunk, which is a privilege extended to women who are at least fifty years old and/or disabled. As soon as I sat down, I heard a collection of footsteps; really more like a herd hoofing it up the hall like rushing cattle. I turned to see inmates rushing by my room toward the cafeteria.

My bunky (a term used for inmates occupying the upper or lower bed of the same bunk) leaped down from the top bed and said, "C'mon, it's time eat!" In what felt like an engagement in the childish frolic of follow-the-leader, I followed her. However, she was maneuvering her way so fast through the crowd that she reached the destination before I did. By the time I arrived, most of the inmates were already lined up from the cafeteria counter, all the way up the sidewall and against the back wall of the room. There were only two inmates behind me. Perhaps I was too overwhelmed, a little depressed, or simply void of appetite by the time I reached the counter. In any event, I wasn't hungry, so I just took an apple, which was handed to me by one of the inmates working behind the counter. I also picked up a plastic cup and filled it with what appeared to be diluted orange juice from the dispenser. I looked for my newly acquainted bunky. Once I spotted her, I walked toward the table where she was seated with other inmates. Cautioned by my bunky not to drink the juice, I asked why not? Her answer disgusted me; she informed me that those in the know never drink anything from the juice container because the machine had roaches in it. That gave me the creeps and throughout my incarceration I never considered drinking any beverages I didn't purchase from the commissary.

A group of women seated at a rectangular table welcomed me with smiles as they raised their hands and waved me toward the table, showing me there was an empty chair to sit in. *What a kind gesture*, I thought, though I was a bit skeptical. The counselor and case manager had informed me of the culture and warned me about a few things, which included how to deal with inmates offering me things like food, candy, cosmetics, or any type of assistance. They both emphasized the importance of denying any type of supportive gestures, as it could lead to trouble. This reminded me that I was now in prison and that the motto of inmates was "no one does anything for nothing." Wherein an inmate offers to do your laundry, make your bed, or tidy up after you, even do your hair, they would be expecting something in return. Even with such thoughts lingering in my head, I still accepted the seat at the table, which apparently the women had saved for me. The cafeteria was always crowded. Later I would learn that it simply wasn't true that inmates only do nice things for another inmate seeking something in return.

Anyway, there were not enough seats to accommodate all of the inmates if everyone elected to eat their meals in there at the same time. Many inmates chose to avoid eating cafeteria food, if not for every meal, for most. Rather than eating food issued by the FBOP they made their own meals. They prepared meals from groceries purchased from the commissary and/or stolen from either the commissary or the kitchen.

By day's end I was exhausted and eager to retire for the evening. My lumpy bed actually seemed inviting regardless of how uncomfortable the mattress appeared to be. All six of the inmates were in the dorm and dressed for bed. I located my prison-issued ankle-length nightgown made of T-shirt material. There were no private dressing areas of course, so my options consisted of either undressing in the dormitory in front of five people or changing in the ladies' room, where I'd encounter other inmates taking showers and changing as well. Turning my back toward the inmates and facing the wall where my bunk was stationed, I first placed the nightgown over my head, covering below my knees. Without putting my arms into the sleeves, I used the nightgown as a makeshift curtain and began to unbutton my blouse, removed my top, bra, panties, and pants. Now, I was ready to lie on top of the covers and fall asleep. No sooner had I laid down a voice over the intercom shouted, "Counts! Counts! Counts time! Let's go, ladies!"

Clueless, I simply followed suit and joined the other inmates in standing by our assigned bunks. Utter silence fell over the entire prison with only the sound of correction officers walking, as they went from room to room. Only one of the officers entered our dormitory and proceeded to count us. We were only able to resume activities once the officer left the room. Letting out a sigh of relief, I went back to my itchy blanket. The next thing I heard was, "Lights out!" Immediately following, the entire building went dark, leaving only a dim overhead stream of light throughout the corridors. There was just enough illumination to see exit signs and to make your way to the bathroom during the night. As I lay there in my solitude, the explosive reality that I was really in prison hit me. I suddenly felt extremely weighty, like I was trapped beneath a tractor-trailer. My breathing became labored and I began to feel claustrophobic. As my eyes welled with tears, a sense of hopelessness and despair enclosed me like a cocoon. Easily I could've wailed long into the night. Instead, however, I turned my body toward the wall in an effort to hide my emotions from the other women, to suppress my cries so that no one would hear or know my pain.

In the midst of my sadness, the power of my inner voice emerged and said, *Wipe those tears from your eyes. Pull it together, and don't surrender your will to enemies and those who seek to oppress you. Don't shed another teardrop.* My job was to stay healthy and give them only what they had the power to control. They only had jurisdiction over how much time I would serve. But I had the power over *how* I'd served that time. Determined not to succumb to the delight of the evil persecutors, I pulled it together and never allowed my spirit to sink that low again. That's not to say that I did not have some disturbing moments throughout my incarceration. Nothing minimizes the fact that I was in prison. My liberties had been taken away; I was separated from loved ones and the comforts of the freedoms I once knew.

Rita's Rule # 22

In good times remember to reflect upon the bad times, and in bad times remember to reflect upon the good times, for surely both will come again.

Small things taken for granted outside of prison become big things for inmates. Getting permission to call home and visitation privileges felt like hitting the lottery to me. After listing the names and providing detailed information of individuals you want permission to communicate with, inmates must wait for Federal Bureau of Prisons [FBOP] approval. My first opportunity to call home came about a week after being admitted into prison. As I held the phone to my ear, I waited intensely for the taped message informing the recipient that the call was from a federal prison to conclude. In addition, it provided directions on how to reject the call and avoid receiving any future ones from the inmate named in the message. I was extremely eager to speak with my son, Azim, whose voice I had already heard when he answered the phone. Of course he couldn't hear me until the auto-message finished.

Azim was beyond elated to hear from me and expressed how much the family was concerned about my well-being. He was relieved when I assured him that I was fine.

"Don't worry, son, I got this," I said with confidence.

"Great, Mom, I knew you could handle it. It's just that I began to worry when we didn't hear from you after several days. So, how are the women responding to you? Are they treating you with respect or what?"

"They've been extraordinarily kind and helpful," I told him. "I'm already viewed as a sister, mom, and friend to several inmates. Many of the younger women, and boys, also refer to me as Mom."

"Wait! I thought Danbury was a women's prison!"

I let out a mischievous chuckle and said, "That's correct. It is for women only."

Azim laughed. "Wow, Mom, that's funny. I get it!"

He knew I was talking about gay women, specifically the type who projected a masculine demeanor and image. They loved me and treated me like I was their mother. Marla, who resided in the same dorm as I, was in her early twenties. After returning from a segregated house for beating another inmate, she was assigned to my dorm. The incident earned her a reputation for being tough. Marla occupied an upper bunk across the room from me. Apparently believing her own hype, she made the mistake of speaking rudely to me. Before I could respond, and believe me I would have checked her, my bunky, Zee, leaped down from the bunk above my head. With the speed of lightning she was all over Marla. Zee was about five-foot-nine, lean and muscular, built like a star NBA player.

She was a very open proud lesbian who would've been attractive as a female but acted like, looked like, and dressed like a dude. Marla was a bit shorter than Zee. She was a chunky Jamaican woman who thought she was tough. I was the oldest woman in the dorm. In addition to her just coming into our dorm, she was unaware of the type of relationships I had with Zee and others throughout the prison. Perhaps, due to my age, she thought I was someone she could bully.

Whatever she thought, her impression was drastically altered after Zee knocked her across the room. Marla didn't realize had Zee not dealt with her, she would have found me to be more than a worthy opponent. Beneath my bed I kept a sock loaded with rocks. It was for the sole purpose of busting any would-be assaulter in the head. Surely, anyone foolish enough to attack me would be the recipient of repeated blows with my protective sock! Never was it my intention to start a fight, but in no way would I ever permit anyone to get away with hitting me. An inmate bragging about whipping Ms. Ali's ass was out of the question, and my special sock ensured that.

Rita's Rule # 23

Always stand up to bullies regardless of where you encounter them. Remember, it's not how tough you are. What matters is your willingness to fight. Bullies are cowards and will back down when they sense you're not fearful of them.

You see, as an observant person, I paid close attention to my new surroundings. In particular, I assessed the demeanor of the women. As opposed to engaging in frivolous dialogue, I sat quietly. From this vantage point, certain character traits of specific inmates became abundantly evident. Subsequently, I knew from their actions, conversation, even body language who were aggressive, arrogant, mean-spirited, nosy, gossipers, and troublemakers, as opposed to those who were kind, intelligent, and in the know. Obviously, Marla was not wise enough to determine I was not someone to disrespect.

Rita's Rule # 24

Never underestimate an opponent, particularly when it comes to initiating a physical altercation. Assuming someone is easy prey or cowardly because they exhibit the qualities of a reserved demeanor, are educated, and have been exposed to a privileged life is a serious error. Acting on these notions could be costly in the least, and physically harmful at worst.

It's imperative that I don't leave the impression that older women being accosted, or attacked by younger inmates, was a frequent occurrence. In my experience, for the most part, younger inmates actually treated elders like parents and older women treated them like their children. Overall, both federal prisons I spent time in were environments conducive to inmates getting along with each other. We women shared what few extra amenities we had with each other and supported each other during difficult times.

For instance, when an inmate's loved one died, we did our best to comfort the grieving woman. When any woman was denied the opportunity to see a parent, spouse, child, or sibling when they were dying, or to attend the funeral service, was devastating. Missing out on memorable occasions such as loved one's birthdays, marriages, births, and other events, relegated many of the women to tears and emotional trauma. These are the type of occurrences that make serving time intolerable.

Recalling my first Mother's Day at Danbury Federal Prison, my heart ached for the women. Hearing the sobbing of many inmates was a most depressing experience. In spite of heartfelt efforts of the inmates to comfort each other with homemade arts and crafted flowers, cards, and sharing meals together, nothing compensated for mothers being ripped away from their children on any day, let alone Mother's Day.

Factor in additional traumatic events such as spousal abandonment, minimal, if any outside support, no visitors, no money to purchase commissary items and the harshness of incarceration alone. The forthcoming examples are mere fractions of hardships female inmates shared with me serving their prison sentence.

*   *   *

Jazz had been incarcerated for close to twenty years and was in her early forties by the time I came to Danbury. She admitted to having been involved in drug trafficking but was never convicted on any violence or gun-related charges. Regardless of having not murdered or injured anyone, receiving such an extensive sentence deprived her of a woman's God-given ability and right to ever experience the joys of motherhood. By the time she would be released from prison, her biological clock would have long since come to an end. Due to the length of her sentence, she was originally incarcerated in the building down the hill from the camp. That's because initially her incarceration required a higher security level. After serving many years down the hill without ever being written up for any type of infraction, her security ranking was finally low enough for her to be transferred to a prison camp.

*   *   *

Miss June was a feisty, petite, medium brown African-American woman. She and her daughter were accused of theft for continuing to receive Miss June's husband's social security checks after his death. Miss June and her daughter's offenses were found out by the social security department within a year of her husband's death. So, for a few thousand dollars, and a first offense, she and her daughter were sentenced to prison time.

It was customary for younger inmates to accommodate some of the older ladies by carrying their commissary purchases back to the dorm for them. In prison, there's always a line to stand in for everything you need, from food to soap to mail. On this particular day I saw Miss June in the commissary line. I'll never forget how she looked and what she'd told me on that day. She appeared to be very tired and weak. I asked her if she needed me to carry her items back to the dorms and she said, "No, one of the younger inmates is going to do that for me."

"Okay, then, but are you feeling okay?" I replied.

Then she gently put her hand on my forearm and said, "Actually, I don't feel well at all and I know I'm going to die in here."

That response shook me to my core. Naturally, that was something I did not want to hear nor did I want to believe it. "No, Miss June, you are going to be fine," I said.

"Look, I'm a nurse. I recognize what's going on in my body," she insisted. "I need my heart medicine, and the FBOP is not providing the exact prescription, the kind I was taking before I came here."

Attempting to reassure her I said, "I believe they will have all that straightened out in a few days, or so." I could tell she didn't take an ounce of confidence in a word I'd said. Her defeatist look bore witness to it, as she simply shook her head no. A few days later Miss June died of a massive heart attack. The entire inmate population was grief-stricken by her unnecessary and preventable death, as well as the cruelty inflicted upon her by the FBOP.

One of the women in my dormitory encountered the same type of problem with medication. She kept complaining of a headache because of not receiving her blood pressure medication. It wasn't long before she had a stroke and was transported to a nearby hospital. We were told that she was okay but never saw her again. Another woman in our dorm who occupied the bunk above me continued to scream out in agonizing pain. Nothing was done until a group of about twelve inmates approached the corrections officer on duty that night and insisted that something needed to be done. Nonchalantly, the insensitive male officer finally called 911 and she was taken out in an ambulance.

Recurring stories of women who broke no laws themselves but were affiliated with men who committed crimes are common in prison. Many of these cases were with white women involved with black men. Some admitted to engaging in unlawful activities with their men while others professed to be innocent. They were victims of federal punishment because they could not or would not cooperate with the feds. Of course cooperating takes on a whole new meaning when the feds are involved. If you lie or go along with a prosecutor's version of events, you have officially cooperated.

I can't emphasize enough the depth of cruelty that occurs in women's prisons. Wherein friends, husbands, and children abandon incarcerated women, it is understandable why holidays are sad days for inmates. All things considered this begs the question, when is enough, enough? As a matter of common practice, the federal government incarcerates individuals for a first offense. The vast majority of their sentences result from individuals seeking some type of mercy from the feds that will lessen their prison time. As if that's not enough, many inmates are required to pay some type of restitution while they are incarcerated.

When family members put their hard-earned money on the inmates' books so that they can purchase commissary items, the FBOP automatically docks a percentage of the money. Upon release to a halfway house, inmates are required to obtain employment. They must give the halfway house 25% of their gross income while they are staying there. Hypothetically, if the inmate earns $400 a week, the halfway house automatically gets $100 off the top. As well, deductions for social security, state and local taxes are deducted from the $400. By the time the inmate receives her cut, it is substantially less than what they earned.

After serving halfway house time, most convicted felons are placed on supervised release. During that period inmates must continue to pay restitution. In my case it was for three years. Finally, the long-awaited day arrives when you're off of supervised probation and can finally get on to resuming your rightful place among society. But, not so fast... the mark of the beast remains. Or should I say, the feds remain. You are forever typecast as a convicted felon. Getting a decent job, even for the most educated, is no longer within reach. Essentially, the federal government has stripped you of everything and there's no way to ever make you whole and complete again in this society.

So again, I ask, when is enough, enough? Is it justice to compel someone to do all of the above and still never allow them to obtain normalcy again? From my perspective, the answer is an obvious NO! Such extreme punishments, particularly for first offenses, do not fit the crime. What are even worse are the mind games and manipulation tactics executed by the feds to break your spirit.

Generally, inmates are provided advanced notice of their release dates. This is done based on time served or if they are leaving to go to the halfway house. All the fellow inmates chip in to make sure that the person who's leaving looks their best on departure day. During the days leading up to an inmate's exit, it is customary for them to be primped and pampered by other inmates. The joy of each person leaving fosters good feelings throughout. Like those remaining, I always cheered for anyone's release. Naturally, it was a joyous occasion as well as an encouraging reminder that my turn was coming someday.

Anyone—innocent or guilty—convicted of a crime is stereotyped as a lowlife individual. You're believed to be a liar if you profess or claim your innocence. This image is projected not only through societal norms, it is perpetuated in the media as well as through entertainment sources. Think about it. There are countless movies and stories on TV where someone professes to be innocent. Detectives, federal agents, prison guards, and law enforcement officials always have the same attitude toward the person claiming to be innocent. "Yeah, yeah, everybody in here is innocent," they say with a sarcastic smirk. Images like this desensitize society into believing that everyone charged with a crime has actually committed it, or at least has done something for law enforcement to pursue them. Such sentiment is unequivocally false. It has become commonplace for innocent people to be convicted of crimes they did not commit.

* * *

Out of all the inmates I met during my two different incarcerations, at two separate prisons, only two women said they were innocent. The others stated with conviction that they did whatever the crime was. They viewed accepting responsibility as a necessity and wore it with pride. Statements like, "Look, I ain't even gonna lie about it. I knew what I was doing and took a chance on getting away with it. Ain't no reason to be whining about it now because I did the crime and now I gotta do the time. It's as simple as that." Inmates feel that's the least they can do to make amends for having made wrongful decisions in the past and see it as a way of moving on and reclaiming their dignity.

To impose lifelong punishment on inmates because they've made a mistake, is simply another way of dehumanizing them. Far too many people tend to believe the worst, particularly as it relates to affiliates of law enforcement. Therefore, some will question the extent of how often inmates are subjected to unnecessary cruelties once they've been convicted of crimes. In anticipation of such skepticism, I have provided documentation from extensive research on prison life contained in articles and data. However, for the purpose of confirming facts pursuant to wrongful convictions and incarcerations, I'll refer you to excerpts from the writing of a former female corrections officer, Liz Webster:

"University of Virginia law professor and expert on identifying wrongful convictions of the innocent, Brandon Garrett's registry alters conventional wisdom about how innocent people get convicted. For his 2011 book, *Convicting the Innocent*, Garrett identifies eyewitness misidentification as the leading cause of those wrongful convictions (as have others). But the larger pool of cases reflected in the registry reveals other trends."[1]

According to University of Michigan law professor Samuel Gross, "Perjury or false accusation is the leading cause of wrongful

---

1   Webster, Liz (2012) https://www.thenation.com/article/how-many-innocent-people-have-we-sent-prison/

conviction. Roughly 50 percent of the cases involved African-American defendants." Gross believes that the cases in the database are just the tip of the iceberg. He has also referenced the *Proceedings of the National Academy of Sciences* for noting that 95 percent of crimes such as burglary, car theft, tax fraud, and drug possession are felony convictions that are the result of plea bargains, with no formal evidence ever presented, and most never bother with an appeal.

INMATE CLASS SYSTEM

Those who have never experienced prison life are probably totally unaware that there is a class system beyond the walls of these institutions. Status has a lot to do with the quality of how one spends their time incarcerated. High-profile individuals often have an easier time than some inmates. They are perceived to be, and often are, persons of influence, financially better off than most, and supported by family as well as friends. This puts them in a position to compensate inmates who receive no outside support and must live off the meager rations supplied by the prison. Similarly, inmates of lesser profiles who receive continued outside support are also privy to the best that prison life has to offer. The same holds true for younger, attractive women and/or those with the gift of gab and who have "swag." Then there are those who lack any special talents, are poor, and have no one putting money on their books. These individuals have to rely on the charity of other inmates looking out for them. Correction officers show favoritism to inmates according to their prison social status.

Among the things that impressed me most during my incarceration was seeing how inmates look out for each other. Bucking the FBOP's policies of not sharing with other women was regularly practiced. Wherein someone had the means to purchase extra items from the commissary, they would look out for their buddies by purchasing something for them. This meant a lot to those who had no money to purchase snacks, cosmetic items, and other necessities. Secretly, an unauthorized welcoming committee, comprised of inmates, would collect items from the general population and/or an inmate leaving the prison. Items such as toothpaste, soap, deodorant, combs, brushes, shower shoes, and so on would be given to incoming inmates. Like radar they automatically spotted those in need of help.

I once asked why no one ever gave me anything upon my arrival. I was informed that, first of all, they knew I was coming to Danbury. Second, it was obvious I didn't need any help because I was wearing a pair of Gazelle glasses when I arrived. Though I hadn't paid any attention to how I'd been perceived, I found the statement to be clarification of how observant many of the women were.

Needless to say, not everyone incarcerated is a person of means, notoriety, young, attractive, or popular among the inmate community. Young attractive inmates were recipients of special favors from corrections officers, particularly by male and lesbian officers. Overt continuous flirting and sexual contact between some officers and inmates were common. I knew for a fact that some female inmates spent countless hours alone with male corrections officers. To be fair I can't say with certainty what went on behind closed doors; I simply wondered why they indulged in such activity in the first place. Discriminative special privileges provided to inmates because they appealed to specific correction officers not only goes against FBOP policy, it's morally reprehensible. Here, I must insist on a word of caution to any judgmental reader who may harbor damnation upon inmates who willfully engage in such activity. Before condemning them I beg you to consider their situation and why they may consent to providing sexual favors for male correction officers. There are many reasons why lots of sexual encounters occur in prison.

In a 2014 article by Ava Vidal, she states that sex in prison is commonplace: the male inmates just hide it more than girls do.

As a report warns, female inmates are being coerced into sex by staff in return for favors like alcohol and cigarettes. Former prison officer Ava Vidal suggests that sex behind bars is commonplace in both male and female prisons (both among inmates and between inmates and staff) but the women are far more open about it.

It should also be noted that not all sexual acts perpetuated by prison guards upon female inmates are consensual. There are many incidents of male guards raping women, which are not reported. Victims might fail to report the assault due to fear of repercussions from the perpetrator and/or administrators turning a blind eye. From my perspective the entire justice system must be held accountable for allowing such atrocities to repetitively occur. Issues of this sort could be at best eliminated or at least substantially reduced through implementing simple precautionary measures.

Step one would entail discontinuing the practice of male correction officers guarding female inmates.

Step two is equally as easy and would require placing cameras in all private areas where guards could have their way with inmates. Surveillance devices need to be in offices, all common areas of prison facilities, dormitories, and strategically placed in lavatories, where many unlawful acts occur. Installing cameras in the open area of the lavatories, but not the actual toilet stalls or shower stalls, would go a long way in preventing sexual contact between inmates as well as staff. In spite of the corruption, inmate favoritism, and predatory behavior by some guards, the inmate population contains some really remarkable women.

Hustling was another means of survival for certain women. I'll never forget the day that I was approached by an inmate nicknamed Harlem because she was from that section of New York. Harlem had a beautiful dark complexion and was of average height with humongous boobs that hung nearly to her waist, not because they were flabby, but because they were just that huge. She wore her very short black hair slicked down to her scalp. African-Americans jokingly refer to this type of hairstyle as fried, died, and laid to the side. A few days into serving my sentence I was approached by Harlem.

"What's your pleasure?" she inquired.

Based on her looks and my close observation of her, I got the impression she was a lesbian, so I was quite guarded in my response. "My only pleasure is to do my time and get out of here as soon as possible."

My cold negativity was apparent to which she responded, "Whoa, sister, I'm not trying to come on to you. I was talking about what you want from the commissary." Harlem went on to explain that purchasing commissary items from her would be substantially discounted. Running down a list of choice items, she said, "I can get you chicken wings, flour, sugar, tomatoes, and vegetables." My assumption that she was referring to cooked food from the cafeteria was immediately crushed when she clarified that she was talking about fresh chicken. "And the price includes keeping the chicken preserved until you're ready for it," she concluded. Since I didn't eat chicken or want to get involved in any rule-breaking activities, I simply declined her offer.

Sometime later I became knowledgeable of various tactics used by inmates to make living with limitations a little easier. Nonperishable items were stored in a number of hiding places, including the ceiling. Cleverly, they hid perishable items stored in containers packed with ice in secret location throughout the prison compound, which I will not reveal. Ice was readily available from two ice machines near microwaves strategically located at both ends of the dormitory. Unless I witnessed it myself, I would never have believed that so many things could be cooked in a microwave. The necessity for home-style recipes definitely stimulated the inventive spirit among inmates. They actually fried chicken wings in the microwave, as well as prepared numerous other delicious dishes. Among the most popular meals were macaroni and cheese, chicken lo mein, fried rice, and, believe it or not, pound cake! In what can only be described as a remarkable display of genius, the inmates would purchase sandwich cookies with vanilla icing in between, remove the icing and put it into a separate container. They'd pulverize the cookies, add vanilla-flavored coffee creamer to the improvised flour, and blend these ingredients with other items confiscated from the cafeteria. After adding water to the dry ingredients, the batter was placed in plastic bowls and cooked in the microwave ovens. When cream cheese and butter were added to the icing extracted from the cookies. Believe it or not, it made for a delectable treat. Seriously, the cakes were as delicious, if not better tasting, than any I'd had in or out of prison.

*　　*　　*

Prior to incarceration I had never tasted mackerel before. There was one woman from the Caribbean islands who made the best curried mackerel ever! It was absolutely incredible and tasted so much like curried chicken that at first bite I spit it out into a napkin because I don't eat chicken. Once I realized it was in fact mackerel, which came in aluminum pouches like tuna fish and packed the same way, I enjoyed it immensely. Other inmates made it as well, but nobody made it to be as delicious as she did. Seasoned to perfection and smothered in gravy with sautéed onions and bell peppers over rice, the dish made you forget you were in prison for a minute. Actually, the inmates took such pride and had such enjoyment in cooking that the experience was more like recreation than meal preparation.

Speaking of recreation, Danbury also offered recreational activities overseen by the corrections officers who ran that department. Again, the creativity of the women was extraordinary. I was so inspired by the gorgeous items they made with yarn and knitting needles and crochet hooks that I, too, took up crochet and knitting. The garments they made could compete with any store-bought garments, easily. These ladies whipped up dresses, tube tops, sweaters, handbags, hats, shawls, bikinis, and just about any other garment imaginable. Long before I ever saw a boot constructed of yarn, the inmates were already making them. Using the bottoms of rubber flip-flops, they would punch holes all around the border, remove the thong portion, and weave yarn in and out of the holes to make the foundation for the boot. Then they'd proceed with crocheting the yarn into the shape of a boot. Tassels and other accents, also made from the yarn, would be added for extra flare. The final product could compete with any *Vogue* fashion boot. Mostly, these activities took place in the recreation areas where televisions were stationed.

Danbury had two common areas inside the dormitory. The smaller TV room, generally occupied by younger inmates, was located on the lower level of the floor. Eagerly after the end of each working day, about twenty of them would rush to the TV room to watch *106 and Park*. They knew all the latest songs and dances from watching the show. Most of them could dance quite well themselves, so I learned from seeing them dancing here and there throughout the dormitories. However, they really blew me away with their talents when they'd perform during shows they'd put on for various occasions. In an attempt to pacify the inmates, during the holidays Danbury would allow them to put on performances. We were all entertained by inmates singing, dancing, and performing skits.

The second TV room was located in the actual visiting room. It was a huge space on the second level with the only other room being the office of the warden. Inmates could purchase items from the vending machines stationed in that location. This was considered a privilege because we had access to this area from the time we got up until lights-out at night. Generally, this was not available to prisoners. The exception was during approved visitation time; someone had to be visiting the incarcerated person. Unfortunately, many inmates had no one coming to see them. However, during times when the weekly movie was selected by Danbury, or something like the Grammys or BET award shows were shown, the TV room was filled to capacity. The aroma of fresh-popped popcorn, purchased from the commissary and microwaved by inmates, dominated the air as the women intensely watched their favorite shows.

One thing still baffles me today, however: I could never understand why anyone incarcerated wanted to watch reality shows about others in prison. The mere thought of anyone capitalizing on the misfortunes of prisoners sickened me to my stomach. Nonetheless, the vast majority of inmates loved watching these shows. They would even point out someone on the show who they'd known before coming to prison, or someone whose path they'd crossed in one prison or another. Just as I wouldn't watch such shows during my time in prison, I've continued to refuse to watch them outside of prison walls.

Even though having my liberties taken away was nothing I ever imagined would happen to me, I made the best of the situation. Every day there was something to laugh about. Some of the inmates were hysterically humorous. They would have us laughing to the point of tears. We'd be holding our aching stomachs from laughing so hard. To find gut-busting laughter in prison was a blessing. Couple that with the fact that I had no problems getting along with the population there too. Therefore, things could not have gone better for me, right? Perhaps not!

Ordinarily, I was the well-respected, well-liked mother or senior in the group. No one would dare cross me the wrong way until a disagreement between one of my roommates got out of hand. It escalated to the point where the only thing left to do was go to blows, as they say-fight!

The prison rules forbade us to exchange personal items in the way of giving gifts or loaning anything to each other. Nonetheless, we did anyway since this rule was held in disregard more so than honored by the inmates. So, I had loaned a pair of sneakers to a young roommate until she was able to purchase her own. However, a time came when she was getting transferred to another prison and had packed up to leave. I noticed that she had packed my sneakers in her bag, too. So, I said, "Excuse me, those are my sneakers in your bag, right?"

"You gave those to me," she responded.

"Uh, no. I loaned them to you. Remember? It's okay, just leave them in my locker," I said, wanting to avoid an argument.

Shortly afterward the door flew opened and she threw my

sneakers into the room and yelled, "Keep your fucking sneakers, you old bitch!" and slammed the door and ran.

Like a lioness after prey, I went after the vulgar mouthed youngster. Angered to the point of wanting to kick her ass, I rushed down the stairs after her. Before I could reach her, several inmates intervened and stopped me from going any further. The young woman made no attempts to connect with me as she continued to rapidly walk further away from where I was being held back by other inmates. All I had left was my mouth as I yelled out, "Old bitch I may be but I'm about to kick your young ass! Stop running! Come on back here!" She sped up and ran with the wind, not looking back as I continued to summon her back. "That's okay, you've got to bring your ass back here sometime and I'll be right here!" I assured her.

Still not responding she headed straight to the guard's office and tattled like a child. He expressed shock about my conduct and sent word for me to come to his office. In addition he insisted that I be the bigger person and apologize, which I refused to do. With no viable option but to separate us, he sent the other inmate to another dorm. By the next morning the inmate had apologized and all was forgiven. But that didn't prevent the captain from ordering me to his office as well. Dude was so short, I thought he was sitting but he was actually standing behind a desk. Holding back my laughter, not because he was of dwarf size, but because he looked just like the character from the movie *Leprechaun in the Hood*. He was freckle-faced with orange/reddish hair which matched his red, flustered, angry face. The tiny captain spared no words as he began with, "Ali, there is no point in lying because I know what happened! You're just like all the other lesbians around here. You gave that younger woman shoes, then got mad because she left you for somebody else younger. The two of you had a lover's quarrel and almost got into a fight! Now tell the truth! Isn't that how it happened?"

Pissed off though I was, I still managed to avoid doing or saying anything indicative of how I really felt. I had to bite my tongue in order not to call him a little sawed-off bastard and slap some sense into him. He had a face perfectly ripe for slapping. Women know the kind of man I'm describing: the kind of guy who never quite measured up to other men on an average level socially in high school or college—the kind who basically despised women—an unattractive loser in every way, too frightened to stand up to his male peers so he picked on and berated females. Standing before him and maintaining my model inmate status, aside from my recent outburst, I simply shook my head and said, "That's the craziest thing I've ever heard. I will not permit you to continue to verbally accost me. I'm done responding to you. You can do whatever you want to do, but I'm done."

Looking back, I'm not proud of getting on that level. However, I knew one thing for sure and that was that sometimes it was necessary to make brutal assertions. A person with that young inmate's ghetto mentality would never have responded favorably to courteous language.

For the record, let's be clear, it was never in my nature to be a tough girl, but I was never a punk either. While I sought to be respectful to authority, I wasn't going to accept being disrespected by them.

Rita's Rule # 25

Play the hand you're dealt, and put your words in terms and on a level that the subject of your comment can understand. Sweet words don't reach evil persons, as they take it to be a sign of weakness.

Entering Danbury Federal Prison Camp, I wasn't sure what to expect, so my mind was already set; I wasn't taking any beat-downs. Don't forget, at the first opportunity I had gathered up rocks and put them into a sock that I kept hidden. But later I replaced the rocks with batteries and combination locks that I had purchased from the commissary. For the purpose of a makeshift weapon, I found that these items were better. Never was I a person looking for a fight. I was the person who wanted to avoid them whenever possible. But taking me for the stereotypical fragile, light-skinned girl with long hair was a mistake on the part of anybody assuming I was just a pushover. My loaded sock was my special surprise for anybody who earned a good Rita pummeling. Trust me, getting busted in the head with a sock full of metal objects would soften the toughest tyrant.

12

ANTICIPATION OF RELEASE

Anticipation of being released from prison is a constant thought for anyone in such situations. Halfway house provisions are far more desirable than incarceration and highly sought after by inmates. Right around the time of my sentence, the FBOP had just started to permit inmates to have six-month halfway house stints. Nonetheless, prison administrations were reluctant to give most inmates that amount of halfway house time. Overpopulation resulted in some inmates' bunk beds being stationed in the common areas of dormitories. Even with a constant flow of inmates entering the prison, the administration continued to engage in holding inmates as long as possible. Somehow, I must've slipped through the cracks because I was given six months in a halfway house.

Remaining cautiously optimistic, I always imagined leaving the prison, but a point had come when nothing that the feds would do shocked me. Wondering if I would meet the same fate as other prisoners who looked forward to their release date, I was prepared for anything. Inasmuch as I had been privy to see happy women say their good-byes and head down the hill to be released or go to the halfway house, I never trusted that I'd be released early. I'd also seen those who had completed their time and were scheduled to be released from both institutions only for them to return to the camp minutes later devastated and crying profusely. Their explanation was that the feds were waiting for them to present them with new charges. Worst, now the women would have to fight the new charges from behind prison walls. It's just another example of the low tactics imposed upon helpless individuals by the federal government. It defies reason that the feds could not have brought new charges well in advance of the day an inmate thinks they're being released. But, no, that would be too humane, and that's not within the thinking of some cruel federal agents.

I thought about it with every step I took toward the release station and during the process of completing the paperwork. To be clear, I wasn't fearful. Not in the least. As far as I was concerned, I was prepared for whatever unjust treatment or actions the feds had up their sleeves.

Mixed emotions overwhelmed me as I was showered with hugs and embraced by those I was leaving behind. Certainly, I wanted to get on with my life, but I also felt a sense of sadness for leaving behind so many good women who had been supportive and kind to me. I couldn't help but worry about them and pray that they would also soon return to their loved ones. Our final good-byes were interrupted when the correction officer politely reminded everyone that I had to go because I had to be at the halfway house on time. A sigh of relief came over me as I walked out of the doors of Danbury Federal Prison and entered the car with my son and daughter. Time was certainly of the essence not only because I had to surrender to the halfway house, but I wanted to see my husband before doing so. What happened next was another one of the feds' nasty, immature tactics.

Undoubtedly, it was no coincidence that after losing his appeal to the Third Circuit Court, my husband was ordered to self-surrender on the same day I was released from Danbury. It was another personal vendetta action on the part of the federal government, and their cronies, to frustrate or cause my family as much pain as they were empowered to do. Shamsud-Din was scheduled to turn himself in to the Federal Detention Center at 7th & Arch Streets in Philadelphia at two o'clock in the afternoon. I was released from Danbury that morning around ten o'clock.

Literally, I arrived in front of the gate which leads into Latham Park, where our residence was located, in just enough time to see Shamsud-Din. He was waiting in front of the park with several other carloads of family members and well-wishers to greet me. He got in the car with me and rode to the halfway house, where I surrendered and we said our farewells. The caravan of cars proceeded to follow him to the detention center, where members of the Islamic community and family wept as he entered the compound. Our four-year-old grandson Rafi, named after his deceased uncle Rafi Ali, was devastated. He broke away from his father, Azim, and tried to enter the building with his grandfather. Certainly that was a hurtful moment for Shamsud-Din, who was extremely close to his grandson. Nonetheless, his spirit was not broken, nor could it ever be broken by the injustice he faced because of his devout faith in Allah (SWT).

Routinely, individuals convicted of nonviolent offenses in the federal system serve time in federal camps. Generally, they are designated in nearby facilities in an effort to enable family members easier means of visitation. According to the Federal Bureau of Prisons (FBOP) guidelines, inmates are encouraged to maintain constructive and healthy relationships with family members. This is perceived as a means of correction, rehabilitation, and preparation for inmates to reenter society. However, when they want to stick it to you, they go out of their way to place you as far away from home as possible. Such was the case for my husband, who the feds sent all the way to Fort Worth, Texas.

There was absolutely no justification for sending someone from Pennsylvania to Fort Worth, Texas, when there were so many available institutions much closer. How vividly I recall the day he was sentenced to eighty-seven months in prison. My attorney came to my home after leaving the courtroom and reiterated Shamsud-Din's fate, in that he was given a lot of time and ordered to pay an enormous amount of restitution. As if that was not bad enough, she tearfully said, "Rita, you know, this is a death sentence for a man his age, and the government expects him to die in prison."

Her statement jolted me and I felt a heavy weight fall on me. But it only lasted momentarily as I was hastened to recall the reality of Shamsud-Din's spiritual and physical strengths. At that point, I comforted the attorney. "Don't worry, he won't die in prison. He's strong and in better physical shape than most men half his age." She described violence perpetrated by gangs or individuals in prisons as a major concern for my husband's safety. I was not concerned for my husband's well-being because I knew that wherever he was incarcerated, the inmates would admire him. That is precisely how it was during his prison stay, as confirmed by the inmates, guards, and officers we encountered when visiting him. Of course, though, before I would visit him in prison, I had to complete my own prison sentence.

ENTERING THE HALFWAY HOUSE

Arriving at the halfway house, I encountered brothers as soon as I walked in the door. They greeted me with words like, "We got you, Sister Faridah," referring to me by my Islamic name. Offers of a cell phone, snacks, clothes, toiletries, etc. were at my disposal should I be inclined to accept them. Graciously, I thanked them but had to politely decline their generosity. Primarily, I had to say no because cell phones were prohibited as well as accepting gifts from halfway house residents. Having never been a violator of rules, I had no interest in doing so then, or prior. I had never had a write-up or any disciplinary actions taken against me throughout incarceration, halfway house time or while on supervised release. The incident with the young lady and my shoes was the closest I'd come and that was enough for me.

Time spent in the halfway house was short for me because I had gotten a job offer. Fatimah Abdul Haqq, wife of Luqman Abdul Haqq, aka Kenny Gamble, provided me with an employment opportunity. With my extensive experience in public relations, event planning, and political savvy, I was more than qualified for the position she offered me. Working for Fatimah, in the public arena again, was great because of her far-reaching community outreach programs. In conjunction with her husband, they had successfully refurbished an entire community. The opportunity to work on planning events and engaging with prominent public figures came easily to me; it was a familiar element. Providing low-income housing and developing charter schools thrust Fatimah into a position of prominence and visibility.

Hiring such a high-profile convicted felon was a courageous endeavor on Fatimah's part. Yes, courage is to be emphasized here because she was fully aware that some might react negatively to her offering me a professional position of employment. Since my early twenties I had been self-employed and not having to answer to a superior. Adjusting to being in a subordinate position as opposed to being in the leadership role came easily enough for me. I was determined to do a good job for Fatimah, not only because she was my employer but because I was also grateful for the opportunity.

Of course my task was made easier as a result of the respect, kindness, and consideration awarded to me by a supportive friend. Having a job while in the halfway house is a game changer. There were two opportunities that allowed me to reacquaint myself with some semblance of normality. I was blessed to have friends who were in a position to hire me. Remember, I was in the halfway house twice and both times I had job offers. Another person who provided me such an opportunity was a brother in the Muslim community who was like a son to me.

Proprietor of an electrical and mechanical contracting business, Jamal Johnson offered me employment both times that I was in the halfway house. At some point, while serving time in one of the facilities, I did work for him for a few months. To this day I don't believe Jamal really needed to hire me. Aside from answering the phone and attending to a bit of paperwork, there wasn't much to do. Thus, I suspect that he gave me the job because he wanted to ensure I was okay and in good standing at the halfway house. Established relationships like the ones I had with Fatimah and Jamal were an enormous help to me. Not everyone is fortunate to have support of this kind. For many transitioning from prison to halfway houses, and reentering society, it can be far more difficult. Despite the reasons, whether my help was really needed, or if I was offered a position simply to help me during a time of need, I'll probably never know. The point is, I was fortunate enough to be offered positions that I needed to comply with the halfway house requirements. And, I did just that. In any event, I shall forever appreciate the support I received from two of my cherished friends.

Rita's Rule # 26

Always put forth your best efforts in a position of authority or servitude. It takes a good subordinate to be a good leader and vice versa. Being in the position of a subordinate or leader requires diligence and good listening skills, which are major components of competent leadership.

With a secured job, paying restitution, and no violations, I was looking forward to being released from the halfway house soon. One day, I was awakened from a sound sleep by the annoying clinking of an object hitting against the metal frame of my lower bunk bed, so I turned my body toward the disruption. Rubbing my eyes with both hands in order to focus on the hazy image before me, I still could not make out who or what stood before me. A dim vision of a person began to slowly come into view through a beam of light piercing through a small overhead window directly across the room. Hearing the familiar sound of my case manager's voice enabled me to identify who it was. "Are you okay?" she asked me. I had no idea why she posed the questioned, but I answered, "Yes. Why?" Automatically, my mind pondered if a family member had been injured or abruptly died. Sitting straight up in the bed, I clenched my teeth while pressing my hands over my rapidly beating heart. I anxiously inquired again, "I'm fine. Why do you ask?" However, I was totally unprepared for the response that followed.

Quickly the case manager assured me that there was no problem with any of my loved ones. Then she caringly apprised me that the third circuit had overturned my sentence. She was referring to the first sentence imposed by Judge Fullam. This meant that Kiki and I had to be resentenced because the U.S. attorneys had successfully achieved their goal. With a Republican politically dominated appeals court, they were confident of winning. More than anything the feds wanted more jail time for me. They wanted Kiki to go to prison as well. Again, I found the timing to be a calculated, coordinated effort by the feds to inflict additional anguish upon my family.

Finding ourselves before Judge Fullam again was surreal; it was like déjà vu. Being reassessed by a judge who was favorable to us, in a courtroom full of supporters overflowing into the corridors directly outside the courtroom, reduced the tension somewhat. However, all that quickly diminished after hearing the arguments from prosecutors and our defense attorney, which resulted in Judge Fullam sentencing me to a year and a day of incarceration, and Kiki to six months. Strangely in his concluding remarks the judge reiterated his belief that he still considered us to be good people.

Even more compelling were Judge Fullam's comments about my situation. Looking straight at me he leaned forward and expressed his disdain for how I had been sentenced three times on virtually the same charges. In his opinion this was triple jeopardy and he advised me to appeal the sentence. He also suggested that Kiki appeal her sentence as well. He then provided us with two proficient public defenders to put forth legal arguments for the two of us. Before adjourning the courtroom procedures, Judge Fullam inquired if we needed time to attend to our affairs before surrendering to the FBOP. Against the U.S. attorney's objections, Fullam permitted us thirty days to attend to personal and business concerns.

While still seated at the defense table, Kiki whispered to me that she wanted to go immediately and just get all of this nonsense behind her. Rightfully so, she was annoyed with being mandated to serve the six months. Neither of us understood why, after Judge Fullam expressed belief in our innocence, we were now facing a first incarceration for Kiki and a second one for me. I understood why she wanted to just get it over with, but I talked her into taking thirty days to attend to our affairs. She reluctantly went along with my suggestion as we conveyed our agreement to our defense attorney, who was still in the huddle with us.

Kiki and I met separately with our court-appointed attorneys, however, in comparison of our discussions it was revealed that our meetings rendered the same results. Both attorneys were devoted to work hard in our defense, and to overturn the third circuit's decision against us. Notwithstanding their sincere desire to help us, they were compelled to serve us a brutal dose of reality. Any hopes we had of overturning the appeal, and finally putting an end to the feds' brutalization of our family, were shattered. The probability that our appeal would be rejected at the next level was zero. It became even more evident when the attorneys explained that Judge Fullam was looking out for us. According to both attorneys, six months and/or a year and a day was actually considered a gift in the federal system. In addition, Judge Fullam, at age eighty-two, was fully aware that he might not be on the bench by the time our appeal to the next circuit was rejected. The likelihood that another judge would preside over our case was concerning to Judge Fullam. As the attorneys explained, at that point, we would most likely receive many years of incarceration as the prosecutors were seeking. The consensus was that it was better to just do the time, get it over with, give the feds their pound of flesh, and move on with our lives. From our perspectives rolling the dice on an appeal was not an option. Thus, we left the courtroom with another defeat but maintained our dignity.

A few days later Kiki learned that she was pregnant. Immediately upon hearing that, I recommended that she petition the court to postpone her self-surrender date until after delivering her baby. Inconceivable? Not at all. A common practice in the federal prison system is to permit co-defendants in the same family to serve their sentences consecutively. This is a little tidbit of information I picked up while serving time at Danbury. A rare act of humanity by the federal system that is relative to husbands and wives who are co-defendants.

There was a woman in the dorm next to me who was just about to complete her sentence. She had been convicted of committing a crime with her husband, who she had three children with. As opposed to the two of them serving time concurrently, the judge presiding over their case allowed the husband to stay home and watch the children. Upon her release she would watch the children while her husband served his time. The benefits of this should not be understated because separation of parents from the children has a devastating effect on everyone. Poor kids. They not only suffer the devastation of being separated from their parents, they are often the subject of ridicule and banter from their peers, in addition to judgmental adults.

Aside from the concerns of being pregnant in prison, I was also aware of the inhumane manner in which pregnant prisoners are treated, not by fellow inmates, but by the federal prison system itself. Naturally, I hoped my daughter could avoid the potential experience. Confirmation of her pregnancy was immediately passed on to her public defender, who then petitioned the court. Preferably, the first option was to remand her to six months of house arrest. If not that, then at least allow her to have the baby before going to prison. By that time I would be out of prison and able to care for the baby until its mother would return home. Confronted with U.S. attorneys who basically despised us for being African-Americans of prominent status, the prosecution objected. I always felt that they hated us because they considered us uppity niggers who lived better than most. For that reason they were determined to put us in our place. Irrespective of my belief, I was headed back to prison, and regrettably, so was my daughter. For what it was worth, Kiki and I were mandated to serve our time together at Alderson Federal Prison Camp in West Virginia.

PREPARING TO SERVE TIME

In preparation for self-surrender, I conducted an estate sale. Void of enthusiasm, perhaps even bewildered, I watched as our family possessions were sold at a mere fraction of the original cost. Our home was full of deal seekers bidding for furniture, a concert grand piano, works of art, clothing, china, jewelry, fur coats, designer bags, and so on. Among the purchasers were strangers as well as people we knew.

I recall a Muslim sister tearfully saying to me, as she held one of my Chanel designer bags in her hand before bidding on it, "Sister Faridah, are you sure you want to part with this bag and so many of your personal items? You act like you're never coming back."

"Oh, I will come back, but my life will never be the same," I told her. And my words to her were not born out of self-pity. It was far from that. The fact is, I was never attached to material things or wealth. My status as an outstanding, law-abiding citizen was most important to me, so the possibility of being forever tainted in the eyes of some, was a tremendous concern for me. Regaining my positive public image of integrity would be next to impossible. So, it was comforting to think that those who knew me well would never view me in that negative light. Self confidence in my good character was a source of strength.

ALDERSON FEDERAL PRISON

Just about everything that needed to be attended to had been done before Kiki and I were to surrender to Alderson Federal Prison. Mariah Carey's music on the soundtrack "Touch My Body" was my favorite, so I played it repeatedly during the days leading up to our surrender. Now, before anyone gets fixated on thinking that it was because I wanted someone to touch my body, just stop with the dirty thoughts. It had nothing to do with that. I just like the beat!

On the morning of our journey to West Virginia, we continued playing Mariah Carey songs. It was a way of keeping Kiki and me focused on a few more hours of having a free life. Azim and his wife, Jahaira, were obviously disturbed at the reality of their mother and sister being subjected to prison life—again. Azim and Jahaira gave Kiki and me the tightest embrace as we stood in front of the entrance to the prison. I knew Azim's heart was breaking and I could barely look at Jahaira as her eyes filled with tears that she did her best to hold back. Neither Kiki nor I looked back at the car as they pulled away. Though we didn't express it, I believe she felt as I did. It was better to focus on what was in front of us as opposed to what we were leaving behind.

Except for being incarcerated with my daughter, nothing about the intake process, dorm placement, or imprisonment at Alderson differed from Danbury. News of our designated arrival had already reached the inmate population. We were high-profile individuals, which naturally generated substantial interest, particularly as it related to Kiki since she was carrying Mike Tyson's baby. I had schooled her on how attentive, protective, and caring the inmates were at Danbury. If these ladies that we were about to encounter were anything like them, she would be okay throughout her pregnancy. Well, the reaction to her being pregnant while incarcerated was just as I had told her it would be. True to form, the women at Alderson did the same thing for Kiki. Consistently they showered her with various fruits, snacks, beverages, and cooked foods that were snuck out of the cafeteria by the inmates working there. They also made crocheted and knitted items for her unborn child. Kiki appreciated their efforts but declined their offers. She preferred they distribute the items among inmates who were in need of them.

Generally speaking, there was very little conflict between the women imprisoned at Alderson. However, there were two incidents that I vividly recall. First, an inmate was struck in the head with a large rock by another inmate. I can still hear the piercing scream of the injured victim and visualize her being carried from the recreation area by a group of inmates. The altercation ensued as a result of a lover's quarrel. The assaulter caught the victim cheating with another female inmate. Incidentally, the injured woman spent a few days in the hospital, and the perpetrator was removed from the camp. The second encounter took place in the dorm occupied by my daughter, me, and four other women. A verbal confrontation between two inmates resulted in everyone in the room getting involved. One of the women was about five-foot-eleven, and the other one was petite and pregnant. Out of common decency and fairness we had to intervene. After a bit of shoving, predominantly directed toward the bigger, more aggressive inmate, we separated them. Once everything seemed to calm down, we all prepared for bed directly after the ten o'clock count. As I sat on my bunk, it felt a tad bit moist, which was concerning because I knew I hadn't spilled anything on it. Then I noticed something dripping from above me; it was coming from the bottom of the upper bunk. *What in the heck is causing this?* I thought.

As I pondered what was going on, my bunky — the larger aggressive woman from the prior described conflict — leaped onto her bunk and in a flash, jumped back off. Her bare feet hit the floor with a resounding slap, obviously due to the force of her oversized body. "What the fuck!" she yelled out. "My entire bed is saturated with something!" Apparently, someone had poured buckets of water over her entire mattress after the tussle. After it was over, we'd all left the room for a while. Some of us had gone outside to take in the warm late summer air. Others adjourned to the common area television room. Apparently, the culprit did the damage then and she was never found out. The bunky suspected everyone, though. Even worse, the bunky was relocated to another less favorable dorm, for which she was highly pissed off. Realistically, the culprit could have been any number of inmates, especially since she was disliked by most of the Alderson prison population.

Rita's Rule 26

Treat people with respect and avoid conduct that is of an intimidating nature. It is better to be liked and admired as opposed to being feared. When forced to coexist among strangers, sharing the same living quarters, it's imperative to develop friendships. That way you'll have allies in a time of need.

In the case of the wet bed — had the disliked inmate had allies, that probably would not have happened to her. The dorm we occupied was called the fish bowl because the outer wall and door leading into the main area of the dorm was constructed of see-through glass. In light of all the constant activity, there's no way that someone didn't see a person or persons, carrying a large container full of water, who obviously climbed up the bunk and poured the water all over the bed. This sort of thing just doesn't happen without collaboration, and it certainly doesn't go unnoticed.

Rita's Rule # 27

Bullies may be able to bully some of the people some of the time, but there's no bully that ever gets away with bullying all of the people all the time.

I don't want to leave the impression that prison life was torturous for either my daughter or me. As far as incarceration goes, federal prison camps are the lesser of the evils when losing one's liberties. Depending on the mentality of the correction officer, the treatment varies; some are caring, others are indifferent, but too many of them are outright cruel. There are mean-spirited guards in the system who go out of their way to make life miserable and are despised by inmates, while humane guards are revered.

For example, there was a female guard who the inmates had a great deal of regard for. She used to announce when she was leaving the dorm to go take a smoke. Several inmates would follow her outside. The correction officer would light up one cigarette after the next, take a puff or two, and then toss them to the ground. Once she turned her back, the inmates would pick up the lit discarded cigarettes, stand close to an exterior wall, and smoke them. You can bet these inmates had this particular CO's back; had there been a violent breakout of any kind, they would have protected that guard. This is an important concept to mention since there are no officers with guns in the federal prison camps. They don't even carry nightsticks.

The next example involves an inmate in our dorm who was a very attractive young Caucasian woman. She had devised a plan to get transferred to a camp closer to her home. Boastfully, she went on about how a particular male guard was attracted to her. Her plot was to get him into a compromising situation wherein she could formally complain that he made sexual advances toward her. Surely, she believed this would force the administration to accommodate her transfer request. Since the male guard in question was one assigned to our dormitory, we all knew him to be a gentleman and no one took the inmate's threat seriously. In fact, we thought it was hilarious; she had to be joking. It wasn't until she was transferred that some of the inmates were interviewed by members of the prison staff. That's when we learned that the inmate had actually carried out her evil plot.

Personally, I felt offended that she had the tenacity to tell us about her plan, as it made us accessories to the fact. Call it what you will—snitch, informant, or whatever—I feel the inmates did the right thing by telling the truth when interviewed. The male officer had always treated everyone respectfully and exhibited a kind demeanor toward the women. In other words, he treated us like he would want his wife, daughter, mother, or sister treated if they were incarcerated; it mattered not that he was employed by the Federal Bureau of Prisons. He was a decent man and did not deserve to be lied on or set up. He was facing the possibility of a reprimand, termination, or worse, being charged with a criminal offense. However, due to the inmates' honesty he was spared the hardship of any of the above options and was still in the same position at Alderson when I left. Possibly, this is among the most important stories I've shared in *Triple Jeopardy* because it indicates what I know to be a fact about incarcerated women. The fact is that the majority of the women are good people who try to do the right thing regardless if they indulged in a life of crime prior to going to prison or were one of the rare ones, like myself, who were unjustly incarcerated.

Without a doubt the happiest day for me while serving prison time was the day that my daughter completed her six-month sentence and left Alderson. We all rejoiced for Kiki. For her, returning to a life of freedom was bittersweet because she was leaving me, her mom, behind. The night before her departure the entire dorm participated in a celebratory going-away feast. Everyone was happy for her and prayed for a healthy baby. Kiki left on Halloween 2008 and delivered a healthy baby girl on Christmas Day 2008. Ironically, the baby girl who was named Milan, after the city in Italy, was born on her father's deceased mother's birthday.

Since Kiki's pregnancy went several days beyond her due date, obviously Milan was meant to be a gift to her father. Incidentally, Milan greatly resembles Mike, as noted by one of his friends who refers to her as a pretty Mike Tyson. Not long after Milan's birth, I was released from Alderson. On that freezing day, January 6th, 2009, I headed to a halfway house in Philadelphia for the second time. Kiki brought Milan to visit me at the halfway house before returning to Las Vegas to resume her life with Mike. A plan was in place for me to join her upon my release, which was scheduled for early April of 2009. Under the circumstances, things were going well. I just wanted April to get here already.

THE UNEXPECTED

Approximately three weeks before I would have completed my time at the halfway house, out of nowhere I woke up one morning in excruciating pain. It was a sharp, moving pain that felt like my internal organs were being pricked with a hot, piercing object. Relegated to a fetal position, my breathing was labored and I could not move without increasing the pain. Attempting to wait it out, in hopes that the condition would subside, was to no avail. Hearing my moaning alerted two of my roommates, who informed the officials that something was wrong with me. An ambulance was summoned immediately. Still immobile when the ambulance attendants arrived, I welcomed the medical attention. Finally, I thought I would be taken care of, but such was not the case. The two attendants seem to scorn me instead. They treated me with utter odium and insisted that I get up and walk to the ambulance. I pleaded with them to put me on a stretcher. When they refused to, I asked if they had a wheelchair, which they also denied me the use of.

My only alternative was to lie there and possibly die, which I felt would happen if I did not get to the hospital, or struggle my way to the ambulance. No exaggeration, I literally rolled over the bed while holding onto the frame until my knees reached the floor. In the midst of trying to crawl, I couldn't go any further. Seeing my struggle the workers in the halfway house and residents lifted me off the floor and placed me in an office chair with wheels. Not even the worker's angry comments to the ambulance attendants softened their disposition toward me. Once I was placed in the ambulance, they still denied me the stretcher. Instead I had to sit on a side bench where I felt every bump in the road as we traveled to the hospital. One of the attendants sat directly across from me sneering at me instead of attending to me or offering an ounce of compassion. Far too weak to offer any verbal defense on my own behalf, I prayed to get to the hospital in time.

Arriving at Temple University Hospital changed everything. The emergency room doctors admitted me immediately after an expeditious examination. They sedated me prior to conducting any further tests because I was in too much pain. Clinical testing revealed an internal bleeding which resulted in me having to undergo emergency surgery. Several days would pass before I was coherent enough to comprehend what had happened since I was under heavy sedation.

During my stay at Temple University Hospital, I was properly and humanely treated. There was no guard at my door, nor was I handcuffed to the bed in my private room. I'd been put on a ward with regular patients, too. This semblance of normality was refreshing to me, as it rekindled my faith in society, and wherein I'd believed that people were predominantly kind. Surely, if left solely to the two Caucasian male ambulance attendants, I would not be alive. I had never been treated so inhumanely in my life. My treatment was truly subhuman. I questioned if animals were treated worse.

I'm convinced that their ill will toward me was not only racial; I felt their warped perception of me being a corrupt person would not allow them to treat me any better. Had it not been for my condition preventing me from getting their names, I would have reported them. The doctors explained that I'd gotten to the hospital in the nick of time. The ambulance attendants' hesitance could have caused my death. Any longer and the infection would have spread to my heart and killed me. Of course that didn't matter to them. Their blatant attitudes confirmed that I was just another worthless nigger who committed a crime and deserved to suffer and die.

*   *   *

In preparation for my release date, the hospital communicated with the halfway house, and relayed the attending physician's recommendation, that I be sent home. The halfway house administration agreed that my recuperation should take place at my sister Zaynah's home, where she could take care of me. Not only did they not want to take the responsibility of caring for someone in my condition, but they were also concerned with liability. Passing on their concerns to the FBOP, the halfway house officials concurred with the doctor's recommendation and sought permission to release me to home confinement. A request of this sort is not unusual; the FBOP can grant such requests at their discretion.

Consistent with their never-give-the-Ali-family-any-breaks policy, the FBOP ruled against the halfway house and the doctor's advice and ordered me to return to the facility. Yes, you read that right. Even though I only had scarcely three more weeks before my release date, they still denied any humane accommodations for me to recover in.

After leaving the halfway house I stayed with my sister Zaynah for three weeks. She waited on me hand and foot as I was still bedridden. Finally, I was released from home confinement and placed on supervised release, which would take place in Las Vegas. Here's when I had my conflicting emotions. It was hard leaving my sister, who I loved dearly and had spent nearly every day of my life with. I was also leaving my son, his wife, and their two sons Antonio and Rafi. On the other hand, I was going to spend time with my daughter, who I also loved dearly. The bright side was that being in Las Vegas would afford me the opportunity to help care for my newborn granddaughter.

13

LIFE IN LAS VEGAS

Mike and Kiki met me at the airport with Milan. I sat in the back of the SUV with my infant granddaughter who, of course, was strapped in her infant seat across from me. She was so beautiful with her little round, plump body and silky, straight black hair. I could barely keep my eyes off her. Indeed, I loved being able to be there for my daughter, granddaughter, and Mike. I also loved traveling throughout the world with them, staying in five-star hotels, and dining in the best restaurants. But I often laughed about living in their home because it reminded me of being back home in my parents' house. Life was easy but definitely different with Mike, Kiki, and Milan. Sometimes I chuckled because Kiki reminded me so much of my mother and Mike reminded me so much of my father! Family has always been a priority for me. That remains so still today.

THE JOYS OF FAMILY

My deeply imbedded love for family is unwavering, but so is my love for Philadelphia, the city of my birth, and the East Coast in general. Relocating to Las Vegas was not even a thought until Milan came along. Even though I'd been released, I remained under federal supervision and needed permission to transfer my residency. The original plan was for me to have an extended visit to see my latest grandchild and to help my daughter now that she'd been initiated into motherhood. Well, I ended up living with Kiki, Mike, and Milan for two years. During that time their baby boy, Morocco, was born. World travel with the Tysons was frequent and somewhat challenging with Milan barely a toddler and Morocco still an infant. Mike's world-class celebrity status was a blessing. It made the process of getting through customs and security and maneuvering through various countries much easier.

We were treated like royalty just for being associated with Mike. Choosing a specific incident would not adequately convey the extent of amenities bestowed upon us, which was befitting for dignitaries and elected officials. The security that surrounded us, the fans and friends around the globe thronged us throughout our travels. Since there are far too many events to cite in the confines of this book, I'll simply mention a few examples.

ADVANTAGES OF BEING ASSOCIATED WITH A CELEBRITY

Visiting Poland is something I will never forget. We were supposed to stay at an undisclosed location in the center of town. Somehow, the word got out about where Mike Tyson would be lodging and in no time there was a sea of people surrounding the premise of the hotel. Security drove us around in circles for more than an hour before coming to the realization that the crowd was not going to disperse. They were eager to see Mike Tyson regardless of how long the wait. Concerns of an enthusiastic crowd unintentionally injuring one of us, particularly the babies, caused the security to relocate us to another undisclosed property. Just so that you get the concept of what I mean by security... envision a slew of men in dark wear. Imagine a motorcade. There were cars with security in the front and back of our vehicle, along with men on motorcycles riding along both sides of our vehicle, and men running alongside the slowly moving convoy of vehicles.

Similarly, we received intensified security in other countries as well. Italy was no exception. Protecting Mike Tyson was an extremely serious matter. I was already in one of the vehicles when I needed to relieve myself after having drank nearly a quart of water shortly before the plane landed. Generally, I'm not a huge water drinker, but flying for many hours tends to dehydrate me, so I tried to make sure I took in plenty of water. Initially, my thought was to just wait until we got to our hotel. To be on the safe side I asked the driver how long the ride was to our lodging destination. Apparently he didn't understand me because he didn't speak English, at least not well enough to respond to my question. Fortunately, Kiki spoke some Italian, which she learned while living in Florence, Italy, during her junior year of college. Simultaneously, after she conveyed my concern to the driver, he summoned one of the security who was running alongside of the slow-moving motorcade. Suddenly and abruptly the security brought the whole company of cars to a halt. He opened the door, extended his hand into the backseat of the limousine, and helped me out of the car. "Come, Ma," was about the only thing I understood him say except for "Mike Tyson's mama," which he said to the other security men. The rest he conveyed in Italian as the men accompanied me to the ladies' room. The only other thing I understood was when the same security person said, "Wait." So I did. Then two of the security men cleared the entire ladies' room so I could use it alone. When I realized what was occurring I attempted to tell the gentleman, "No, no. Don't make anyone leave. I'm fine. I can go in there with everyone." My words held no merit as they hustled several women out of the ladies' room, some of who shot me some perplexed looks. I can't be sure what they were thinking, but I assume they were wondering, who the hell is this woman that we have to be ushered out of the ladies' room for? It was certainly not my intention for that to happen and I can understand the women might have resented it. Moreover, I am under no illusion that the treatment I received had anything to do with my importance. I knew full well it had everything to do with me being the mother-in-law of a famous icon.

Traveling at that level definitely has its perks. Staying in the best hotels, and even castles throughout Europe, would be a dream come true for many. I'm more of a hotel kind of girl and preferably a bright one. The first trip abroad with Mike, Kiki, and Milan, who was less than a year old at the time, was an experience that cannot be overstated. We were in a large arena filled to capacity with impassioned British Mike Tyson fans chanting, "Mike! Mike! Mike!" The roar of British accents chanting his name reverberated in our heads as it rang in our ears. It was truly unbelievable. Entering the venue required maneuvering us through a secured entrance, of course. Once we were in, the crowd shouted non-stop, prompting Mike to appear on stage. Once he appeared, the crowd exploded in cheers and applause. I was used to people expressing praise for Mike, but the magnitude of this overzealous crowd was intense. He addressed the audience very candidly about his life in general. He recognized Kiki and then shocked me by introducing me to the audience, too. He said, "Oh, and my mother-in-law's here, too. After just getting out of prison, she's traveling with us." Possibly, he meant to say more but didn't get a chance because of the loud outbursts from the audience. I had never been ashamed of having been in prison, particularly since I was unjustly incarcerated. However, I didn't perceive it as a badge of honor. Consequently, void of the crowd's awareness of what can only be described as a federal persecution, I was prepared for boos from the audience. However, in that very instant, I received a warm reception generally associated with how rock stars are greeted. Of course it was only in the moment. But, to my utter surprise they erupted into cheers and clapping as they yelled out, "Yay, Mike's mom! Yay, Mike's mom!"

Nonetheless, the affirmation from hundreds of adoring strangers demonstrating genuine regard for one who's labeled a convicted felon, was a phenomenal experience. While I can't state with certainty the reason for the applause, it was a comforting acknowledgment. From my point of view, I believe it confirms that societal perceptions have changed about the injustice of so-called justice systems, globally.

Friends and acquaintances often ask me what it was like living with Mike and Kiki and traveling the globe with them. For the most part I assume it was pretty much like any other mother/mother-in-law living with their married offspring and their spouse. Traveling with them or even attending events locally, is phenomenally different. The fascination of seeing people from all walks of life admiring Mike and going crazy at the sight of him is extraordinary. At the same time it's humbling to witness the genuine love that is shown to him despite the challenges and obstacles he conquered, which many others didn't survive. Similar to Muhammad Ali, Mike Tyson is revered globally by many, including other celebrities.

People often inquire what my life is like post-prison. They ask how my reentrance was into society after being labeled a convicted felon. Fortunately, I live a quality life as a result of loved ones and supporters. For me, my prayers have always been for my children to be God fearing, to have regard for humanity, to be productive and successful. Observing the development of these traits in Azim and Kiki was assuring to me that they would continue to achieve great heights, be good parents and spouses. This is my greatest joy. Who could ask for a better post-prison life? I may be ill-labeled but seeing my family flourish and receiving love and acceptance from them, my husband, and my dear friends is more than I can ask or wish for. In many respects, my life is not so different than before. Meeting and/or working with celebrities is different now because most of my contacts with them come by way of my children now. Whereas, when they were growing up, they met powerful, influential icons through my husband and me. In that way our roles have changed.

As I conclude this portion of the book, perhaps it's a wild guess, but I'm just assuming by now some of you are anticipating much more elaboration about Mike Tyson. After all, he is my son-in-law and I have had the privilege of having a close relationship with him. Knowing and loving him as a son, husband to my daughter, and father of my grandchildren is a cherished experience. Technically, he is my son-in-law but my heart makes no distinction. I love him as much as I love my biological son, for the heart knows no difference.

At this point, I'm sure you're eager to hear more fascinating stories and episodes that I've shared or witnessed during the many years I've been around Mike. Well, hopefully you won't be too disappointed because this is just about the most I'm going to convey about the Tysons. It's definitely not because I'm void of countless episodes that I could add, but respectfully no one can tell Mike's stories as well as he can. His books and sold-out one-man shows are evident of that. Mike and his wife have their own stories to tell and they do it best. I have my story to share and that's what this book is intended to convey.

*   *   *

Even with all the joy I had from being with Mike, Kiki, Milan, and Morocco, I still missed my son Azim, his wife Jahaira, and their sons, Antonio, and Rafi. They were still living in the suburbs of Philadelphia when I first came to Vegas. I only got to visit them once or twice during those years, and it was really hard on me. Never was I more grateful than the day that they finally moved to Las Vegas. My emotional cup of family attachment was filling more with each relative who moved to Vegas. And the blessings keep coming. It's even better since my granddaughter Mikey also moved to Las Vegas. It's great for me because I get to spend a lot more time with her. I can always count on her to hang out with her old grand mom, whether it's going to a show together or taking in a movie. My grandson, Miguel, also resides with Mike and Kiki now. So I see him a lot and that's wonderful. As much as I would love having all my grandkids, great-granddaughter, and family in the same city, it's not possible. They're spread all over the country. I am so proud of each of them and humbled by their love and affection for me.

Even though I raised Azim and Kiki and played an intricate role in raising my nieces, Asia, and Sakina, I didn't have to travel long distances with them. Besides, for the most part, whatever vacations or fun activities I did with the kids, my sister Zaynah was always with us. That made it so much easier for both of us because it was two adults with four youngsters. Traveling with Milan and Morocco out of the country, along with their parents, was a bit more challenging, but quite adventurous. As a matter of fact keeping up with day-to-day tasks pertaining to their schedules was more challenging than I perceived it would be.

Early on when Milan was a mere toddler and Morocco was still an infant, trips abroad required both of them being pushed in strollers. Milan and Morocco started flying at the age of about one-month-old. Milan's adjustment was a bit easier, but Morocco had a more difficult time because he had suffered from severe colic. I was so grateful to have Farid Barnes and Darrell Francis around to pitch in. Both of them had been longtime friends and employees of Mike. They were both good with the children and regarded as part of the family. Regardless of Milan's mood, whenever Darrell would say, "Hey, Milani Poo," she would immediately smile and raise her arms up for him to pick her up. Poor Farid had it rough with Morocco, who was very attached to him. On those long trips, when Morocco would cry, Farid would pick him up and walk back and forth from first class, where we were seated, to the end of coach repeatedly until Morocco would fall asleep. Kiki had to appreciate that as much as the rest of us because it allowed us to get some rest in the comfort of seats that transformed to beds on international flights. Today Milan is ten, Morocco is eight, and they are world travelers. Long gone are the challenges described above, but our family ties and friendships remain in full force.

Darrell and Farid's presence made daily life less stressful; they ran errands and screened phone calls and guests seeking to enter the gated community where we resided. When traveling, they would communicate to the security teams locally, as well as abroad, prior to and during our trips. They made sure that transitioning the entire Tyson family went smoothly and safely. It was a major convenience to just get in the car upon our arrival in a different country and head to the hotel while Darrell and Farid made sure all of our luggage was secured and brought to the various hotels.

On a more personal note, I enjoyed them so much because we got each other's sense of humor. So in those quiet moments when we weren't hustling and bustling, we could always count on each for a good laugh.

LOVE AND ADMIRATION

There is no way that the benefits of my life's journey would be complete without the love and support of family. I have been truly blessed with a wonderful devoted husband, caring children and a loving family. Recently, I was reminded of what an extraordinary family I have. On May 10, 2019, I attended the graduation of my granddaughter Saeedah Ali, where she received her doctorate degree in dentistry from Howard University. Since we are both Dr. Ali's we joked about taking a photo together showing a commemorative momentum that Howard University had provided her. It was a wooden hanger with a wire bottom that had been configured into the script: *Dr. Ali.*

On Saturday, May 11, 2019, I attended my grandson Amir Tyson's graduation at American University, where he received his bachelor's in communications. The highlight of the evening manifested when I sat at the table and noticed the placement cards with Mom on one and Pop on the other. Holding back tears of elation, I gently wiped away a few drops that had managed to escape my eyes. I was overwhelmed with a sense of joy and belonging at the realization of Dr. Monica Turner (Mike Tyson's former wife and mother of his children, Gina, Rana, and Amir) acknowledging me and my husband as Mom & Pop.

From the very moment I met Monica approximately eleven years ago, I loved her as a daughter. "An exceptional woman" doesn't begin to describe how warm, kind, and caring she is. I had barely been out of the halfway house and made the transition to Las Vegas when I first met Monica. Aside from the fact that she was Mike's ex-wife, I was meeting her for the first time as the mother-in-law of her ex-husband. I wasn't sure how the situation would go. Much to my delight things could not have gone any better. In addition to Monica and Kiki regarding each other as sisters, Monica has been such an inspiration to me. She was among the first persons to encourage me to write this book.

Knowing that Monica is a pediatrician, I naturally assumed that she was a caring person. However, her sensitivity toward me was beyond that of mere niceties. It was as if Monica had a built-in emotional detector and realized that even though I appeared to be adjusting to my new life, it was nonetheless challenging. She was correct. I was grappling with the idea of forever being stigmatized as a convicted felon, and the impact of that on my family, even though I did not discuss it with most people. However, Monica was so engaging that I felt an immediate connection to her and was able to freely express my anxieties. She was extremely concerned for my well-being and took the time to not only listen, but to encourage and reassure me that I was still a person of great value. Over the years, we have become closer with every family vacation or gathering that we were both a part of. Seeing her, Mike, and Kiki work as a team of constructive support and influence on their children is one of the great pleasures of my life. It's the reality that love of God, family, and humanity supersedes all adversities and is a prescription for a successful and happy life.

SO, RITA, WHAT ABOUT THOSE CELEBRITIES?

Quite often I was asked about the celebrities I'd known through the years. People would be so curious as to ask for details about specific celebrities. "So, Rita, tell me, what was so-and-so like when you met him or her?" they'd ask. These inquiring minds wanted to know if celebrities were as they appeared to be from a distance or were they sporting fake public personas.

By no means do I want to give the impression that I am the know-all and be-all for the celebrity population. I'm no authority on them, but I am a proficient judge of their character based on what I have observed from decades of working with various entertainers, famous individuals, and high-profile people. Therefore, I feel safe declaring to you that first impressions go a long way.

I've met some stars who were standoffish or downright nasty, so much so that they are not worth mentioning. However, the vast majority were not in that nasty category at all. Instead, they were quite charismatic and too many to mention. I will tell you, though, that some of them captured my heart immediately.

Snoop Dog was one of them. This man illuminates a room upon entering it. He is so much more than talent; his aura is extremely positive, warm, and engaging. Snoop has that special light that only comes from a higher power. Mike and Snoop already knew each other and were friends. I recall meeting him in Los Angeles during a promotion of one of Mike's video games. We were all in a VIP-holding- room when Snoop arrived. He didn't just walk into the room. No, not Snoop. He glided into our presence and brought with him considerable warm feelings that made us all feel that he valued us. I was holding Milan, who was about six months old at the time. She wasn't very happy this day as she fussed and whined a bit. The place was noisy, crowded, and dimly lit. Making matters worse, Milan was a breast-fed baby who wouldn't take a bottle. Rocking her was fruitless but it was all I could do until Kiki returned to the area. When Snoop came over to Milan, he placed her little hands in his, looked her straight in the eyes, and said, "Mike, is this your baby? That's a pretty baby," Snoop repeated several times. Instantly, Milan stopped crying and began to smile. Then she had the nerve to laugh and coo for Snoop as if she'd known him forever!

Another celebrity of interest was Flavor Flav, who was a bundle of optimistic energy. Shamsud-Din and I were blown away by his enthusiasm to meet us. Azim brought Flav by our home one day while they were on their way to an engagement. While I had always liked Flav from afar, I now had a chance to understand why he was revered by so many. He is an extraordinary kind and caring person who truly loves humanity. Now, I actually have to credit Azim, who most call Osh, with meeting the fabulous Flavor Flav. Flav is the only one I know who calls Azim the great and powerful

Oz. An impromptu visit by Azim and Fav surprised my husband and me. Fav was so excited to meet us. That's how humble he is; he treated us like we were the stars and he the fan. I knew he was a gifted artist, but I learned how extremely well versed he is on current affairs. When and wherever I see him, he rushes to embrace me and say, "Mom, are you all right."

Being the mother of Mike, Azim and Kiki causes my socially adopted family to continually increase. Many of Mike and Kiki's friends referred to me as Mom. A few of my favorites include Bobby Brown and his wife Alisha, even though I only see them occasionally when we're in Los Angeles. They are always gracious. Nothing about them is pretentious. What you see is truly what you get. In fact, there's a humorous encounter relative to Morocco and Bobby worth sharing.

Over time Milan and Morocco grew to know and love Bobby and Alisha as their uncle and aunt. After years of already knowing Bobby, Morocco became familiar with his talent as an extraordinary entertainer from watching *The New Addition Story* on TV. Morocco loved it and mimicked Bobby's dance moves and sang "Mr. Telephone Man" for months. This was major for Morocco because he's not easily impressed. One day the children received an invitation to attend Bobby's son Cassius's birthday party. The timing was opportune since we all just happened to be at our California residence, where Milan and Morocco received intense tennis training during the week. As a result we were close enough to get Morocco and Milan to the party with ease. Their grandfather, who they affectionately call PopPop, drove the kids to the gala.

When they arrived at the venue, they were greeted by Bobby himself, standing out front. When everyone exited the vehicle, Pop Pop approached Bobby with a smile. "Mr. Bobby Brown, meet Mr. Morocco Tyson," which drew laughter from both men. Of course Bobby knew exactly who the kids were. However, Morocco didn't seem quite as engaged as one would have thought he should be since he had been around Bobby several times. Seemingly, Morocco would have been a little more enthused seeing Bobby up close and personal after watching the biopic. "Morocco, aren't you happy to see Uncle Bobby?" Pop Pop asked him.

"Yes," Morocco whispered to Pop Pop, "but where is the *real* Bobby Brown?"

It was quite apparent that Morocco was expecting to see the actor, Woody McClain, who portrayed Bobby in *The New Edition Story*. The two men quickly went into a thorough explanation about real life versus portrayals and that Uncle Bobby was indeed the real Bobby Brown. Only then did Morocco finally recognize and truly understand Bobby's star status.

Remarkably, the innocence of the children and their genuine affection for their loved ones has nothing to do with celebrity.

By the way, I'm still waiting for the chance to taste some of Bobby's fried fish, which I hear is delicious. He was well informed about my love for fried fish and promised to fix some for me when I visited his home. Unfortunately, I have yet to make it there. So, Bobby if you're reading this, you need to know for certain that I'm coming for that fish!

* * *

Al Be Sure is another one of my adopted sons. Fortunately, I see him more frequently since he, too, lives in Vegas. I always tease him about being my go-to celebrity when I have guests come in to town. But on the other hand, many of my friends expect to see Mike Tyson, which isn't usually possible. For several reasons I don't press Mike about meeting my friends because I don't want to impose on him. He's always busy with travel, and while he would be kind enough to accommodate my request, I never want to take advantage of my relationship with him.

Even as it relates to taking people to Al's house, I wouldn't take advantage of him either — no way. Al stays busy, too, as his career is still in full swing; he performs before large audiences regularly and hosts a radio show. Regardless of his hectic schedule, Al checks on my husband and me regularly and has even invited us over pretty often. In fact, my husband and I had been on one of these invited visits to see Al during a time when we were entertaining out-of-town guests. We'd visited Al on numerous occasions, just to spend time together, or when he was hosting a few guests in his home. We were visiting one night when a group of Al's close friends assembled at his home to watch *Star*, the TV series featuring Quincy, Al's son.

On both occasions Al insisted that we bring our guests with us. It meant a lot to Brother Faruq, who I mentioned earlier on as being the director of operations for the Philadelphia Masjid and SCMS. He and his wife, Aalliyah, who's often described as a mini-me, were visiting my husband and me. That's because she is an all-in, supportive wife, devoted to helping others, a hard worker and go-getter like me. Shamsud-Din and I wanted to do something special with them because they'd always been helpful and faithful friends to us. We took them to see my favorite show on the strip, *Hits Ville*. It's a fabulous rendition of the Motown hits and a must-see performance.

To further address the question of my celebrity affiliations, I've met a host of young celebrities during my travels with Mike and Kiki. And, happily, I've also met some icons from my era. The introduction that brought me the most excitement was to the great Dionne Warwick. I found her to be as smooth off stage as she was on stage. My first encounter with Dionne was like being with a home girl I'd known forever. And by no means am I talking about some ghetto kind of chick. Her demeanor never allowed for that; she was class personified. I'd already known her son Damon for several years, before he brought her by the house to see Mike, who they both had been close to for many years.

Damon is an accomplished person in his own right and beyond that he's also what I call a closet comedian. Dionne was performing in Las Vegas and I wanted very much to see her show. I would have gladly paid any price for the tickets. However, Damon wouldn't hear of it and insisted on providing me with complimentary VIP credentials and seating; my seat was only four rows back from the stage. I was enthralled as Dionne sang like the super star that she is. I knew every lyric and wanted to belt out every word right along with her, but I suppressed my urge. I didn't want to detract from hearing her phenomenal delivery of the songs. She put on a spectacular performance, captivating fans with every note she sang, throughout the entire concert.

*　*　*

Like Damon, I have another *son* who I call my baby boy. We call him Frenchy. I met him while traveling through Europe on one of Mike's tours. Unbeknownst to me, he was a mega entertainment promoter, but upon meeting him I thought him to be a nice person who happened to be competent in his dealings. Oh, but it was more than that; the rest of the family also later met him along the way and fell in love with him. At that time Milan was the cutest chubby baby ever, at less than two years old and barely walking.

Frenchy had the entire wing of the hotel, where we stayed, blocked off with two security guards at the entryway. Since no one could get in or out without being noticed by the guards, it was a perfect and safe walkway for Milan to roam freely from room to room. "I go Frenchy room," Milan would say as she wobbled along. She repeated this back-and-forth throughout the day. She'd arrive at the foot of Frenchy's bed and try to climb up. With some help from Frenchy, she'd finally make it onto his bed where he also had his computer on and in use. Regardless of how busy he was, he would always take time with Milan.

Frenchy has done more than well for himself. His business is thriving and he has properties in Dubai and France, yet he endures hotel stays throughout his travels — that is except for when he is in Vegas, where he has his own room in my home because I insist on having my baby boy home with me when he's in Vegas.

Being associated with Frenchy has afforded me to see a parade of Who's Who on a continuum. As he spent time in my home I became increasingly aware of his promotional expertise. He'd meet many celebs right there in my home, since it was his temporary office while in town, which made it also his meeting place with many of them. He promotes venues with many of the biggest entertainment icons in the world. I was blown away when he got me VIP seating to Diana Ross's concert in Vegas. However, Mike being in attendance was also a factor. Performers and promoters consider Mike's presence at their venues the ultimate honor. His presence was duly noted when Diana Ross spotted him and Milan at her show. There were other celebrities at the show but Diana only mentioned Mike. Surely, she meant no disrespect to the other notables; apparently Mike overshadowed them a bit.

After the show we were just about to pull out of the parking lot when Frenchy received a call informing us that Diana wanted Mike to come backstage. Mike was really trying to get out of the area, as we had left the show before the last song. This is the routine we opt for because it reduces the number of fans who will potentially mob Mike as he's trying to leave—a special concern when he's traveling with his younger children. However, there was no way Mike would not honor Diana's request.

Diana had already changed from her luxurious stage attire when we arrived backstage. She had to be exhausted after her energetic and amazing performance, but that didn't stop her from giving us a warm, heartfelt greeting. She went over to Milan and teased about them having the same hairstyle. As if seeing Diana's live performance wasn't already a life-fulfilling wish, meeting her in person was beyond my expectation.

Never will I forget the pleasure of being in Oprah Winfrey's presence as well, not once, but twice. She came into the green room on both occasions when Mike and Kiki were on her show. Her charisma was totally encompassing. I was holding Milan on my lap when Oprah approached us. After expressing how adorable she thought Milan was, Oprah commented that I must be Kiki's mom. I replied that I was Milan's grandma. Oprah complimented me and said, "Don't refer to yourself as a grandma. You look too young for that." She gave me a smile and a tap on my shoulder, then turned and exited the room.

Mike and Kiki were already on stage with Oprah, being

interviewed, when one of her production crew informed me that Oprah specified that I should be the person to bring Milan on stage when prompted to do so. I said okay. Milan was whining as I stood near the entrance to the stage. In an effort to calm her, I continued to rock her in my arms, to no avail. Milan was about six months old at the time and she wanted to nurse. I was getting really concerned. Taking Milan on stage before hundreds of fans, under bright lights, was not going to go well, I thought. Concurrently, as we stepped out of the dark holding area, directly onto the brightly lit stage, Milan immediately stopped crying. The applause and the cheering audience evidently fascinated her enough to even bring a smile to her little face as if she knew it was all for her. Later her parents and I laughed about the incident and claimed that time as the moment "a star was born." Although that statement was meant as a joke back then, I can tell you today that it was more like a prophecy because those words have manifested into Milan walking that road to stardom. She is a remarkable tennis player who is often referred to as "the next big thing" by tennis legends and trainers.

I have to mention Rodney Jerkins, and his wife, Joy. I love them beyond compare. Rodney is a phenomenal music producer who has written hit songs for Brandy, Mary J. Blige, Whitney Houston, Jennifer Lopez, Monica, and even "Babyface" Edmonds. They couldn't be any nicer to me if I was their biological mother. I remember telling Rodney and Joy about my plans for releasing my memoir. Their enthusiasm encouraged me to get back to completing the book.

While I could acknowledge many more notables that touched me in meaningful ways, I'm going to end this segment with Whoopi Goldberg. Needless to say, she's an amazingly multitalented woman. Whoopi is highly intellectual and speaks truth to power at any cost. I made her acquaintance when Mike appeared on *The View*. I mentioned to her that Milan loved Elmo so she immediately arranged for the puppeteer to bring Elmo to the green room to meet Milan. She was also very engaging toward me and made me feel relevant.

As I conclude this segment, it's imperative to stress the significance of why I mentioned my experiences with the aforementioned notables. First, I've been around many celebrities on a professional and personal level, which surely you realize since you've gotten to this point in this book. I've never been star struck. More so, I was struck by the aforementioned stars because of their demeanor and respect for my family and me. You see, it's no secret that members of my family and I were convicted felons. In social climates some could easily shun us since we have been accused of crimes and carry the burden of these negative connotations. Our innocence matters not. Innocent people get convicted of crimes every day. And, unfortunately, some convicted individuals wear the label of convicted felon like an unseen insignia that still repels some people. Even worse, for many, being a felon is like being leprous. People feel that getting close to us will cause their reputation to be tainted, merely by association.

My interaction with the extraordinary people I've mentioned, and the way in which they highly regarded me, says more about their character than it does mine. They are worthy of recognition beyond their talents and notoriety. A true star is a bright light with a warm heart and a special blessing from God. They radiate beyond the status of stardom. Personal magnitude is real, and I feel humbled and blessed to have been in the presence of so many gifted individuals. I value celebrities like those I've mentioned, particularly after encountering some icons who actually refused to speak to people, not even acknowledging children who nearly worshiped them.

All right, even though I could go further with mentioning notables I love and admire, I'll stop here. Admittedly, I'm namedropping but I don't perceive that as a negative. I feel blessed to have known many of them, and still know some today, and to have simply wisped by some others. Besides, some names are worthy of namedropping and these definitely fit into that category. Moreover, it means a lot to me that they love me for who I am. They consider me the same as they would a family member and a good person, in spite of federal convictions. Most important is the genuine fondness we share for each other, which has nothing to do with their notoriety.

It was no secret that I used to be around celebrities on a personal, social, and professional level. Constantly. Even the feds knew that, which is why they went so far as to spend taxpayer dollars traveling to various parts of the country in order to discuss our case with several of our celebrity friends. They couldn't limit it to Pennsylvania. No. They literally crossed several state lines to harass our celebrity associates who had no affiliation with the Philadelphia Masjid or Sister Clara Muhammad School. Apparently, the feds had two goals in mind. According to what was reported back to my husband and me, the feds didn't even really discuss anything about the charges against us. They were just there to let our friends know that we were really bad people and would be going to prison.

Celebrities weren't the only people they intruded upon; they searched out our dearest friends and supporters in an effort to turn them against us. They launched an all-out effort to castrate us among them. Thanks to Allah (SWT), in most cases their efforts failed. However, one of my son's friends confessed that getting visited by the feds frightened him. According to him, he was told that associating with us would be bad for anyone because it might make the feds look into the prospect of charging them with a crime as well. It was for that reason that he avoided contact with our family for several years. Note, this individual had nothing to do with a community college, was not a member of the Muslim community, and was simply a lifetime friend of my son.

LIARS AND PERPETRATORS

Certainly the vast majority of our friends stood by us and considered the feds' pursuit of us to be unjust. However, I would be remiss to allow the readers to think such was the case for everyone. There were a few people at the school who turned on us. Whether they were frightened by the feds, jealous, or simply liars, it's their burden to bear. In fairness to some of them, getting a visit from the FBI can be a chilling experience. It can make friends turn on friends, spouses turn on spouses, children turn on parents, and vice versa. Everyone's not the same. Where I am strong, some are weak. Where I am weak, others may be strong. That's life. Struggles, trials, and tribulation go on from the day we're born until the day we die. You simply have to keep striving. Give life your best shot.

SHATTERED HOPES

Expectations that my family and I would one day be vindicated of our felony convictions was something I continued to hope for. One option was a presidential pardon. The other was something I had not anticipated. A member of the Masjid, henceforth to be referred to as Nedi, who always called me Mom, had actually been working with the federal government to bring down my husband. It was revealed in court during Shamsud-Din's trial that Nedi was being paid over $80,000 a year to get dirt on my husband. I met Nedi after he was released from prison and he started coming to the prayer services. Rarely was there a time when I saw Nedi that he didn't ask me for money — small amounts of $20 or $30 was his general plea. I would always give him more than what he asked for because I thought he really needed the money. I even gave him a job working at the school in the cafeteria. Later Nedi wormed his way into working at my husband's office in his collection agency.

The sister he was married to at the time said something I should have taken heed of. She told me that her husband was a paid informant for the federal government, but her statement didn't bother me. I knew we weren't involved in any illegal activities, but because I was aware that they were having marital problems, I took the wife's discernment to be derived out of her frustration with him. As the trusting and sometimes naïve person I can be at times, I was blinded by Nedi's continuous betrayal by someone who pretended to regard me as a mother. But then again, perhaps he wasn't pretending to regard me as a mother. Realizing what a scumbag, liar, and ingrate he was, I think he would have done the same thing to his own biological mother.

Rita's Rule # 28

Never give in to sentiment, because feelings for an individual could cloud your judgment. Listen to what is being said and do your due diligence to observe the situation objectively.

Much later when confronted with the reality of imminent death, Nedi reached out to my husband. On his deathbed he pleaded with my husband to forgive him for conspiring against us. Nedi said it bothered his conscience because he knew we were honorable people and that the feds forced him to go along with their plot or go back to prison. In addition, Nedi recalled that my husband had always been kind to him, and particularly so when he had done his mother's eulogy at Nedi's request. Being the compassionate man Shams was, and continues to be, he accepted Nedi's apology and prayed for him, as he requested. Days later, at Nedi's request, James Binns Esq. and Adib Mahdi scheduled a visit with Nedi. It was for the purpose of recording his dying confession. When informed that Nedi wanted to clear our name and reveal what the feds had done, I was elated with the news. On the morning Nedi was to expose the government's unlawful tactics, I could barely contain my joy. Anxiously, I waited with all the enthusiasm of a child anticipating opening gifts on Christmas morning. "Mortified" best describes the letdown and anger I felt when I learned Nedi passed minutes before the sonographer arrived to tape his confession.

Nedi had known for months that he was terminal. Easily he could have cleared our names and been a powerful contributor in exposing the feds' attack on our family. When conveying my contempt for Nedi in my reluctance to ever forgive him, Azim attempted to console me with the following:

"Don't be upset, Mom. For whatever reason it wasn't meant to be. Surely, Nedi wanted to rid himself of the evil sin he committed by working with the feds to harm two people who were good to him and the Muslim community. I think Allah (SWT) rejected his effort to right his wrongdoing and called him to an immediate judgment. On his dying day I think Allah (SWT) said, 'No, you don't get the chance to clear your reputation and rid yourself of your sins; you're coming to me right now and I will judge you. You don't get the chance to be forgiven or to rid yourself of such a heinous sin."

Azim's words sent a chilling feeling through my entire body. Such a powerful statement coming from my son jolted me back into a humane position. Instantaneously, I forgave Nedi and prayed for his soul because I realized that it's important to forgive.

Rita's Rule # 29

The power of forgiveness is the ultimate force, more powerful than holding a grudge. Forgiveness begets forgiveness. Those who seek forgiveness from Allah (SWT) for their sins must have the humility to forgive those who offend and commit sins against them as well.

14

FORGIVE? YES. FORGET? NEVER.

This next immoral person is such a reprehensible person that he can never be trusted. Forgiving a man who l shall refer to as Bradford is a bitter concept to accept. He worked for me at the Sister Clara Muhammad School during my tenure as Assistant Director of Education. This refers to someone who had fallen from grace in the Islamic community. According to reliable accounts he was fired for stealing thousands of dollars, from the Masjid and the school, to support his crack addiction. I don't recall how many years he was cast out of the community because I was not active myself from 1976 until 1990. During that period he would often enter my beauty salon complaining of being hungry and asking for money. Never was there a time that I denied him money. On more than a few occasions I even did two of his daughters' hair free of charge. Fast forwarding to year one of my working at the school. I summoned Bradford to the school. He was smelly, dirty, and trembling in need of a dope fix. Appealing to what I hoped was his higher self, I offered him a job in the school. He was so emotionally and physically fragile, he professed a fear of not being capable of carrying out any type of employment task. Reassuring him that I had the confidence in him to do so, he accepted my offer to help him pull it together.

Bradford was in dire need of housing for himself and his youngest son. Victor Rashid was a member of our Masjid who owned multiple rental properties. Fully aware of Bradford's reputation for being a crack-head, Victor resisted any notion of renting a property to him. Only after pleading with Victor and convincing him that Bradford had changed his ways did Victor consider my proposition. Only after assuring him that I would be responsible for paying the rent, and that brothers from our Masjid would keep a watchful eye on Bradford, and his property, did Victor acquiesce to my request.

Using my personal American Express credit card, I completely furnished the house for Bradford as well as bought clothing for him and his son. Without exaggeration I purchased and filled the house with every essential from linen, dishes, flatware, television, toiletries and more. Waving tuition for his three younger children was another gesture of my good will toward him. Even when Victor Rashid, informed me that Bradford was still getting high, I continued helping him. Victor wanted him out of his house, but I pleaded with him to let Bradford stay and promised to get our addicted brother in to a drug rehab program. Realizing the need for Bradford to get help, I contacted a friend of mine named Ronald Tyree (AKA) Beetle, which he was affectionately called by close friends from Germantown. Ronald immediately admitted Bradford to the rehab facility, where he was the director, at no cost to Bradford.

Unbeknownst to us Bradford had placated my husband and me for years. In conjunction with being propped up by the feds and their media disciples, Bradford, along with his son-in-law were conspiring to execute a coup to take over the masjid and school. Though a small man in stature his Napoleonic complex and overinflated ego was always apparent. As well, his evil nature and inclination toward pedophilia were not readily known throughout the community. Upon the realization that he was going to testify against me and was the federal government's star witness, my attorney, Garland Giles, obtained a police background check on Bradford. There it was in black and white print that Bradford had been charged with and convicted of child molestation. Disgusting, right? Well, evidently not to the feds. They preferred to overlook his deviant character in exchange for Bradford's willingness to conspire with them to convict me, and my family members.

More appalling is that after circulating copies of Bradford's police record, it's now suddenly nowhere to be found. Miraculously, Bradford's arrest and conviction record is no longer readily accessible to the public. Hmm... let me guess... the feds took care of their star witness and traitor to the Islamic community, and awarded him with expunging his record. How else could he get a professional position working at one of the universities? In spite of the apparent expunging of Bradford's record, myself, and others still have a copy of it.

Regardless of favors bestowed on Bradford by the feds and gifting him help to hide his true self, copies of his police record still exist with many. Believe it or not he still has the audacity to sashay around the community, skinning and grinning, as they say, shaking hands and forcing himself on decent people who he knows despise him. Bradford is fully aware that Muslims are required to return the greetings offered by another Muslim. So he takes full advantage of that in order to perpetuate an image of a humble believer. What really matters is that Bradford knows what he did, and above that, Allah (SWT) knows. Incidentally, after a court decision in their favor, Bradford, along with a small group of his followers, did finally take over the school. However, as the saying goes, you reap what you sow. Their tenure was short-lived. Another group of people took them to court and were successful in their coup against Bradford and his group. More than ten years have passed, and the school has changed hands several times since my husband and I left. To date, the building still stands and there has been no successful reopening of one of the most outstanding Islamic educational facilities to exist. All the boards, the large membership, bickering and backstabbing continues to plague the membership too. Too many big I's seeking to take advantage of the masses keeps the community in disarray. Unity amongst the believers is challenged by individuals in leadership positions seeking to enhance their own personal and financial agendas.

Rita's Rule # 30

Abstain from evil practices in this life as your evil deeds will catch up with you, if not in this life, in the hereafter.

Honestly, I've been so far removed from the activities of the Philadelphia Masjid and Sister Clara Muhammad School that I rarely think about my tenure there. Not now nor ever have I endured one moment of grief about not being assistant director of education for the school.

For the few professed Muslims that bought into the feds' and Bradford's plot to disrupt and divide the Islamic community, they prevented advancements from occurring. I had obtained provisional approval for a charter school focused on Middle Eastern Studies. Interest was high. Potential applicants from various ethnicities throughout the city were excited and desiring to get on board. In addition to that, there were negotiations between Shamsud-Din, investors, and elected officials about constructing *The Muslim Mall of America* near 69th Street. Neither venue would have discriminated against people who were not of Islamic faith. However, both projects would have contributed to enhancing better understanding of Middle Eastern culture and strengthen relations between Muslims and the community at large.

Incidentally, I want to emphasize why I used Nedi and Bradford as names to conceal the identity of two unsavory characters. It's not because of any legal concerns, simply stated, they are both such perpetrators of evil that I could not bear to write or see their real names throughout my book. The thought of either of them is repulsive and relegates me to feeling like I need to take a thorough shower in an attempt to wash them from me. Simply put, I know of no one with lower characters than them.

While I loved the progress I made during my tenure at SCMS, I'm more proud of the progress the students made. Established relationships between them and me are what I cherish most. They have gone on to become professionals and outstanding adults. Their affection for me remains strong. Their affection for me is a reminder that I provided them with excellent academic, social and professional skills that have thrust them into success. Neither time nor distance has diminished the bond shared between my students and me. One only has to witness them showering me with affection when we come in contact with each other, to understand the truth I'm telling here. I will always remember the love they showed for me as I grieved the loss of my dear sister, Zaynah. They loved her, perhaps even more than they love me, if that's possible. She departed this life on September 17, 2018, and with only two days' notice there were at least a thousand people in attendance for her janazzah (funeral). No words can express how uplifting it was seeing all her students, their parents, Muslims, Christians, and loved ones who paid tribute to my baby sister — my best friend. Of course I shall miss her every day for the rest of my life. But I'm comforted knowing she was truly loved in life and has gone on to glory. That time will forever be cemented in the archives of my mind, spirit, and the depths of my soul.

On a personal note it was gratifying to witness the harmony and unity of the broader Islamic community. Muslims came from various parts of the country. You see, that confirms that the Islamic community's humanity and love of Allah (SWT), and my family never wavered. In spite of the federal government's attempts to disrupt and distort the truth, the Islamic community continues to support and love us. Surely the feds would deny that their pursuit of us had nothing to do with hatred for Muslims. Nonetheless, let's keep it real. It's a known fact that some of the powers-that-be in America are not in favor of the expansion of Islam.

Instead of embracing Muslims who also loved this country, some, not all, governmental authorities prefer to castrate us; deprive us of our vitality and power. It would be better for our country, and individuals in powerful positions, to embrace Muslims who also value our country. Working together would go a long way in protecting each other from outside perpetrators who seek to harm Americans. I just want to remind anyone, who may have a tainted view of Islam, that Islam means peace. Muslims share the same monotheistic beliefs as Christians and Jews. We are better working together to advance principles in the belief of one God.

ACHIEVING LIFELONG GOALS

For me, achieving a lifelong goal meant obtaining a doctorate degree. Truth be told, it was the only thing that sparked my attention when forced to attend reentry classes. In what amounts to a waste of taxpayers' money, inmates are mandated to complete a series of classes to qualify for release. Inmates complained. They didn't pay attention in class. They also slept during class. Honestly, everything discussed in the classroom could've simply been explained by counselors or case managers aside from a classroom setting.

After days of attending a variety of classes, all that was of interest to me was learning that convicted felons could enroll in a degree program. This was of particular interest because I was aware that in some states, individuals reentering society are denied the right to vote and are rendered ineligible for gainful employment. Seeking employment was never an option for me, regardless, because I had no plans to work for anyone other than myself. Earning a doctorate degree would enhance my efforts to better comprehend business and leadership applications in today's market.

I began researching universities to determine which one best suited my needs a few months after I moved to Vegas. Scheduling time for attending classes and completing assignments was a major consideration for me. Globetrotting with Mike, Kiki, Milan, and Morocco necessitated having some flexibility. Ashford University was perfect for me to earn my master's degree. Under the cloud of a convicted felon label, I was still unsure the university would admit me. Getting directly to the point pertaining to my conviction and incarceration, I conveyed my circumstances to the admissions recruiter. In turn, he shared something with me of a personal nature.

Ironically, his mother had recently been mandated to Danbury Federal Prison. She was an older Caucasian woman and he was quite concerned about her safety. I reassured him that federal prison camps were about as safe as any lockup situation. This brought some immediate relief to the young man. Further dialogue led to me schooling him on the things to tell his mother about how to go about getting the best job. I also identified correction officers who would be the most helpful to her, and provided names of inmates I had been close to who would look out for her. The enrollment counselor and I stayed in touch during the entire time I was at Ashford University. His mother was helped by my suggestions, too, which of course made me feel pretty good.

Rita's Rule # 31

Integrity matters. Regardless of how you think someone will perceive any negative impressions of you, it's best that the truth be known. At the very least you will have been honest and that quality is self-serving.

Toward the end of completing my first semester in the master's program at Ashford University, I began the process of looking into PhD curriculums. Time was critically important because I wanted the transition from my MBA program to a doctorate program to be seamless. I called the first university from the list of contenders I had compiled and enquired about what PhD disciplines they offered. Unsatisfied with the response I called the second college on the list and rejected it as well. I continued to research universities simply through a process of elimination. Walden University was third on the list, and I asked the same question of the academic recruiter who answered the phone. Upon obtaining some information about my academic level, the interviewer began to discuss possibilities with me. My insistence on enrolling in a discipline that would render the most expeditious result apparently prompted him to enquire why that mattered so much to me. I explained that I wanted to change my title ASAP. "Oh," said the gentleman. "May I ask what your current title is?"

Jovially I blurted out, "Convicted felon!"

He erupted into hysterical laughter. Whether it was my comedic directness, or not shying away from my situation, that tickled him so, it matters not because he obviously appreciated my candor.

"Hey, look here, ma'am," he said, "since you're gonna keep it real like that, I'm gonna keep it real with you. With your current master's degree being in business management, you should consider getting a doctorate degree in business administration." He went on to advise me to change my present discipline at Ashford from business management to a master's in Business Administration. Amending my degree program in that manner would let me avoid having to take five courses at Walden because I would have completed them at Ashford University.

Determined to succeed in my studies at Walden University, I never missed a course and maintained an outstanding academic status. Attending the required residencies, I met people from all over the world and established relationships with instructors and administrators that I continue to maintain today. Challenging and difficult, though it was, I'm so happy that I chose Walden to complete my doctoral studies. Inshallah (God willing) I will continue to contribute to the academic forum through writing scholarly papers for peer review and committing to impact positive social responsibility. Moreover, as a proud alumnus of Walden University who has earned the distinguished title of Doctor, I shall use my credentials to help others. Supporting individuals who have been incarcerated and are trying to move forward in life, is a priority. Future goals for me include lobbying the government to restore voting rights for convicted felons, working with corporations to employ persons reentering society, and working with academics to educate and help them gain skills suitable for today's employment markets. In addition to having a doctorate degree, I am also a certified life coach specializing in relationships and corporate leadership training. This expertise awarded me the opportunity to continue to contribute to society in a positive way.

DIFFERENT STROKES FOR DIFFERENT FOLKS

Here's some food for thought relevant to triple jeopardy. On March 13, 2019, Paul J. Manafort, Pres. Donald Trump's former campaign chairman, was charged with mortgage fraud and more than a dozen other felonies. An admitted news junkie, I watch Fox News, CNN, and MSNBC every day. To gain a broader perspective on diverse opinions about current events, I fluctuate between the aforementioned cable news channels. For several days I observed pundits arguing on behalf of Mr. Manafort's constitutional rights being violated by the New York state attorney charging him with virtually the same charges that he had already been convicted of in federal court.

How ironic, I thought, as I heard a slew of pundits express outrage that this was double jeopardy. The majority of commentators tended to agree, adding that the odds of New York State being able to actually prevail with such a case against Mr. Manafort, was highly unlikely. They were adamant that double jeopardy is against the law and that such charges would not hold up in the appellate court. Whether or not their point of view will manifest is yet unknown. My guess is that by having so much public attention brought to this matter, Mr. Manafort has a much better chance of receiving a fair outcome, unlike in my case. Unike Mr. Manafort, I was not a globally known political icon, nor was I wealthy. Worse, I had no support from the media presenting exculpatory information about me or my family. There was no media coverage fostering a public debate wherein any commentators could alert the world of what equated to triple jeopardy in my case. To the contrary, negative media continued to be a driving force to assist the government's persecution of me. To them, I was just a lone African-American woman being persecuted and subjected to triple jeopardy. Also, considering the numerous counts that Mr. Manafort was convicted of, and sentenced on, were far more than what I was unjustly convicted of. Yet, my sentence was much harsher than his. This illustrates a distinct difference in how persons of lower means are treated by law enforcement and even some media that's supposed to be non-biased.

For some skeptics who may perceive Manafort's case to be different from mine, let me further explain. Here's the problem, and what makes our situations similar. The NY state attorney's charges against Manafort included some of the same charges he was convicted of by the U.S. government, plus crimes which supports the premise of double jeopardy. In addition, the NY district attorney charged Manafort with state crimes that differ from federal convictions which he was sentenced for. This is precisely what happened in my case. Again, if you recall, I outlined prior how I was charged with the same crimes in a superseding indictment, wherein the government added charges different from the original counts. This caused me to be sentenced on three separate occasions. Normally, regardless of what an individual was convicted of and/or served time for, the same offense would not be added on to something they were already being punished for. If, in fact, the government's new charges against me were legitimate, there is no way that my sentence should have included crimes I was already sentenced and punished for.

NOT INNOCENT OF ALL CHARGES

Ignorance of the law is no excuse and to that point I have to be honest. I did commit a crime when I embellished a pay stub to obtain a car loan. It was in July of 1998 when I went to the Mercedes-Benz dealership in Cherry Hill, New Jersey with someone who was interested in purchasing a new Benz. I wasn't even in the market for a new car but was lured in by impulsiveness. What the heck, it was time to upgrade my 480 Benz sedan for a 500. I wanted to surprise my husband with a new car for our anniversary. Knowing I was due to come into a large sum of money in October, I planned to pay the remaining balance of $87,000 off in a few months. But like I said, instead of waiting a few months I did something really stupid. I had one of the workers make up a pay stub for me reflecting enough income to qualify for the car note. I had very good credit, which I have always maintained throughout my adult life. So, with that and the down payment I had enough of the financials to be approved for the car note. I had no idea that embellishing one's income was defrauding a bank because it was never my intention to defraud anyone. Even though I paid the car off as intended in just a few months, the feds charged me with bank fraud. That was added to the superseding indictment, which was the only charge that was different from the prior charges I had already been sentenced for regarding the Philadelphia Community College. They knew I paid the car note off because they had in their possession evidence of it through receipts supplied by the lender. They could have obtained the information from the bank, as well. Nonetheless, I was ordered to pay $87,000 in restitution for a car that was already paid for. As if prison wasn't enough punishment. At least I paid the bank back, but the feds charging me $87,000 in restitution for something I already paid for amounts to nothing more than blatant robbery as far as I'm concerned.

Not only that, before I was ever charged with it, my attorney told me that it was something the feds were looking into. Immediately, I owned my car purchasing "crime." I never denied it, and that was even before I was charged with it. But my confession wasn't satisfactory to the feds. For me to admit to something that I was guilty of, even though I was ignorant of the law pertaining to that specific crime that I never intended to commit, was of no effect to them. As a consequence I was more than willing to accept responsibility for that. Obviously that's not what they wanted. They wanted to humiliate me, deplete my financial resources, and use anything they could to put me in prison for as long as they could. And, they did just that.

By the way, my husband had nothing to do with, nor did he know anything about how I obtained the car. Like I said, it was a surprise for him. There was nothing on any tapes or paper trail or anything that involved him in any way regarding me purchasing that car. But that didn't stop the feds from charging him with defrauding the bank for the same car when he was also wrongfully convicted on other unrelated charges. For the record when he finally went to trial and was convicted on multiple counts, that was the only thing the jury found him not guilty of.

LASTING IMPRESSIONS

An oversaturation of negative and distorted media accounts presenting my husband, Azim, Kiki, and me as deplorable characters undoubtedly leaves a lasting impression. Those who know us, love us, and support us will never acquiesce to believe deceptive assertions propagated by certain members of the U.S. government and their media disciples. For that I thank Allah (SWT) over and over again. Of course, there are some who believe anything presented by law enforcement, or media exchanges, is true. For that matter they're probably not reading this book anyway. While I was quite aware of the media coverage about us that saturated Philadelphia, and a few stories that went viral, most people have no interest in retaining such information after so many years. Whether good or bad the lasting impression of what occurred to our family still exists with some.

As I stated earlier, celebrity status only excites me when it represents the outstanding accomplishments of the individual associated with it. Such is the case with my regard for renowned attorney Mark Geragos, with his professional contributions as a legal media consultant and his work as a defense attorney, who I have admired for decades. When Kiki informed me that she was rushing off to a business meeting with Mark Geragos, I immediately questioned, "*Thee* Mark Geragos?" to which Kiki replied, "Yes, why?" She didn't have to explain her response. She was somewhat surprised that I asked about him and already knew him by name. Between Mike, Kiki, and Azim, they were always meeting with high-profile individuals pertaining to business as well as social circumstances, but it was not customary for me to enquire about any other meetings.

"You know me," I said. "I'm no celebrity groupie but I'm so impressed with Mark Geragos as a defense attorney. He's just awesome."

With that, no further words were exchanged between Kiki and me. Shortly after she left, my cell phone rang displaying her name as the caller. Surprisingly, it was not her voice on the other side of the receiver. "Hello, Rita, this is Mark Geragos."

Familiar with his voice from seeing him on TV numerous times, I responded, "I know, I recognize your voice. It's an honor and a pleasure to be speaking with you."

Immediately Mark stated, "I had no idea Kiki was your daughter."

I assumed he was being humorous, because he couldn't possibly know who I was, while on the other hand Kiki had gained notoriety as Mike Tyson's wife. In that respect it was more likely that I would be identified as Kiki Tyson's mother rather than Mark identifying her as my daughter. My identification in that order had become rare, if not nonexistent. That gave me a good laugh. "Yeah, right," I said.

"No! No! Seriously, I'm not joking. I know exactly who you are," he insisted.

"R-E-A-L-L-Y?" I said, shocked.

"Yeah. I was actually in Philadelphia during the time of your trial and leading up to it. I observed you and your family going to and from court and was privy to all of the media frenzy surrounding your case. I thought you all carried yourself with such dignity. Even though I had already met Kiki, I had not until just now put the connection together and realized you were her mother. I think you're a remarkable person that's been through quite an ordeal. I found your case and all the media coverage very interesting. It would be my pleasure to sit down and talk with you sometime over lunch. I look forward to meeting you and not just because you are Mike and Kiki's mother."

After thanking Mark for his kind words and confirming that I would love to meet with him, I told him I was considering writing about the experience. I wanted to get his opinion on whether he thought it would be something worthy of capturing the attention of readers. I felt motivated to proceed with telling my story after Mark said he thought it was something that would be of interest to many. To put it mildly, I was inspired by the encouraging words from such a brilliant legal mind, and I knew in that instant I had to tell my compelling story. As of yet I still have not had the pleasure of meeting Mark Geragos in person, and he has no idea how much he lifted my spirit on that day. The thought that a man of his stature would take time out of his busy schedule to speak with me, knowing I was a convicted felon, and still treat me with such regard meant more than words can express. Whether or not I ever have the opportunity to make his acquaintance in person, I shall always cherish the privilege of speaking with him. The mere fact that he was considerate enough to regard me as a person of substance is a reminder of the good of existing humanity. It would be wonderful if everyone would see individuals reentering society as worthy of forgiveness and to be given a second chance to live a normal life, particularly since some individuals, like me, were wrongfully convicted.

So many times throughout this whole ordeal I wanted to lash out at the feds and others for lying on us — members of the media, particularly Katie — but I maintained my dignity. Just as Mark Geragos noticed how my family conducted ourselves, others have also noticed.

Rita's Rule # 32

Always present yourself in a dignified manner under any circumstance regardless of how you may be tempted to lash out or act out. Maintaining your dignity will take you further than wallowing in emotional outbursts. Remember, you never know who's watching, and the image you project will leave lasting impressions.

By now I feel confident that I've provided readers with a compelling story with content beyond merely my opinion. For anyone who may think I've been hard on Republicans, the FBI, U.S. attorneys, and other government officials, let me clarify. First and foremost, it's imperative to note that I'm not conflating the conduct of individuals with the policies of our great institutions. Not now or ever have I defined persons as good, evil, bad, or negative based on anyone's political affiliation, job, or status in life. Thus, it's essential to convey that I'm not suggesting, nor do I want it misunderstood, that all Republicans are bad people or that Democrats are flawless. Factually, I had no way of knowing what political persuasion any of the FBI or U.S. attorneys were. What I do know is that during the time that my family was under constant political attack and character assassination, the Republican Party was in charge. I also realize that while very few people may use their positions of power to wrongfully convict individuals, the vast majority of Republicans, Democrats, or Independents, for that matter, are good, law-abiding citizens. It's also possible that if the situation were reversed and some rogue Democrats were seeking to bring down Republican operatives, and we were Republicans, perhaps the outcome would've been the same.

Seriously, I must emphasize the fact that I wholeheartedly believe the unjust persecution and prosecution of me and my family members were driven more by personal ambitions than loyalty to a political party. The politically aware individual that I am, I have lived long enough to witness affiliates of the Republican and the Democratic parties launch unfair investigations against adversaries. One only has to read news articles, or watch news outlets on TV, to observe political pundits of both parties distort realities to fit a narrative they want to project as truth to the public. Thank goodness for those who provide honest commentary regardless of their political affiliations. MSNBC commentators Chris Matthews, Lawrence O'Donnell, and Rachel Maddow; Fox News commentators like Brett Baier, Andrew Napolitano, and Chris Wallace; and CNN's Wolf Blitzer, Jake Tapper, Don Lemon, and Anderson Cooper are among my favorites. I don't always agree with them, but I can rely on them to convey an honest interpretation of what they perceive the facts to be. As a news junkie, I record their shows to ensure that I catch each episode. I also find myself arguing with the TV when I disagree with them. In actuality, while some of their views are liberal and some are conservative, what matters is the information they provide. The ability to be open to discussions of different points of view broadens one's perspective.

Rita's Rule # 33

Never be reluctant to amend your position when clear evidence contrary to your opinion is imminent. Maintaining an open mind is far more empowering than having a closed perspective. Circumstances often change, and as life evolves, you must be willing to adapt.

MSNBC commentator Michael Steele, former lieutenant governor of Maryland and chairman of the Republican Party, had a profound impact on me and made me consider becoming a Republican. During his tenure as Republican Party chair, he changed the game. He made the Republican Party appeal to a younger and more diverse group of African-American professionals like myself. The consensus among many of us was that his position as the chairman solidified that there was more acceptance of

African-Americans among Republicans and that it was not a party of exclusion. Because of Mr. Steele many African-Americans began to look at Republican candidates in a favorable way and voted for Republicans from the presidential candidacy to local elections. I'm not alone in admiring Michael Steele for his accomplishments as a brilliant attorney and former elected official, but I would also add that the man has charisma—or as a younger hip-hop generation would say, "The brother got swag."

I'm also not alone in feeling a great sense of disappointment when he was voted out as the national Republican chairman. Why? Many people wondered, why change course when there was never a greater appeal to the broader, diverse electorate than when Michael Steele was the Republican Chair? Perhaps some in his party didn't like the fact that he was an honest broker. Michael always tells it like it is; whether you agree with him or not, he tells the truth. Unfortunately, there are far too many politically influenced persons who are devoted to *party* over *principle*. We see it every day from Democrats and Republicans. In my particular case, it just so happened that Republicans were in charge during our fall and conviction. However, some of the people I described here, who actually lied on my family and worked with the feds to convict us, were Democrats and so-called friends. In this regard, it would be complete naïveté to think or suggest that politics was the only factor. It is quite apparent that certain individuals involved in the persecution of my family were driven by their own dishonest aspirations of winning at any cost.

CONCLUDING STATEMENT

Why, you may ask, have I written about a situation that has long passed? The simplest explanation is that closure requires a thorough assessment and facilitating resolve of all circumstances. Of course, when you are targeted by the federal government, as my family has been, there can never be complete closure. You live with the constant threat that the feds could at any time launch another attack on you. The government has the wherewithal to indict an innocent person at will. With a 97 percent conviction success record and unlimited financial and legal resources, very few individuals have a chance of fighting back. Even when we elect to do so, it's never a fair fight. Unless you bow down to them, confess to the crimes you're charged with, guilty or not, you are subject to the whims of prosecutors and federal agents. Again, I must emphasize not all federal agents or prosecutors are plagued with thoughts of exercising demagogic powers over victims. However, in the case of innocent persons like my family and me, it only takes a few unscrupulous agents or prosecutors to label you a felon. Combine that with the public scrutiny that comes from potential employers. Add to that the inability to even join certain social organizations. When you put these unreasonable pieces together it becomes clear to see how you can be haunted and denigrated by a federal conviction for life.

In our particular case the media also played a role in ensuring that no one would forget that we were charged and convicted. Ten years after the fact, one of the Philadelphia news outlets wrote a lengthy article reminding readers that it was the tenth anniversary of taking down the Ali family. Surely after ten years, the writer could have had something else to write about. But for media minions who work in conjunction with the federal government, it was essential to remind Philadelphians of their victory. Moreover, it was near the time my husband was to be released from federal prison to a halfway house facility. Obviously, the writer was hoping to stir up feelings of animosity toward us. Why they continue to try to turn people against us, particularly our supporters, indicates a deeply rooted obsession to torment us or, at worst, break our spirits. They must be individuals void of spirituality because they lack the fundamental ability to recognize strength in individuals. So, for the media minions and the feds who persist in trying to break my spirit, understand this: *You didn't create me and therefore can never break me. My strength comes from a higher power that goes far beyond your earthly abilities or control. Regardless of whatever you have the power to do, I know that when God is with you it matters not who is against you.*

I didn't feel compelled to write about this incident because I'm traumatized by the unprecedented, unjust burden of being convicted three separate times on virtually the same charges. And, I cannot delude myself into thinking that what the federal government did to my family and me should be ignored. I have a responsibility to myself, my family, my friends and supporters to finally tell the truth about what occurred. Believe me, I wanted to speak out from the very moment the bogus charges were revealed in the press.

Incidentally, the first notification I received telling me that I was under investigation by the feds came by way of the press. On the advice of my attorneys, I never commented before, during, or after the events took place. I thought about it for years but suppressed writing about it because it involved other individuals who may have moved on and would prefer that I not mention them by name. No one understands that more than I do, because it was a humiliating and horrific time. I have substituted some identities with different names. However, that doesn't alter the facts of what took place.

Frankly, another compelling reason for writing the book is my compulsion to let people know, straightaway, that I am a convicted felon when they first meet me. That's because I don't want anyone to find out later and then feel as though they were deceived. I always let people know so that they can make an intelligent decision to be associated with me or not. Once I tell them, naturally they want to know what happened, which drags me down memory lane and much chatter about details of the case, my husband's case, etcetera. Surely you can imagine how tired I am of telling the story, but not ashamed to do so. In short, writing this book tells the story for me once and for all. I'll still apprise new acquaintances of my felon background, but I have the ability now to refer them to the book so that they may read a comprehensive account of my journey. Aside from that, writing my story has been therapeutic and a comfort to release suppressed feelings.

Rita's Rule # 34

Only you possess the power to free yourself of the harmful acts of others against you. Don't suppress your feelings.

Long after I've departed this life, I will have left a legacy of an African-American woman falsely accused and deliberately persecuted by certain members of the federal government. Generations to follow shall regard my efforts as nothing less than courageous; they'll read of a woman who proudly stood on her convictions. Though I was knocked down, beaten down, lied on, and humiliated, I stood strong. Like great champions Muhammad Ali and Mike Tyson, I overcame getting knocked down by getting back up. And, still I rise. My generosity, kindness, and goodwill toward humanity shall ever be etched in the archives of history. And I will go before Allah (SWT), not as one of perfection but as one who tried to do her best. In spite of vicious efforts of the federal government to force me to admit to a crime that I did not commit, I stood my ground. Yes, while they had the power to put me in prison, they could never imprison my soul. Not then, not now, nor shall I ever say I did something I did not do.

How will the federal government's evil, racist, and anti-Muslim representatives be remembered? While they bask in the ambience of their wins of incarcerating many who they know are innocent, they suppress the reality of their immoral conduct. For them it's simply about destroying their targeted prey by using the power of their positions as federal agents, U.S. attorneys, and others, to take away people's liberties. But they too shall face their Creator and be judged for every ill will and unjustified act they perpetrated on God's people who were unable to fight back. Society will remember them for the cowardly, inhumane, and unjust villains they are. Given the choice, I choose my position over theirs any day. As a believer in Allah (SWT), I must forgive them. Therefore, I pray, God have mercy on their souls.

In spite of the pernicious conduct on the part of government officials to my family and me, I still believe in our justice system overall. I still love my country and prefer it over the other nations of the world, even the ones I've been privileged to visit. I also believe that there are many honest law enforcement officers in the federal government who do operate with integrity. Therefore, it's imperative that I convey that in no way do I mean to cast disparities on our outstanding institutions. Instead, I'm exposing the individuals who attacked us, the Ali family. This is my *mommy dearest* moment where I get the opportunity to rectify the lies and distortions that have been told about my loved ones; my family.

Rita's Rule # 35

Always act from your higher self and never succumb to the whims of temptation though that path may render temporary relief from a substantial challenge in the short run. In the long run you will wrong your soul. All intelligent life has a conscience. Whether we choose to adhere to our moral compass or surrender to lesser temptations, we will be rewarded or punished for our deeds.

To quote the profound lyrics from a Billie Holiday tune: *"It's cost me a lot but there's one thing I got; it's my man. Cold and wet I'm tired. You bet. All of that I'll soon forget with my man."* Okay, strike that. I'm really not tired nor wet! I'm more like Whoopi Goldberg's character Celie in the movie *The Color Purple*. After suffering, being ridiculed, treated like dirt, at the end she said, "I'M STILL HERE!"

So...triple jeopardy equates to *three strikes but I'm not out*. I'm still here.

Rita's Last Rule — STAY POSITIVE! STAY UP!

Shamsud-Din and Dr. Rita Ali FOREVER.

Acknowledgments

How do you thank individuals who have impacted, and continue to impact your life in such a profoundly positive manner when words are inadequate? Well, that is precisely my task in acknowledging my sincere gratitude to my family, friends, and supporters. Completing Triple Jeopardy has been a milestone for me. It was accomplished through due diligence on my part. However, the encouragement, technical and professional input from others has enabled me to bring the project to fruition. My daughter *Lakiha (aka) Kiki Tyson* actually provided me with the concept of adding life coaching tips throughout the book; a personal touch that I call *Rita's Rules*. My son *Azim Spicer* consulted with me and encouraged me to keep going and tell my story in my own words. Throughout the entire process of developing this book I have consulted with them and relied on their professional skills and vision for telling my story. Azim actually came up with the subtitle for the book, also.

I owe a heartfelt note of appreciation to **Dr. Ahmed Muhammad** who I first encountered when I attended Montgomery County Community College. He has been and continues to be a powerful source of support. He was the Dean of Central Administration, which I found particularly impressive because he was a Muslim and African American. Prof. Muhammad is a world renowned, brilliant, academic scholar and known for being a man of integrity. He has provided me with excellent advice since my days as a student and continued to advise me on the development of *Triple Jeopardy*. I am honored to have the advantage of his expertise, as an academic writer, to proof my work. His input adds to the assurance of producing a quality product.

Richard Beck is another academic scholar who assisted me early on in the process of structuring this book. As an experienced writer, Rich read portions of my very rough draft early on. He directed my attention to excellent techniques for sharing my personal and professional experiences in a comprehensive manner. He also enlightened me on strategies to transform my academic writing skills into content conducive to writing a memoir. His objective to elevate my story from good, to an exciting read, has been a tremendous asset.

Noted author of several self-help books and motivational speaker, *Stacey Speller,* who is like a younger sister to me, empowered me with information pursuant to all the tools for self-publishing. She has always been an extremely talented person with extraordinary charisma and communication skills. Though a kind and caring person, Stacey is an accomplished professional who can be relied upon to tell the truth. Therefore, when she said I had a compelling story that must be told, I knew she took my writing seriously. Naturally, that was encouraging. Her perspective really impacted me because of her successful career as an author. As a novice to the complexities of writing, publishing and promoting written works, Stacy's knowledge and experience was essential. She not only discussed the best methods for facilitating how to approach various tasks, she provided a written detailed description, too. Her outline included contact persons, companies, websites, phone numbers and everything I needed to know about how to move forward. Actually, my first editor, Nhat Crawford, came as a result of Stacy's recommendation.

My acknowledgements would not be complete without mentioning **John Howard, PhD,** who I consider family. Originally, I contacted John while working on my doctorate degree to tutor me in a statistics course. It had been decades since I had taken statistics as an undergrad student. John had a doctorate degree in physics, and was a professor at UNLV (University of Las Vegas). My initial impression of him was that of a young Caucasian male barely out of his teens, who must be a genius to have mastered science on a doctoral level. Though still quite young to have such impressive credentials he was a bit older than my initial impression and married with children, he just looked much younger. Immediately I felt a motherly attachment to him, and often teased him about being his African-American adopted mama. John continued to work with me beyond completing the statistics course. As fate would have it, John was far more than a brilliant scientist, he's also fully adept in all aspects of English. He was a tremendous help to me when writing my dissertation because of his skills in research and editing. Regardless of how many times I would read over pages, and make corrections, John would always find and correct even the slightest error. Completing my dissertation required considerable research, and providing references in an APA format. The process is very tedious and must be void of any errors. I was fortunate to have John proof all my writing before submitting them to my committee chairs for final approval. I owe him a sincere note of gratitude for helping me get through the process, which would have taken much longer without his professional input. On a personal level John always encouraged me to persevere, particularly when I would become frustrated and/or overwhelmed. Confirmation of his regard for me as a mom was evident when he introduced me to his lovely wife Erica, their two daughters when they joined me for family gatherings at my home with the rest of my family. Naturally I adopted them into the family as well. I could not have asked for a better instructor, tutor, friend and bonus son. As it pertains to this book, I would not feel comfortable releasing it without John contributing to the editing process.

Phenomenal writer, **Larry Solomon (aka Ratso)**, who collaborated on two of Mike Tyson's New York Times best-selling books, also advised me on *Triple Jeopardy*. I was privileged to get to know Larry during both times he spent months observing Mike in his natural surroundings. As a consequence, he was able to witness Mike's relationships and interactions with his wife

Kiki, their children and me. During that time Larry became like an extended member of our family. I loved his appreciation of my cooking as well as participating in a plethora of conversations with him pursuant to national and global affairs. I learned a lot about Ratso's humanity, social and political points of view in conjunction with his exceptional intellect. Simply stated, I truly value him as a friend and master of written words. With that in mind, I sought Ratso's expert opinion about the need to obtain a ghostwriter or not, and if I needed one, could he help me find someone. He accommodated me by offering to read some of my earliest chapters. Admittedly, I felt a bit intimidated to forward my writings to such an experienced writer who I knew to be a man of great integrity. If my work lacked the ability to capture and hold the attention of potential readers, Ratso would certainly express that harsh reality to me. I was more than elated when Ratso insisted that in no way did I need a ghostwriter. He emphasized that my writing was more than sufficient to tell my story. In fact, he convinced me that no one could convey it with the authentic passion that I could.

My publicist, *Joann Migano*, is more than deserving of my acknowledgement and appreciation. She has done a phenomenal job facilitating plans to expedite the launching of *Triple Jeopardy*. Jo has devoted considerable time and effort to contact relevant individuals to review the first ARC (Advanced Reader's Copy) of my book to receive feedback from them. In spite of the fact that I'm not one of her celebrity clients, Jo expeditiously responds to all of my emails, phone calls and concerns. Due to her personal aspirations of good will towards others, Jo has taken an interest in my work that exceeds professional goals. She believes in my project and my potential to inspire others who are confronted with similar problems, to move beyond feelings of hopelessness and despair. My fondness for Jo also exceeds our professional relationship. Jo is like a daughter. She's family to me.

I'm eternally grateful to everyone that helped me achieve the completion of this literary journey, particularly my son-in-law *Mike Tyson* for commenting on my book by way of his blurb.

Being an ardent reader, that makes his assessment of *Triple Jeopardy* extremely significant. Seriously, Mike reads more than anyone I've ever known. Though family bonds are important, Mike would not provide a comment, which essentially equates to an endorsement, in my book based on personal ties. His millions of national and global fans, and social media followers, trust his judgement. They regard him as brutally honest and will regard his statement as authentic. Moreover, Mike's comment adds validity to *Triple Jeopardy* as a page-turner worth reading.

And, last, but never least, **Nhat Crawford** is an amazing author of several books who undergirded me on my road to authorship by consenting to do my first edit. As a first-time author I was privileged to work with such an experienced writer. Nhat's guidance empowered me with knowledge, which enabled me to focus on the essential components of this manuscript. Nhat spent weeks, days and many hours pouring over my words to ensure that the story was being told with the richness and structure it deserved, without taking away my voice, like too many editors tend to do. Her input enabled me to present my story in a manner that would profoundly connect with readers. Prior to writing this memoir I was already a fluid writer as a former columnist, academic administrator and in my capacity to convey written concepts through the lens of obtaining a DBA (Doctorate Business Administration). However, the transformation of those writing styles to express emotions, differs. Early on, Nhat pushed me to write from my heart, write with passion so readers will envision each experience portrayed in the book. My confidence grew every time Nhat confirmed that she felt like she was in the moment with me when she read and

edited each adventure I wrote about. Nhat spent a significant amount of time familiarizing me with the publication process. Beyond attending to my professional concerns, Nhat's actions and comments conveyed a sincere sense of caring about my personal wellbeing and that I'd be able to connect with readers from my heart.

A million heart-felt thanks to you all!

About the Author

Young Rita Ali, a novice convert to the religion of Islamic, was no stranger to controversy. She was no stranger to posh living. Although well-coiffed, she never backed down from a fight, either. A woman in pearls and diamonds who possessed beauty, brawn and brains was a rare threat in her hometown of Philadelphia, Pennsylvania. Unlike most of the newsmakers that hailed from this forward city, she found her footing in business and excelled among the renown for decades. However, one day on her path to the next level upward, Rita found herself in *Triple Jeopardy*; being falsely accused of a crime, and sentenced on it three times. Heartless Federal investigations unleashed terror on her family as they sought to unseat her and all the good she'd done in the Muslim community and society at large. Sentenced to prison — thrice — during a period when most middle-aged women are enjoying the most creative time of their lives, Rita was being afflicted by the cruel malaise of injustice, fighting for her legacy and to maintain the structure of her family. *Triple Jeopardy* is no pith at all. It is the tell-all that recalls her moments up until she enters the dark corridors of the U.S. legal system. Some would say that *Triple Jeopardy* is an unorthodox memoir that will no doubt leave the reader reeling as they journey with Rita through her years of glorious productivity to heartbreaking losses, and the fight back again.

About Dr. Rita Ali in the words of Murad Muhammad

I would be remiss not to acknowledge Dr. Rita Ali for her contribution to the sport of boxing. She apprised me that she was writing a book and wanted to share how I decided to promote the first championship fight in the City of Philadelphia in over thirty-two years.

When we discussed her idea to schedule this major boxing event in Philadelphia, I honestly had no interest in the endeavor because Philadelphia was not known for major televised Boxing productions. Yes, Philly was already ripe with The Flyers, The Seventy-Sixers, The Phillies and The Eagle's great talent; not to mention talented Boxers the likes of Smokin' Joe Frazier, George Benton and Slim Robinson, etc. Being the gentleman that I am, I did not want to tell her that the sport of Boxing was not a lucrative investment in cities like Philadelphia. Be that as it may, she convinced me that she had the ingenuity and ability to bring it to fruition; she envisioned a fight being held in Philadelphia.

I chose the Spectrum [as the venue] and she agreed. I decided to promote a World Title Fight between WBA Light Heavyweight Champion, Dwight Braxton (aka Qawi Muhammad) vs. former WBA Light Heavyweight Champion, Matthew Franklin (aka Saad Muhammad), that would be a very entertaining and lucrative fight for the city and the sport of Boxing. I said, "Rita, if you think you have the skills to be my personal Administrative Assistant/ Public

Relations Representative for such an event in Philadelphia, then let's get it on." And she did just that!

I booked the Spectrum and produced a fight promotion that surpassed our wildest imagination. How? Because it was televised nationally on ABC with the legendary Howard Cosell as the fight announcer, as well as televised internationally to over two (200) hundred countries on six (6) continents, in addition to an overwhelming crowd at the Spectrum. It was a great fight for the Spectrum as well. So much so, that in acknowledgment of me, and the event, the Spectrum placed a neon plaque on its wall of *Greatest Events* right up there with the likes of world-renowned basketball players, the Harlem Globe Trotters, etc., which Rita was responsible for; in addition to the key to the City of Philadelphia, which I humbly accepted. When I received the replica of the Liberty Bell, I jokingly said in my short acceptance speech, "Why did you give me a cracked Bell?"

I would like to acknowledge and give sincere thanks and much credit to Dr. Rita Ali for her spirit, her foresight, and her confidence and belief in me, and even herself. It was a tremendous success. Because she believed in me, together we created a memorable event that can be relived for generations to come due to the magic of modern-day technology. Yes, I was the Promoter, the Producer and the Creator of the event, but it must be acknowledged and understood by present and future business entrepreneurs that men have limited ability to achieve success without the partnership of women.

To my beloved sister, Dr. Rita Ali, keep on keeping on! Peace and Love!

> MURAD MUHAMMAD,
> Boxing Promoter Extraordinaire
> *The 'Greatest Young Promoter of All Times.'*

References

Vidal (2014).
https://www.telegraph.co.uk/women/womens-politics/
10662145/Women-prisoners-Sex-in-prison-is-commonplace-the-
male-inmates-just-hide-it-more-than-girls.html.

Yant, M. *Presumed Guilty: When Innocent People Are Wrongly
Convicted*. Prometheus Books (1991).